THE POLITICS
OF
CHRISTIAN ZIONISM
1891–1948

PAUL CHARLES MERKLEY

FRANK CASS
LONDON • PORTLAND, OR

First published in 1998 in Great Britain by
FRANK CASS PUBLISHERS
Newbury House, 900 Eastern Avenue
London, IG2 7HH

and in the United States of America by
FRANK CASS PUBLISHERS
c/o ISBS, 5804 N.E. Hassalo Street
Portland, Oregon, 97213-3644

Website http://www.frankcass.com

Copyright © 1998 P. C. Merkley

British Library Cataloguing in Publication Data

Merkley, Paul Charles
    The politics of Christian Zionism, 1891–1948
    1. Zionism – History – 20th century 2. Christian Zionism –
    History – 20th century 3. Jews – Restoration
    I. Title
    320.5'4'095694'09041

ISBN 0-7146-4850-7 (cloth)
ISBN 0-7146-4408-0 (paper)

Library of Congress Cataloging-in-Publication Data

Merkley, Paul Charles.
    The politics of Christian Zionism, 1891–1948 / Paul Charles
Merkley.
        p. cm.
    Includes bibliographical references and index.
    ISBN 0-7146-4850-7. – ISBN 0-7146-4408-0 (pbk.)
    1. Christian Zionism–Great Britain–History.   2. Christian
Zionism–United States–History.   3. Zionism–United States–
History.   I. Title.
DS150.5.M47   1998
320.54'095694'041–dc21   98-13351
                                                              CIP

Typeset by Vitaset, Paddock Wood, Kent

Contents

Abbreviations

ACPC	American Christian Palestine Committee
AFL	American Federation of Labor
AHS	Abba Hillel Silver
AMF	American Messianic Fellowship
APC	American Palestine Committee
AZEC	American Zionist Emergency Council
CCP	Christian Council on Palestine
CDTH	*The Complete Diaries of Theodor Herzl*
ChW	Chaim Weizmann
CIA	Central Intelligence Agency
CZA	Central Zionist Archives
DCA	*Dictionary of Christianity in America*
ECZA	Emergency Committee for Zionist Affairs
EJ	Eddie Jacobson
EZI	*Encyclopedia of Zionism and Israel*
FDR	Franklin Delano Roosevelt
FDRFA	*Franklin D. Roosevelt and Foreign Affairs*
FDRL	*Franklin Delano Roosevelt Library*
FDRPL	*Franklin Delano Roosevelt: His Personal Letters*
FRUS	*Foreign Relations of the United States*
HST	Harry S. Truman
HSTL	Harry S. Truman Presidential Library
ISA	Israel State Archives
JHS	Jewish Historical Society
KJV	King James Version
LDB	Louis D. Brandeis
LLDB	*Letters of Louis D. Brandeis*
LPChW	*Letters and Papers of Chaim Weizmann*
NAACP	National Association for the Advancement of Colored People
PPAFDR	*Public Papers and Addresses of Franklin Delano Roosevelt*

PPF   Pro-Palestine Federation
PPPHST   *Public Papers of the Presidents: Harry S. Truman*
RN   Reinhold Niebuhr
SSW   Stephen S. Wise
SSWP   *Stephen S. Wise Papers*
TH   Theodor Herzl
UNSCOP   United Nations Special Commission on Palestine
WCP   World Council on Palestine
WEB   William E. Blackstone
WH   William Hechler
WWP   *The Papers of Woodrow Wilson*
WZO   World Zionist Organization
ZAL   Zionist Archives and Library
ZOA   Zionist Organization of America

Acknowledgements

My interest in this theme traces back to the experience of living with my wife and our four children in Jerusalem during the first four months of 1981, while I was a Visiting Professor in the Religious Studies and the American Studies Departments of the Hebrew University. Financial support for that trip was provided by the Canada-Israel Foundation and my University, Carleton University, Ottawa. Since then I have returned several times. In 1992, the Canada-Israel Foundation and the Department of Graduate Studies and Research again supported me when I spent two months working at the Central Zionist Archives in Jerusalem, and for this I am very grateful. My research visits to the Jewish Historical Society in Waltham, Massachusetts, the Zionist Archives and Library in New York, the Franklin Delano Roosevelt Library at Hyde Park, and the Harry S. Truman Library in Independence, Missouri, were supported again by my University, and also by a US Government grant in aid of research administered by the Embassy of the United States here in Ottawa. I received generous help by telephone from the Harvard Law Library, which I have not visited. I have come to expect a very high level of efficiency, courtesy and goodwill from librarians and archivists, and I am grateful to all who have helped me. I think, however, I should add my voice to the chorus of Truman scholars who will tell you that the prize for all-around-competence-added-to-Midwestern-friendliness goes to the Harry Truman Library.

I wish also to thank The Canadian Seminar on Zionist Thought, especially Professor Michael Brown of York University, for inviting me to present some of my work to them in Montreal and Toronto in November, 1992.

For valuable discussion or for help in reading portions of my early material I am most grateful to Dr Carl Herman Voss, Professor Yaakov Ariel (formerly of the Hebrew University, presently at the University of North Carolina, Chapel Hill); David Pileggi and Kevin Crombie (both associated with the Anglican Church of Christ in Jerusalem); my colleague Professor

Ray Jones; Charles Brown (on Reinhold Niebuhr); Jan Willem van der Hoeven and Stan Goodenough of the International Christian Embassy in Jerusalem; and Miriam and Halvor Ronning of the American Institiute of Holy Land Studies, Jerusalem.

During recent visits to Jerusalem I have stayed at the St Andrews Hospice (Church of Scotland) where I always enjoy the company of the Reverend Colin Morton, Carol Morton, Alexis Darg, and the gracious household staff. For company during my 1992 visit I thank John Zemba and, in a very special way, Richard Mattersdorff.

Special thanks are owed to Helga and Matti Jaakkimainen.

And first, last, and above all, my wife Gwen. At the beginning of our marriage, she shared in my graduate school penury; and in recent years has made sacrifices of a different kind to make it possible for me to take my several research visits. I could not have got though all of this without her loyalty. Further details can be found in Proverbs 31:10–31.

PART ONE

'HERE I AM': THE HERZL/HECHLER PARADIGM

1

Theodor Herzl and William Hechler

A few days after the first copies of Theodor Herzl's *Der Judenstaat* appeared in the windows of the Viennese bookseller *Breitenstein*, William Hechler, a British clergyman, passed by. Shortly after that, on 10 March 1896, he presented himself in Herzl's study.

Years later, Hechler's own recollection was that he began the interview by announcing, 'Here I am!' 'That I can see', was Herzl's reply, 'but who are you?' 'You are puzzled', Hechler observed. 'But you see, as long ago as 1882, I predicted your coming to the Grand Duke of Baden. Now I am going to help you.'

Here we have the first encounter between the official (Herzlian) Zionism and Christian Zionism. This (10 March 1896) is the moment; this (the study of Theodor Herzl) is the place; these are the protagonists in that first encounter. Both are authors of recently published pamphlets – Theodor Herzl, of *Der Judenstaat* (*The Jewish State*, 1896) and William Hechler of *Die bevorstehende Rückkehr der Juden nach Palästina* (*The Restoration of the Jews to Palestine according to Prophecy*, 1882).[1]

In truth, if this scene had taken place just a few months earlier, it probably would have frightened Theodor Herzl to death. This day, however, Herzl first felt a rush of exaltation; then he began at once to calculate how this strange man could be put to use for his work.

Herzl had always thought of himself as a thoroughly modern man, respectful of the ultimate authority of science. He knew that what he had proposed in *Der Judenstaat* was an absolutely reasonable, indeed scientific answer to the Jewish problem. It had required a heroic effort of imagination; but that made it more, not less, scientific. In planning and carrying out the project, he had experienced an exhilaration which was of an utterly different kind from that which he had known in the conception and execution of his literary work – his essays and his plays. He had been alternately exalted and frightened by what was happening to him. In a moment of extreme exaltation, he told himself, 'I believe that for me life has ended and world history has begun.'

We know the details of all this because Herzl began a diary exclusively dedicated to recording his thoughts and deeds as he pursued the goal of the Zionist state. On the first page, he fixed the title: *Book One of the Jewish Cause, begun in Paris, around Pentecost, 1895.* He began: 'For some time past I have been working on a task of infinite grandeur.'

It was not a mystical experience at all, he was sure. He believed that he had thought through more rigorously than anyone else had done the political and moral forces at work in the world, and then brought these insights to bear specifically upon the situation of the Jews, the most difficult moral and political question of the day. This was what gave him the authority to approach men like the Jewish philanthropist, Baron Maurice de Hirsch, head of the Jewish Colonization Association, whom he had bluntly told to his face, just a few months before the pamphlet was completed, that he must call off his plans for settling Europe's Jews in places like Argentina, and throw all of his resources behind Herzl's program. To another, Herzl wrote a few days later that he was thinking a good deal lately of Savonarola. Yes, he was himself much like Savonarola, as described by the poet Lenau: 'Lightning strikes, I am God's knight./The solemn bond shall stand forever.'

If we can guess that this tone frightened his interlocutors, we know that it frightened Theodor Herzl even more. 'I was often afraid of going mad these past few days', he confessed to the diary. In June, 1895, Friedrich Schiff, a journalist like himself but also a medical doctor, sat stunned while Herzl read to him the draft of his 'Address to the Rothschilds', then in tears urged him to burn it and get medical help at once.

It is just as well that readers of the finished pamphlet, *Der Judenstaat*, did not know about the fantasies which had occupied Herzl during the weeks when he was drafting the text:

> First I shall negotiate with the Czar (to whom our patron the Prince of Wales will introduce me) regarding permission for the Russian Jews to leave the country.
>
> He is to give me his imperial word and have it published in the official gazette ... Then I shall negotiate with the German Kaiser. Then with Austria. Then with France, regarding the Algerian Jews. Then, as need dictates.

Meanwhile, he must prepare the Jewish people for their Exodus, under his own direction:

> In the twenty years 'before it becomes known', I must train the boys to be
> soldiers ... The Exodus under Moses bears the same relation to this project
> as a Shrovetide play by Hans Sachs does to a Wagner opera.

There will have to be a Temple:

> The high priests will wear impressive robes; our cuirassiers, yellow-trousers
> and white tunics; the officers, silver breastplates

We shall need a constitution:

> We shall probably model the constitution after that of Venice and profit by
> her bad experiences by preventing them ... The first senator will be my father
> ... When I thought that someday I might crown Hans [his son] as Doge and
> address him in the Temple in front of the country's great men as 'Your
> Highness! My beloved son!', I had tears in my eyes.

Is it really easier for us than it was for Herzl's contemporaries to answer
the inter-related questions of the reasonableness of the project and the
sanity of the author? In our thinking, but not in theirs, there is the knowledge
that the Jewish State came about. Can a thing come about and not have been
thinkable? And if it was thinkable, was it not by definition reasonable?

THEODOR HERZL BEFORE 1896

Did all this have a religious meaning? He did not think so. He had never
been 'religious', by his own or others' reckoning. Born in Budapest, 2 May
1860, he had been circumcized on the eighth day, and given the Hebrew
name, Zeev, the Hungarian name, Tivadar, and the German name, Wolf
Theodor. Theodor's father, Jakob, had sprung directly from a strictly
orthodox family, a family of peddlars. Beginning life without advantages,
he had become a wealthy merchant and the president of a bank. It was a
thoroughly assimilated family, proud of their fluency in German, their
literate learning, and their patronage of the arts. The Herzls' Temple was
the newly built Dohany Street Synagogue, a Reform instititution. (In fact,
they lived next door to it.) Here on 3 May 1873, the family celebrated his
Bar Mitzvah. Apart from that occasion, Theodor's religiously indifferent
family had taken him from time to time to synagogue on Sabbath, but by
the time he wrote *Der Judenstaat* he had not been to prayer for years. His
earliest schooling, up to the age of ten, had been in a school for Jewish
children, where there had been a modest amount of religious instruction.
In recollection, he always insisted that he had hated it. Thereafter, he had
attended only secular schools.

Shortly before his death, Herzl told Reuben Brainin about a dream he
had had as a boy of twelve, in which the Messiah appeared.

> He took me in his arms and carried me off on wings of heaven. On one of the iridescent clouds we met ... Moses. (His features resembled those of Michaelangelo's statue) ... Then the Messiah called out to Moses, *'For this child I have prayed!'* To me he said, 'Go and announce to the Jews that I shall soon come and perform great and wondrous deeds for my people and for all mankind!' I kept this dream to myself and did not dare tell anyone.

Did he, then, come to believe in the Messiah? If he did, he never admitted it in plain words. He supposed (he told Brainin) that the Messiah of his dream stood for something else: perhaps for modern science and technology, which were really redeeming mankind! 'There and then I decided to become a great engineer.'[2]

The family moved to Vienna in 1878, where Theodor attended the school of Law of the University of Vienna. There he found a student body caught up in the new spirit of ultra-German nationalism. With this coincided the beginnings of a popular anti-Semitic trend, which led, among other things, to the formation of an anti-Semitic political party, the Christian Social Party, whose leader, Karl Lueger, would later become the city's Mayor.

It is striking, in view of all that would follow, how unaware Herzl remained during those student years in the face of the new anti-Semitism. He made a heroic effort to be accepted as a German among Germans to the point of joining a duelling fraternity, turning himself almost into a caricature of the type of the privileged German youth, but in spite of these efforts, the time came when he had to take a stand. When his fraternity officially attached itself to a newly organized anti-Semitic society he reluctantly submitted his resignation. In that letter he speaks sorrowfully of anti-Semitism as 'this reactionary fashion of the day', and makes it clear that he remains determined not to burn his bridge to solidarity with the German youth: 'Since, to the best of my knowledge, my record contains nothing dishonorable, I am counting on an honorable dismissal.'[3]

As late as 1893 he was asked to give his support to a newly organized Society to Combat Anti-Semitism in Vienna (whose membership, incidentally, included prominent Christians as well as Jews). Yet he refused. 'Half a dozen duels', he wrote in reply, would quickly settle the hash of the few anti-Semitic disturbers, 'thus greatly elevating the social position of the Jews'. In the meanwhile, 'the Jews would have to shed those peculiarities for which they are rightfully being criticized'. Conversion to Christianity, he goes on to suggest, would be the best all-round outcome. This was not an impulsive thought. Indeed, he remained a fervent assimilationist virtually to the eve of his conversion to Zionism. 'Crossing the Occidental races with the so-called Oriental ones', he wrote in 1882, 'on the basis of a common state religion – that is the desirable, the great solution.'[4]

Not long after his graduation from law school, Herzl disclosed that his real ambitions had nothing to do with the practice or the study of the law, in which he now had a doctorate. He intended as quickly as possible to become a famous essayist and a playwright, and also very rich. To practice for the first, he became a journalist, first in Berlin, then back in Vienna. By 1889, he was the drama critic of the *Wiener Allgemeine Zeitung*, and the author of two collections of essays, and of three plays which had been performed in Berlin, Vienna, Prague, and even New York. As for the second ambition – to be rich – he had married an heiress, and taken full custody of her inheritance, which he applied to the support of his literary career and his travels. (Later, he expended what remained on his Zionist work – which she despised.)

'Herzl', the American Rabbi Abba Hillel Silver wisely observed many years later, 'came to Jewry by way of anti-Semitism, not by way of Judaism.'[5] It was while Herzl was the Paris correspondent of Vienna's *Neue Freie Presse* that the Dreyfus case broke out. He was present in the court when Dreyfus was pronounced guilty (5 January 1895), and in the courtyard of the *École Militaire* to witness the ceremony of public degradation of Captain Dreyfus, the only Jew on the French Army's general staff.

It now dawned on Theodor Herzl that it was precisely the success of Jewish assimilation that fed the new anti-Semitism. Invited by Napoleon and his spiritual heirs to leave the ghetto and enter into the mainstream of life, to become citizens and disappear as a race, they had in the best of good faith taken giant strides down that path. Yet now when things went wrong – when banks failed or business slowed or agricultural prices were too high or too low, when disturbing ideas occurred in literature or in the political arena, or when disturbing scenes appeared on the stage – people concluded that invisible agents must be behind them. Assimilation meant allowing the Jews to become nearly invisible. Becoming nearly invisible had made them conspicuous. It had become necessary for citizens to seize the Jews by the collar before they disappeared altogether.

HERZL AND HECHLER: THEIR PARTNERSHIP BEGINS

Theodor Herzl was not a religious man:

> I consider religion indispensable for the weak. There are those who, weak in willpower, mind, or emotions, must always be able to rely on religion. The others, the normal run of mankind, are weak only in childhood and in old age; for them, religion serves as an educational instrument or a source of comfort ... God is a magnificent symbol for an enormous complex of moral and legal imperatives, the apparent solution to riddles, the answer to all childish questions.

Nevertheless he was a superstitious man.

Several times in recent days, before Hechler's appearance in his study, he had been struck by how opportunities suddenly opened up for him out of extraordinary coincidences, or, conversely, how a striking coincidence announced that he had missed an opportunity. To take an example from a few days after Hechler's visit, Herzl, having resisted for days the instinct to send a copy of his book to the Baron de Hirsch, is eventually struck by guilt for this neglect of the most powerful potential sponsor of his program. On an impulse, he dispatches a letter together with a copy of the book, only to find that he has acted too late. In his diary, under '21 April afternoon', we find:

> Between yesterday and today Baron Hirsch died on an estate in Hungary ... [W]hat a strange coincidence. This pamphlet has been finished for months. I give it to everyone except Hirsch. The minute I decide to do so, he dies. His participation might have helped our cause to succeed tremendously quickly.

Then, a few hours after the arrival of this news of Hirsch's death comes the news that William Hechler has won him an appointment with the Grand Duke of Baden. Somehow, Herzl knows that this is to be the first step on the road to diplomatic success. Under '21 April, at night', he records:

> I had intended to go to Pest tomorrow morning. Late this morning I received Hechler's call to come to Karlsruhe.
> A curious day. Hirsch dies, and I make contact with princes.
> Now begins a new book of the Jewish cause.

So, we have reason to believe that before he had undergone the exaltation of conceiving and writing his solution to the Jewish problem, and before he had begun to notice how all things seemed to work together so mysteriously for the good of the Jewish cause, Theodor Herzl would not have hesitated to show the door to such a man as William Hechler. That is certainly what any sensible man of Herzl's acquaintance would have done, but had he done so, it is possible to argue, there might never have been a World Zionist Organization, and consequently no Balfour Declaration, no Mandate, no Jewish State. For the fact is that the first political fruit of Herzl's diplomacy was made possible by this man, and without this first fruit, Herzl's program would have been discredited.

Of this initial encounter between Theodor Herzl and William Hechler it has been said:

> Herzl, the visionary, whose dreams had previously found little sustenance within the framework of existing Jewish philanthropists and relief organizations, suddenly discovered the possibility of becoming a *realpolitiker*; this was the pregnant moment when Zionism appeared in the arena of world politics and began to make an impact on world history.[6]

Herzl recorded the event in his diary:

10 March [1896]
The Rev William H. Hechler, chaplain to the British Embassy in Vienna, called on me.

A likeable, sensitive man with the long grey beard of a prophet, he waxed enthusiastic over my solution. He, too, regards my movement as a 'prophetic crisis' – one he foretold two years ago. For he had calculated in accordance with a prophecy dating from Omar's reign (637–638) that after 42 prophetical months, that is, 1,260 years, Palestine would be restored to the Jews. This would make it 1897–1898.

When he read my book, he immediately hurried to Ambassador Monson and told him: 'The fore-ordained movement is here!'

Hechler declares my movement to be a 'Biblical' one, even though I proceed rationally in all points.

He wants to place my tract in the hands of some German princes. He used to be a tutor in the household of the Grand Duke of Baden, he knows the German Kaiser and thinks he can get me an audience.

Hechler's account of the meeting is much more colorful, as we have already seen. In Herzl's subsequent accounts of his dealings with Hechler he abandons the scientific, detached tone. As Hechler passed one after another test of his actual ability to deliver what he promised, Herzl permitted himself to record more and more of the oddity of it all.

The superstitious side of Herzl responded to the magic in the scene. This man knew who Herzl was! Baron Hirsch, for all the similarities in their upbringing – not to mention the matter of their both being Jews – and for all the correspondence that Herzl had heaped upon him, did not truly know who Herzl was. Herzl was the one man in all the world to whom it would make sense that an English Protestant, the Chaplain of the British embassy in Vienna, should have been 'preparing the ground' for him. We can guess that it never occurred to Herzl to ask whether Hechler had ever introduced himself to anyone else in those words: 'Here I am!'

The Reverend William Hechler was a cultivated individual, a person of abundant gifts, well educated, who had held down responsible jobs. In fact, it was the history of his employment that he was now turning over to the service of Zion.

He had been tutor at the Court of the Grand Duke of Baden, and had left behind great goodwill in the family and the Court. (This was the same Grand Duke who had played the pivotal role in aligning the German Princes, so that they would declare in favor of inducing the King of Prussia to become their Kaiser in 1871.) The Grand Duke was married to the only daughter of the late Kaiser, Wilhelm I, and was thus the uncle of the present Kaiser, Wilhelm II. Hechler's Grand Ducal connection, combined with his role at the Embassy of Great Britain in Vienna, gave him extraordinary *entrée* into the highest circles – including the German Imperial Court.

For all of this, however, Herzl had, for now, only the word of this stranger, who was now offering to put everything to the service of Herzl and the restoration of the Jews to Zion; but first, he said, he needed money.

Was it to Herzl's credit that he gave the benefit of the doubt to such a stranger? The point is that in doing so he stepped well out past the limits of trust that a reasonable man would approve, but Herzl had that rarest kind of genius, the kind that recognizes what it does not need to know.

2

William Hechler's Vision

WILLIAM HENRY HECHLER (1845–1931)

William Henry Hechler was born 1 October 1845, in Benares, India. His missionary father, Dietrich,[1] had been born in 1812, in a village near Mullheim in the Grand Duchy of Baden. Raised in the United Evangelical Church, the state church of Baden, Dietrich was educated in the village school. Deeply affected by reading in a magazine the story of Adonirom Judson (1788–1850), the founder of American Protestant missions to Burma and India, he eventually went to the Missionary College in Basle, Switzerland, where he studied under the famous pietist teacher, Johannes Christoph Blumhardt. He was then sent by this Missionary College to an Anglican college in Islington, England, where he studied further, and was ordained in the Church of England in 1844. Shortly after that, he married Catherine Palmer. Now he was ready to fulfill his boyhood dream by sailing to India as a missionary.

After only a short time in India, however, Hechler's young wife died, and his own health declined. Returning on medical advice to England, he joined the London Society for the Promotion of Christianity Amongst the Jews in 1854. In his application for that assignment, Dietrich Hechler wrote that, as a boy, 'One of the wishes I had was that I might be a real descendant of Abraham. I entertained an almost superstitious reverence for Jews, and therefore disapproved of their being mocked or otherwise ill-treated by my schoolfellows.' Now, in 1852, he recalled an earlier conviction that he was meant to be a missionary to the Jews, on which he had, out of weakness, not acted, and so it seemed that, 'Now, the providence of God seems to me most clearly to point my steps to you [the London Jews Society].'

William Hechler, bilingual in English and German from childhood, was raised mainly in English orphanages during his father's absences, and was, like his father, a member of the Church of England. As a boy, he developed an enthusiasm for biblical history, archeology, and maps. He studied theology in London and then in Tübingen, the centre of the liberal-rationalist examination of scripture. Though as well educated as his fellow-clergy, he was not persuaded by the key arguments of the liberals and retained a distinctly creedal, doctrinal, even literalist theology. He served as a chaplain on the German side of the Franco-Prussian War of 1870–71. Then, he went off to be a teacher at Lagos, in the British colony of Nigeria (1871–74), but, like his father before him, he was invalided home from his mission field – in this case by malaria.

Returning to his father's native Baden, he became tutor to the young Prince Ludwig, the heir to the Grand Duke Frederick of Baden. It developed that William Hechler and the Grand Duke were closely attuned philosophically, and, more important, theologically. Quickly, the Grand Duke became interested in the mass of documentation – biblical texts and commentaries, maps, charts, detailed models of the Temple of the past and the Temple of the future – that Hechler was building up, in preparation for the pamphlet which appeared in 1893 (*The Restoration of the Jews to Palestine according to Prophecy*). At Hechler's behest, the Grand Duke built up a massive library of biblical eschatology, biblical history, and archeology. At the Grand Duke's request, Hechler presented sermons and scholarly papers on these themes before the Court and its visitors.

THE PROTESTANT BISHOPRIC OF JERUSALEM

In the years of William Hechler's boyhood and youth – that is, during the generation prior to the formation of the German Empire in 1871 – the Kingdom of Prussia and the United Kingdom were warm partners in the Holy Land. Between 1841 and 1883, their two State churches – the Church of England and the United Evangelical Church of Prussia – shared a single bishopric in Jerusalem, the only Protestant activity countenanced by the Ottoman Empire. This extraordinary project seems to have originated with Christian Carl Josias Bunsen, a Prussian diplomat and churchman, formerly head of the Prussian legation to the Holy See, and married since 1817 to an Englishwoman, Frances Weddington. When he learned that Her Majesty's Government had acquired the unprecedented right to build a Protestant church and operate schools and the whole missionary apparatus in Jerusalem, he was immediately convinced that God had given Great Britain responsibility for the Restoration of the Jews – to be Cyrus *redivivus*. In a letter to William Gladstone, 3 August 1840, Bunsen wrote: 'It is surely impossible not to see the finger of God in the foundation of an English church and a congregation of Christian proselytes on the sacred hill of Jerusalem.'

Bunsen reported these convictions to his King, Frederick William of

Prussia (reigned, 1840–61), another devout evangelical Christian; and he shared with him his dream that the Prussian Church (the same United Evangelical Church in which Dietrich Hechler had been raised in Baden) should become 'the starting point of a worldwide union in which all evangelical Christians at least would be as one, without prejudice to their particular disciplines and liturgies'.[2] Both men sought the conversion of the Jews and their restoration to Israel. Both saw in their Prussian state church (an amalgam of the Calvinist and Lutheran traditions) a pioneer of a new sort of ecumenical Protestant Christianity.

In 1841, the Prussian King sent the Baron Bunsen to England, to propose to the British government the establishment of an Anglican bishopric for Jerusalem, funded in part by Britain and in part by Prussia, with British and Prussian appointees alternating as Bishop, and with all the participating Prussian clergy, including the Bishop, entering, for the purpose, into Anglican orders, and coming under the authority of the Church of England. Out of this would come a national church in Palestine, distinctively Hebrew in language and rituals, but otherwise modeled on evangelical Anglicanism, having the full political support of Prussia as well as England.

As it happened, Bunsen was already well acquainted with the individual best situated to promote this project. This was Anthony Ashley Cooper, seventh Earl of Shaftesbury (1801–85). A member of one of the most privileged of Britain's privileged families, a Tory member of the Commons virtually by right of birth, and then, on his accession to the title, a member of the Lords. He was the nephew-in-law of William Lamb, Lord Melbourne (Prime Minister through most of the period from 1834–41), and the stepson-in-law of Henry Temple, Lord Palmerston (Foreign Minister for most of the 1840s and early 1850s, and then Prime Minister for most of the period 1855–65).

The seventh Earl of Shaftesbury is properly remembered today as the man at the centre of the evangelical (or 'philanthropic') empire of the Early Victorian years – the author of laws for the alleviation of the lot of the workingman, the unprivileged, and the disadvantaged. Less well remembered than the social philosophy of this circle was its philosophy of history and the principles of diplomacy that followed from it. In her discussion of Shaftesbury in her book, *The Bible and the Sword*, Barbara Tuchman provides a check list of Shaftesbury's accomplishments on behalf of the weak – prison reform, criminal law reform, legislation to protect children, the insane, workers, extensions of religious freedom. Then, as if turning to answer the reader's question, 'What has all this to do with Palestine?' she replies: 'The point is that Lord Shaftesbury's zeal for "God's ancient people", as he always styled the Jews, was the outcome of this same entire acceptance of the Bible that had made him a philanthropist.'[3] Shaftesbury and the circle

that he dominated lived in expectation of the End of Times, which they
believed would be immediately preceded by the literal return of the Jews
to their homeland. Biblical literalism, moral earnestness, Christian
philanthropy, and philo-Semitism were all parts of this seamless creed:

> For now the pendulum had swung back again, after the Hellenic interlude
> of the eighteenth century, to the moral earnestness of another Hebraic period.
> Eighteenth-century skepticism had given way to Victorian piety, eighteenth-
> century rationalism was again surrendering to Revelation ... Whenever
> Christians returned to the authority of the Old Testament they found it
> prophesying the return of its people to Jerusalem and felt themselves duty-
> bound to assist the prophecy.[4]

Lord Palmerston, while he certainly showed no signs of converting to the
new religious spirit, confessed that he admired the character of his stepson-
in-law. More than that, he recognized the powerful hold of his views upon
a large part of the public. Thus, he was frequently willing to accede to
Shaftesbury's views on large public issues.

Together, Shaftesbury and Bunsen laid the groundwork for the agreement between the two governments, Shaftesbury acting for Bunsen as
intermediary with the Archbishop of Canterbury, with Prime Minister
Palmerston, and then with Prime Minister Peel, whose Tory government
(1841–46) took over during that year. The purposes of the bishopric,
Shaftesbury wrote, would be both 'political and religious ... a combination
of Protestant thrones, bound by temporal interests and eternal principles,
to plant under the banner of the Cross, God's people on the mountains of
Jerusalem.'

After the necessary Bill was passed through Parliament, in October,
1841, Shaftesbury was given the honour of choosing the first bishop, and
came up with Michael Solomon Alexander, an immigrant from Russian
Poland, a former rabbi, converted in 1925, and now a missionary of the Jews
Society and a Professor in Hebrew at King's College, London. After
Alexander's consecration to the post, in a ceremony at Lambeth Palace, the
residence of the Archbishop of Canterbury, Shaftesbury wrote in his diary:

> The whole thing was wonderful, and to those who have long labored and
> prayed in the Jewish cause, nearly overwhelming to see a native Hebrew
> appointed, under God, to revive the Episcopate of St James, and carry back
> to the Holy City, the truths and blessings we Gentiles had received from it.[5]

And again, on 25 October:

> Had I not been almost accustomed, so to speak, to God's mercies, I should
> have disbelieved it. 'Surely the Isles shall wait for thee and the ships of
> Tarshish first, to bring thy sons from afar and thy daughters from the ends
> of the earth.' [Quoting Isaiah 60:9][6]

Bishop Alexander's mission was not covered in success, however. He was forbidden by the understanding with the Sultan to make converts among any of the population except the Jews; and the Jews were not very responsive. When Shaftesbury heard of the Bishop's sudden death in 1845, he wrote that 'it buries at once half my hopes for the speedy welfare of our Church, our nation, and the children of Israel!' In fact, he briefly wondered whether the whole plan 'was amiss, and not according to God's wisdom and pleasure', an impious effort to determine 'the times and the seasons which the Father has put in His own power.' He wondered: 'Have we conceived a merely human project and then imagined it to be a decree of the Almighty?'[7]

Eventually, however, he rose above these doubts.

Thus, it all made good sense that, when a vacancy occurred in the joint-bishopric in 1883, William Hechler's name was among those proposed for the post. Only a few months earlier, Hechler had produced a book on *The Jerusalem Bishopric* on commission from the London Society for Promotion of Christianity Amongst the Jews, but in the meanwhile Imperial Germany had become convinced that it had outgrown the joint Prussian–Anglican bishopric, among many other inventions of this happy period of British–Prussian goodwill. After some forty years, few converts had been won among the Jews. On the other hand, there was by now a substantial German colony in and around the city, and to serve these the Kaiser's Government now planned to build a new Lutheran church, in the heart of the city, near the Holy Sepulchre.

Hechler was greatly disappointed by the failure of the joint-bishopric; to him, it had been a precious proof of the ability of the Germans and the English to work together in the largest purposes. This was the very heart of his vision for the future of the Jews: his faith that commitment to the promises of God would overwhelm the tribal differences between Prussians and Englishmen, Lutherans and Anglicans. Had he become Bishop of Jerusalem, he would have toned down the policy of seeking conversions among the Jews. Keenly philo-Semitic like his father, he had the twofold purpose of bringing Christians to an understanding that their faith required them to work for the restoration of the Jews to *Eretz Israel*, and of bringing Jews back to their own faith. In a letter to a pastor/missionary in Jerusalem, 1898, Hechler wrote:

> Of course, dear colleague, you look to the conversion of the Jews, but the times are changing rapidly, and it is important for us to look further and higher. We are now entering, thanks to the Zionist Movement, into Israel's Messianic age. Thus, it is not a matter these days of opening all the doors of your churches to the Jews, but rather of opening the gates of their homeland, and of sustaining them in their work of clearing the land, and irrigating it,

and bringing water to it. All of this, dear colleague, is messianic work; all of this the breath of the Holy Spirit announces. But first, the dry bones must come to life, and draw together.[8]

After the sudden death of the Crown Prince Ludwig (1876), Hechler had left the Court of Baden, still very much beloved by all the Grand Ducal family. He served for some years a parish in Ireland, but was back in England when news came of the assassination of Czar Alexander II, and of the terrible pogroms that followed. There he joined with Lord Shaftesbury and others in forming a committee to raise money for the resettlement of Jewish refugees in Palestine. The committee despatched Hechler to Russia to investigate the situation. There he was much impressed by enthusiasm for Zion among Russian Jews. In Odessa, Hechler met Leon Pinsker, and read his just-published *Autoemancipation*. On one crucial point he quarrelled with Pinsker: namely, the latter's willingness to consider some place other than *Eretz Israel* as the homeland for the Jews. As Hechler told it, he took out his Bible and found the passages in Amos, Jeremiah, and Isaiah, and elsewhere that made clear God's plan to bring the diaspora to Jerusalem. Hechler believed that he left Pinsker persuaded. However that may be, we do know that some three years later Pinsker became the President of *Hohevei Zion*, committed to the work of colonization of the Jews of Russia in Palestine.

After his visit to Russia in 1882, Hechler kept up his irenic dialogue with the rabbis, calling them to the support of Zionism, as a requirement of their own faith. He has been credited with winning many observant Jews to Zionism, and with bringing secular Zionists back to Judaism.

HERZL VISITS HECHLER

During the course of that first encounter in Herzl's office, Hechler invited Herzl to his own lodgings where he could show him the research which had led him to Herzl's door. Herzl recorded that second interview in abundant detail:

March 16
Yesterday, Sunday afternoon, I visited the Rev Hechler … He lives on the fourth floor; his windows overlook the Schillerplatz. Even while I was going up the stairs I heard the sound of an organ. The room which I entered was lined with books on every side, floor to ceiling. Nothing but Bibles.

A window of the very bright room was open, letting in the cool spring air, and Mr Hechler showed me his biblical treasures. Then he spread out before me his chart of comparative history, and finally a map of Palestine. It is a large military staff map in four sheets which, when laid out, covered the entire floor … He showed me where, according to his calculations, our new

Temple must be located: in Bethel! Because that is the center of the country. He also showed me models of the ancient Temple: 'We have prepared the ground for you.'

We should linger a bit over this scene. Much that will prove typical of the connection between the political Zionists and the Christian Zionists is here. This is the founder of modern Zionism, the secular prophet of the state of Israel. His manifesto has barely gone out into the world, and already there is so much response to it that he cannot get his bearings. How could he justify the time he is spending down on all fours in the apartment of this Protestant preacher, poring over army maps in search of the right place for building the Temple, listening politely to newly minted hymns in praise of Zion, sung to his own organ accompaniment by the composer?

Herzl's sense – which turns out, against all reason, to be right – is that this eccentric Christian has what it will take to lead him to the Princes:

> Afterwards we came to the heart of the matter. I told him that I have got to establish direct contact, a contact that is discernible on the outside, with a responsible or non-responsible statesman – that is, with a minister of state or a prince. Then the Jews will believe in me, then they will follow me. The most suitable man would be the German Kaiser ... Hechler immediately declared that he was ready to go to Berlin and speak with the Court Chaplain as well as with Prince Günther and Prince Heinrich. Would I be willing to give him the travel expenses?
>
> Of course I promised them to him at once ... At the same time I fully realize that Hechler, whom I don't know yet, may only be a penniless clergyman who likes to travel, and that he may come back with the words that it was impossible to get to the Kaiser ... He is an improbable figure when looked at through the quizzical eyes of a Viennese Jewish journalist. but I have to imagine that those who are antithetical to us in every way view him quite differently. So I am sending him to Berlin with the mental reservation that I am not his dupe if he merely wants to take a trip at my expense ... He considers our departure for Jerusalem to be quite imminent, and showed me the coat pocket in which he will carry his big map of Palestine when we shall be riding around the Holy Land together. That was his most ingenuous and most convincing touch yesterday.

A few days later, Hechler appeared in Herzl's study to report that he had spoken to his contacts in the Kaiser's retinue. He had told them all about Herzl's pamphlet, and his own conviction that this is a sign that 'the time had come "to fulfil prophecy"'. Now he was going back to the Grand Duke to begin to work out the details for Herzl's interview with the Grand Duke and with the Kaiser! Then, 'Hechler asked me for my photograph in order to show it to the gentlemen: he apparently thinks that they would picture me as a "shabby Jew". I promised to give him a photo tomorrow.'

As it happens, on that very day – more wonderful coincidence! – the

Kaiser is actually in Vienna on a visit. This is an opportunity for Herzl, using his skills as a theater critic, to study the Kaiser from a distance, and rehearse in his own mind how he will put to the best effect the interview which Hechler (so improbably) has pledged to arrange. So,

> I went to the opera, sat in a box diagonally across from the imperial box, and all evening studied the motions of the German Kaiser. He sat there stiffly, sometimes bent affably to our Emperor [Francis Joseph II of Austria], laughed heartily a number of times, and in general was not unconcerned about the impression he was making on the audience ... I came home at eleven o'clock. Hechler had been sitting in the hall for an hour waiting for me. He wants to leave for Karlsruhe at seven in the morning.
> He sat with me until half-past twelve making gentle conversation. His refrain: fulfill prophecy!
> He firmly believes in it.

KAISER WILLIAM II

In his memoir of his childhood, the ex-Kaiser William notes his special affection for his aunt and uncle, the Grand Duchess and the Grand Duke of Baden: 'Of Emperor William I's circle, the now deceased Grand Duchess Louise of Baden, the Emperor's only daughter, stood closest to me ... She was an unusual woman, deeply religious, firm in the Protestant faith, but thoroughly tolerant ... Her husband, the Grand Duke Frederick, stood none the less close to me. With his wise counsel and his sustaining encouragement, he was always a fatherly friend.'[9]

William's own religious faith seems to have been both authentic and conventional.[10] (This is not always a contradiction.) There are countless remarks throughout the memoirs on his confidence in Providence. He speaks of the day of his confirmation as 'a great spiritual experience':

> The confession of faith which I pronounced was for me a sacred vow. The ceremony took place on 1st September in the Friedenskirche, and was exceptionally impressive ... My grandmother, the Queen of England, sent the Prince of Wales, who after the ceremony received the Holy Sacrament together with my parents and myself. The ceremony, which moved me very much, is a lasting memory.[11]

Years later, there was to be another even more extraordinary scene, combining these same dramatic elements. In the first days of January 1901, the Kaiser learned that the Queen was dying. Ironically, when the word came he was in the midst of a public occasion chosen for the announcement of his imperial resolve to press on with expansion of the German Navy – the matter which was bound to doom British–German relations. The advice of his Ministers was not to go, as German opinion was then running powerfully against Britain, on account of the Boer war and a diplomatic clash over their spheres of influence in China, but William was determined to carry out his duty as a grandson: 'I have duly informed the Prince of Wales, begging him at the same time that no notice whatever is to be taken of me in my capacity as Emperor and that I come as a grandson.'[12]

Arriving in her last hours, he impressed all in the British court with his earnest and thoughtful manner. He knelt by his mother's side at his grandmother's deathbed. It was he who assisted his Uncle Bertie, the new King, in lifting the body into the coffin. When the King then departed for London for an Accession Council, he requested his nephew to take charge at Osborne. An astonishing moment this: the Kaiser of Germany, interim master of the household of the King-Emperor of Great Britain!

In February 1906, when Britain and Germany sternly confronted each other at the Algeciras Conference, William wrote to his uncle, 'Let us rather remember the silent hour when we watched and prayed at her bedside, when the spirit of that great sovereign lady passed away as she drew her last breath in my arms.'[13]

Scenes like these, which showed the principal figures in the interlocked royal families of Britain and Germany, united in bonds of family, sharing religious celebrations and consolations, spoke powerfully to William Hechler. He was a man of simple piety, but not a naive man. He knew, much better than Theodor Herzl (whom we have just seen trying to peer from out of a crowd into the human reality behind the facade of the Emperor's public appearance) that the Princes of the world, as Herzl had put it in his diary, really were just 'helpless human being[s]'. Their Christian faith and their Christian practice were, Hechler knew at first hand, no better than ordinary, but taking them all in all, he believed that they had been well prepared to grasp the possibilities for putting service to the Kingdom of God ahead of the shorter-term worldly kingdoms that God had given them.

William Hechler belonged to Germany, and he belonged to Great Britain, but before anything he belonged to the Church of Jesus Christ. If Hechler could secure the co-operation of the British and the Germans in this project of Dr Herzl's, he would have vindicated everything that was unique and remarkable in his personal history. It could surely not be for nothing that his German father had sought out and won his English mother; that he himself had been born of these exemplars of ecumenical Protestantism in a faraway mission field; that God had opened up along his way so many extraordinary opportunities for service to both English and German Christians on three continents; that he had been led into the household of a German Prince who was uncommonly sympathetic to his prophetic theology, uniquely situated to influence, on behalf of this same prophetic theology, the Kaiser of Germany – himself the product of exactly

the same background as Hechler – the same mixed blood, the same sort of
sentimental associations, the same intellectual elements!

WILLIAM HECHLER AND THE GRAND DUKE OF BADEN

True to his word to Herzl at their first meeting, Hechler had written a long
letter in English to the Grand Duke of Baden, 26 March 1896:

> May it Please Your Royal Highness,
>   May I venture to draw Your Royal Highness' attention to a very remarkable
> book, which has lately appeared in Vienna, and treats of a subject on which
> I have repeatedly had the honour of speaking to you. I mean the return of
> the Jews to Palestine, foretold by the Hebrew Prophets ... After reading this
> book I called to see Dr Herzl, who was a perfect stranger to me, because I
> was wondering whether the doctor was trying to fulfill prophecy. This would
> be wrong, for God will in His own good time and in His own way bring about
> His wonderful purposes. This was however not Dr Herzl's wish, for he knew
> nothing of the special prophecies on this subject ... With many students of
> prophecy, who can never be anti-Semites, I have for years believed that the
> so-called anti-Semitic movement is the 'woe of Judah', also foretold by the
> prophets of old, which is making the Jews see that they are Jews first, and
> secondly Germans, English, etc., and that this is now creating a longing in
> their hearts to return as a nation to the Land of Promise, given by God to
> Abraham and his children. Is it not also a most remarkable fact that, although
> not long ago there were only about 15 to 20,000 Jews in Palestine, it is now
> reported that there are about 100,000 Jews in the Land of their Fathers?
> Palestine belongs to them by right, for it is the only country in the world, of
> which God has Himself said to whom it is to belong. What startling facts!
> It seems therefore, that the last return of the Jews to Palestine has already
> begun ... It seems that in about a year or two this most remarkable prophecy
> of the angel to St John [Revelation 11:2: '... the Gentiles will tread the holy
> city under foot for forty-two months'] will be fulfilled, and that the Land of
> Promise will then again belong to the people to whom God gave it about 1895
> years before Christ, for this is the biblical date of the birth of Isaac, the first
> Jew born into this world, and he was the son of promise.
>   Knowing the above, Your Royal Highness will easily understand how
> astonished I was after reading this book, written by a well-educated and rich
> Jew, for it is the first serious, quiet and practical attempt to show the Jews
> how they can re-unite and form a nation of their own in the Land of Promise
> given them by God.
>   I cannot help thinking, that if Germany and England were to take this
> movement and such a new state under their protection, and Palestine were
> declared to be a neutral country, something like Belgium, the Return of the
> Jews would become a great blessing to Europe, and put an end to the anti-
> Semitic spirit of hatred, which is most detrimental to the welfare of all our
> nations ... I am sending Your Royal Highness three copies of this book.[14]

A few days later, Hechler returned to Herzl with a progress report. Then, with Herzl's photograph and more of Herzl's money to pay for his expenses, he was off again for Karlsruhe, Baden's capital, where, he told Herzl, he would meet with the Grand Duke and the Kaiser.

THEODOR HERZL AND THE GRAND DUKE OF BADEN

On this occasion, according to Herzl:

> Hechler showed the Grand Duke the 'prophetic tables' which seemed to make an impression.
>
> When the Kaiser arrived, the Grand Duke immediately informed him of the matter. Hechler was invited to the reception, and to the surprise of the court-assembly the Kaiser addressed him with the jocular words: 'Hechler, I hear you want to become a minister of the Jewish State ... Isn't Rothschild behind this?'

Hechler was upset by this, the Kaiser's first response to the proposal that he was offering for His Imperial Majesty's serious attention. Either the Kaiser was not taking this matter seriously, or he was receiving entirely erroneous information about Hechler, his background, and his possible motives. In a letter to the Grand Duke, dated 18 April, Hechler confessed his distress:

> Owing to the most gracious words of His Imperial Majesty the Emperor to me last evening I am greatly troubled in mind, for I have nothing to do with the New Jewish State, as I have no Jewish blood in me, for I am a mixture of pure Schwarzwald and Great Britain; nor have I ever spoken to Baron Rothschild on Dr Herzl's book.
>
> Simply because I have seen for years that, according to God's Holy Word, we are near a Great Prophetical Crisis, have I ventured to write to Your Royal Highness and Lord Salisbury [Prime Minister of Great Britain], besides speaking with my Ambassador, Sir Edmund J. Monson, to unburden my mind and show the wonderful light God is now graciously giving us, as to Daniel of old in Babylon through the Prophets ... The Jewish State is a most serious question as it may be fulfilled in 1897 or 1898, for come it must according to the Prophets and most certainly it will become a great blessing to the whole world. Knowing all this, would it not have been wrong of me to be silent?[15]

Thus, as regards the hope of engaging the Kaiser as the Protector of Zion: 'So far', Herzl concludes, 'the results have been rather meager.'

Then came the astonishing word that Herzl and Hechler both were summoned to an audience with the Archduke.

As they paced the grounds of the Grand Duke's palace, awaiting their interview,

I said to Hechler: 'Remember this fine day, the lovely spring skies over Karlsruhe! Perhaps a year from today we shall be in Jerusalem.' Hechler said he planned to ask the Grand Duke to accompany the Kaiser when the latter went to Jerusalem next year for the consecration of the church. I should also be present then, and he, Hechler, would like to go along as a technical adviser to the Grand Duke. I said: 'When I go to Jerusalem, I will take you with me.'

Everything went extremely well. Herzl was greatly impressed with the Grand Duke, and guessed (correctly) that the Grand Duke was greatly impressed with him. 'I presented the entire plan, which he had actually known only in Hechler's version – that is, in its "prophetic" aspects, which, of course, I don't have much to do with.' In addition to repeating his undertaking to keep the Kaiser interested, the Grand Duke gave his permission for Herzl 'to tell a few trustworthy men in England that the Grand Duke of Baden takes an interest in the matter'. This then led to consideration of the future of the Ottoman Empire. If England and Germany were to act together, Herzl hinted, the thing could even be done without the approval of the Ottoman Empire: 'If Turkey were partitioned in the foreseeable future, a buffer state could be created in Palestine. However, it would be better to think in terms of making the Sultan see the advantages for the continuation of his régime.' This led to speculation about Russia's ambitions in the area. The Grand Duke undertook to try to get Herzl's book into the hands of the Czar. The interview had been an unqualified success.

> What modesty and plain dealing, all around! ... He [the Grand Duke] is of a grand, noble naturalness ... When Hechler took the floor ... and discoursed on the imminent fulfillment of prophecy, the Grand Duke listened silently, magnificently, and full of faith, with a striking, peaceful look in his fine, steady eyes ... I was slightly intoxicated with the success of our conference. I could only say to Hechler, 'He is a wonderful person!'

In the Herzl Museum on Mount Herzl in Jerusalem, the dominating exhibit is the reconstructed study of Herzl's study in Vienna, and there today, hanging directly above Herzl's chair, is the portrait of the Grand Duke of Baden, as it did in the original study ever after the day we have just described.

HERZL AND HECHLER: THEIR FRIENDSHIP DEVELOPS

On the train, as they returned to Vienna,

> [Hechler] unfolded his maps of Palestine and instructed me for hours on end. The northern frontier ought to be the mountains facing Cappadocia, the southern, the Suez Canal. The slogan to be circulated: The Palestine of David and Solomon!

Hechler talked constantly about the Jews and his experiences with Jews, and seemed always to be at pains to parade his philo-Semitism. But sometimes he took the liberty of generalizing about Jewish character in a way that, maybe, Herzl thought, bespoke a certain residual anti-Semitism.

> This man Hechler is, at all events, a peculiar and complex person. There is much pedantry, exaggerated humility, pious eye-rolling about him – but he also gives me excellent advice full of unmistakably genuine goodwill. He is at once clever and mystical, cunning and naive. In his dealings with me so far, he has supported me almost miraculously.
>
> His counsel and his precepts have been excellent to date, and unless it turns out later, somehow or other, that he is a double dealer, I would want the Jews to show him a full measure of gratitude.

Everything about Hechler powerfully affected Herzl. Travelling back to Vienna, Hechler goes on and on about all that must follow, as prophecy is fulfilled. Herzl listens with greater patience than he had shown on that earlier occasion, in Hechler's apartment. Is it possible that, in spite of himself, he is being caught up in Hechler's visions? Is it permissible to guess that he held up his own end of the conversation during that long train ride back to Vienna with some vision-spinning of his own? After all, here he was locked up in the company of perhaps the only man of his acquaintance who would have listened with sympathy if Herzl were to divulge out loud the fantasies we have found in his diary regarding the Temple, the Priests, the rituals that would surround the Jewish 'Doge'.

He grew to trust Hechler more and more. Indeed, frequently, for brief but crucial periods, he virtually entrusted the whole Zionist enterprize to William Hechler, and, though Hechler frequently annoyed and embarrassed him, he never failed him. Biographers of Herzl and historians of Zionism are unanimous in this: he is 'a devoted ally since Herzl's earliest Zionist career' (Sachar);[16] he is 'his first and most loyal follower';[17] he is 'Herzl's Elijah' (Max Bodenheimer).[18]

The Reverend William Hechler was the living embodiment of the path Herzl had not taken – the path of pious faith:

> Of all the people who have been drawn to me by the 'movement', the Rev Hechler is the finest and most fanciful ... He frequently writes me postcards, for no particular reason, telling me that he hasn't been able to sleep the previous night because Jerusalem came into his mind.

From their first moments together, William Hechler had treated him as the most extraordinary man alive. Hechler was the only man Herzl dealt with in those days who looked him in the eye and told him that he was probably underestimating himself!

If Herzl ever told Hechler what he told Brainin – about his dream-encounter with the Messiah (and perhaps he did), Hechler must have urged him to accept the true meaning of the dream, not to hide behind silly 'explanations'. The Messiah was not calling him to be an engineer!

In one diary entry, Herzl registers his suspicion that Hechler hopes to convert him, then to see him used as an instrument for the conversion of the Jewish people, but Herzl was wrong about this. For literalist eschatologists of Hechler's school, the return of the Children of Israel 'in unbelief' was a condition of the inauguration of the last times. Conversion of the Jewish people would follow, not precede, the restoration. Hechler was under no call to convert Herzl to Christianity.

Again and again over the years to follow, Herzl's critics (as, after him, the critics of Chaim Weizmann, Louis Brandeis and Stephen Wise) would seek to cut him down with the same Biblical quotation: 'Put not your trust in Princes!' [*Al tivtechu bi-neddivim*]. Above everything, a Jewish leader ought not to be giving his best energies to the cultivation of Christian zealots – zealots of the very kind that their own coreligionists dismiss as 'fundamentalists', 'End-Times' pamphleteers, who are an embarrassment to their own people!

In the years that followed Herzl's establishment of World Zionism, modern 'political' Zionists were embarrassingly aware of the fact that what they were proposing as a practical or 'scientific' solution to the 'Jewish Question' would be understood by their own pious Jewish brethren as the very plan that the Lord had proposed in the books of the prophets and which He will accomplish at the End of Days – not through human agency but through the agency of the Messiah. What excuse was there, then, for Jewish intellectuals to take seriously and to give encouragement to the Christian counterparts of the Jewish chiliasts to whom they would not give the time of day? Were they so concerned to find friendly Christians to fawn upon that they had to stoop to the bottom of the Christians' own peckingorder to find them?

Herzl shared fully the liberal intellectual's hostility towards religious enthusiasm, but he had come to see himself as an inordinately inspired mortal. This self-discovery opened him to the challenge of responding to other men who are clearly moving under equally extraordinary inspiration – especially when an immediate consequence of their inspiration is to lead them to him!

As his labours on behalf of Zion took him further and further afield from the world in which he was raised, Theodor Herzl would encounter extraordinary confirmations of his own extraordinary gifts. Wonderworking rabbis in Poland would proclaim him. He would live to hear himself greeted as king of the Jews by joyous crowds of eastern European Jews! William Hechler presented Theodor Herzl with his earliest opportunity to confront the fact of his possession by the vision of the restoration of the Jews, and to seek the meaning of the extraordinary powers that this seemed to bring to him – all of this under the cover of his practical work on behalf of the cause, and in the company of a spokesman for the Christian faith, which could not raise a claim to him as Judaism could.

As for Hechler, the promised devotion of his energies and resources to Herzl's cause began that first day of their acquaintance, and never let up for the duration of Herzl's life. When it came time to mark the twenty-fifth anniversary of the death of Theodor Herzl, it was noted by the editors of the English-language memorial volume that William Hechler would prove to be 'not only the first, but the most constant and the most indefatigable of Herzl's followers'.

3

Hechler, Herzl and the Kaiser

On that day in April 1896, when Herzl and Hechler together had discussed their project face to face with the Grand Duke, Herzl had opened up the question of the part to be played by the Sultan. Looking the Grand Duke in the eye, and with Hechler listening intently at his side, Herzl had proposed that Istanbul would have no choice but to accede to their plan.

And so, almost immediately after completing his interview with the Grand Duke, he headed off to deal directly with the Sultan. This was in June, 1896.

To make a long and painful story short: there would be five trips to Istanbul: June 1896; October 1898; May 1901; February 1902; and June 1902. The Sultan was mainly interested in using Herzl's connections with Jewish bankers to get him loans. Herzl had to pretend to have connections with Jewish bankers. Each strung the other out for six years or so, Herzl pretending to be just on the verge of tying up the loose ends of some gigantic loan, but needing a public statement from the Sultan welcoming the Jews of Russia, rescinding all the laws which restricted the rights of Jews to hold land and conduct business, and providing protection against the hostile Moslems – and the Sultan pretending to be ready to do all those things, but not right this week.

The remaining months of 1896 were dreadfully disappointing to Herzl. No further movement was reported from the Court of the Sultan. No response came from the Imperial Court of the Czar to messages which the Russian Ambassador at Istanbul had faithfully pledged to forward there. Nothing came from a letter which Hechler had undertaken to convey to the British Prime Minister, Lord Salisbury. The bankers would not talk to him, and there was nothing new reported from Karlsruhe.

In the meantime, however, Hechler had not let up on his side of the work. On 3 September 1896, he wrote to the Grand Duke of Baden to wish

him a happy seventieth birthday, taking the opportunity 'to report on what
has happened since I was at Carlsruhe', and to replenish the Grand Duke's
supply of his pamphlet on 'The Restoration of the Jews'. He had had several
opportunities since April to deliver lectures on the themes of that pamphlet
before audiences of German and Austrian Princes, where he had found 'a
great interest in the question, "What shall we do with the Jews?"'

> All that this remarkable movement now requires is the public recognition
> and protection of the Sovereigns of Europe. Is this not now possible, after
> the question has been so earnestly taken up by the Jews themselves? History
> repeats itself, and so now also, as at the time of the first Return of the Jews
> from Babylon, the millions of believing orthodox Jews wish to return and
> the money is forthcoming, but some of the rich unbelieving Jews are still
> holding back. However I am sure that they will also join as soon as the Jewish
> State is successful, which it must be according to the Bible, for the Jews are
> then to be a blessing to the nations ... If I could only persuade every one to
> read Dr Herzl's *Judenstaat* and see how wonderfully it agrees with the Bible
> prophecies, and he wrote it without knowing it himself.[1]

As the new year of 1897 began, both Herzl and Hechler had reached the
end of their tethers. Hechler had nothing to show for his approach to the
Christian Princes. Herzl had nothing to show for his approach to the Sultan,
and nothing to show for his approach to the bankers. In this situation, Herzl,
with Hechler in total agreement, now turned his energies to a new project:
the calling of a World Congress of Zionists.

We will not retell here the story of the first Congress – but will only note
that Hechler was conspicuously present – one of three Christians invited
as observers, sitting among the two hundred and four founding delegates.
Afterwards, Herzl summed up its meaning with preternatural accuracy: 'In
Basle I founded the Jewish state. If I were to say this out loud today,
everybody would laugh at me. In five years, perhaps, but certainly in fifty,
everybody will agree.' (The Jewish state, we recall, was founded, fifty years
and a few months later.)

Hechler shared Herzl's enthusiasm for the project, and was often at his
side. En route to the Congress he had written to the Grand Duke: 'It is
simply marvellous how the Zionisten movement [*sic*] has spread in one year
all over the whole world, in spite of the opposition of some of the rich Jews,
who care but very little for the glorious history of their ancestors and still
less, at least most of them, for Jehovah, the God of Abraham, Isaac, and
Jacob, and therefore know nothing of the gracious promises made by God
through His prophets to the Jews of to-day.' He promised to report back
to the Grand Duke.[2]

Back in Vienna, Herzl learned that the Grand Duke of Baden was
expecting a visit from his nephew, the Kaiser. This prompted a letter to the

Grand Duke, enclosing a letter which he asks him to convey to the Kaiser:
'May God, who has set the princes so far above the other people and
enlightens them, be with my truly serious request.'[3] The enclosed letter for
the Kaiser sums up grandly the results of the recent 'Congress of Jews'. It
was called to meet the challenge of Herzl's book (*The Jewish State*); there
were 204 representatives 'from all countries'; they elected Herzl chairman
and adopted a program, of which the chief point is 'the creation of a publicly
and legally safeguarded home for those Jews who cannot or will not
assimilate in their present places of residence'. We know, from other sources,
that the Kaiser had already received a report of the proceedings from his
agents at the Congress, in the margin of which the Kaiser wrote: 'Let the
kikes go to Palestine, the sooner the better. I am not about to put obstacles
in their way.'[4] Herzl, too, reported to the Kaiser that there had been a favour-
able response to the Congress already appearing in influential journals in
the English-speaking world, concluding: 'Whenever and wherever Your
Majesty may summon me for an audience, I shall be at hand without delay.'

A few weeks later, the Grand Duke reported to Herzl that the Kaiser
had requested a fuller description of the Basle Congress, and this Herzl
quickly provided. At last there were signs that the Grand Duke's genteel
lobbying was beginning to succeed.

The Second World Zionist Congress was held at the Basle Municipal
Casino. Observers could see with the naked eye the spectacular results of a
single year of propaganda and organization. Nearly 800 new chapters had
been added to the 117 which had existed in the previous August. Of these
new chapters, 373 were from Russia, and 50 from the United States.
Immediately following the Congress, Herzl and Hechler went together
(2 September 1898) to report to the Grand Duke, who was at his summer
place on Lake Constance.

The Grand Duke had thrilling news for them: the Kaiser had instructed
Count Philipp Eulenburg, his ambassador to Austria (whose intimate
friendship with the Kaiser, some said, made him the most powerful of his
advisors), to hear Herzl's proposals, and report directly to him. The Grand
Duke knew that enquiries were already being made in Istanbul about the
Sultan's attitude toward the idea of some accommodation to the Zionists'
program. Relations were very good between the Kaiser and the Sultan, and
much was expected of a visit to the Ottoman Empire which the Kaiser was
planning to take very soon.

> The Grand Duke conversed with me in the most candid manner about all
> of world politics ... Hechler occasionally broke in with prophetic remarks
> about *the return of the Jews* [English in the original.] The grand Duke listened
> to him with a benign smile, but nodded approval to me when I said:
> 'Such things are beyond my judgement. I can only speak of what I see.'

At this the Grand Duke said: 'Yes, let us consider the matter only as a world-historical matter and not as a theological one.'

The interview with Eulenburg took place on 16 September 1898. In preparation for their discussion, Hechler had set up in a small salon of the German Embassy in Vienna what Herzl describes as 'a Palestine museum', featuring his now-familiar charts, temple models, and plaster casts of ancient relics. Herzl felt that he himself 'made the strongest impression on him when he raised the possibility of England's adoption of the project if Germany should fail to do so'. The mention of England, Herzl guessed, is what did the trick: Eulenburg immediately set up an interview for Herzl with von Bülow, the Foreign Secretary (who became the Chancellor in 1900). The upshot was that Bülow joined Eulenburg in recommending to the Kaiser that he stage some kind of meeting with Herzl, the leader of the World Jewish Congress, during his visit to Palestine, and that he explore with the Sultan the viability of the Zionist program. Herzl was in the Netherlands, en route to London, when, on 2 October 1898, he received the message from the Grand Duke conveying the Kaiser's expression of his wish to meet with Herzl in Jerusalem.

Thus, the moment came when Herzl recalled the promise he had made to Hechler, in the earliest days of their friendship, when Hechler had shown him the very coat he would wear, and the very pocket of that coat in which he would carry his big map of Palestine 'when we shall be riding around the Holy Land together'.

HERZL, HECHLER AND KAISER WILLIAM IN THE HOLY LAND

As we have already noted, the famous visit of the Kaiser to Jerusalem was nominally for the purpose of dedicating the new Lutheran Church of the Redeemer, the first major building to be built by Europeans in the Old City of Jerusalem since the English had completed Christ Church Cathedral in 1849. As we have seen, the decision to build this church followed upon the decision to abandon the joint Anglo-Prussian bishopric – a decision which had greatly distressed William Hechler, along with many other English and German Christians who had drawn hope for future British-German relations from that experiment. For Hechler, therefore, there was a painful side to this moment. For Kaiser William, however, it was a moment of sheer glory. Kaiser William wanted the world to see this project as the beginning of a new era of German presence, not only in Jerusalem, but in the Near East generally. Lest this dimension be lost on the imagination of the world, the Kaiser, in the secret negotiations with the Ottoman authorities preceding the visit, insisted, and the Turks had reluctantly agreed, that a wide breach should be made in the wall at the Jaffa Gate, so that he could enter the Old City on horseback.

There were rumours that the volatile William was actually planning to proclaim himself Protector of the Jews in Jerusalem, with Herzl, representing the Jews, at his side. The stage would be set for this scene by the Kaiser's previous diplomatic conference with the Sultan in Istanbul, scheduled to begin 16 October 1898.

All of this made great sense to Herzl. To his diary he confided:

> To live under the protection of this strong, great, moral, splendidly governed, tightly organized Germany can only have the most salutary effect on the Jewish national character. Also, at one stroke we would obtain a completely ordered internal and external legal status. The suzerainty of the Porte and the protectorate of Germany would certainly be sufficient legal pillars ... Strange ways of destiny. Through Zionism it will again be possible for Jews to love this Germany, to which our hearts have been attached despite everything!

On 16 October 1898, Herzl and the four other members of his official Zionist delegation arrived in Istanbul. There he had his first audience with the Kaiser. To his diary he admits having been too nervous to register everything that was said and done, but,

> The Kaiser, to be sure, made a deep and strong impression on me. Afterwards I tried to capture this impression in the form of a metaphor and could only hit upon the following: I felt as though I had entered the magic forest where the fabulous unicorn is said to dwell. Suddenly there stood before me a magnificent woodland creature, with a single horn on its forehead. But its form impressed me less than the fact that it existed.

When the Kaiser turned to discuss the substance of Zionism, it was clear that he was thinking along the same lines as Eulenburg. 'There are elements among your people', he said, 'whom it would be good to settle in Palestine.' He was convinced that Germany would gain a great deal – in particular, the exodus of the 'socialists' and the 'usurers'. Herzl was a bit discouraged to note that Minister von Bülow occasionally differed from His Majesty on several crucial matters – notably, the degree of malleability of the Ottomans, the goodwill of the British, and the possibility of counting on the goodwill of Jewish bankers. Nonetheless, Herzl came away reassured: the Kaiser was clearly in charge of his Government's policies in these matters, and had the will and the resources to impose the Protectorate.

Then, Herzl headed off by steamer for Cairo, from where he would proceed to Palestine, in time for the agreed public meeting of the Zionists and the Kaiser in Jerusalem.

Meanwhile, William Hechler had gone on ahead of Herzl and the official Zionist party, and was already in Palestine to greet them.

Unlike Herzl, Hechler had no plans for what he must do after returning from Palestine. He was not taking for granted that any of them would return, given that the work they would be conducting in the Holy Land appeared to be establishing the pre-conditions for Christ's return.

A few days before his departure for the Holy Land, Hechler wrote: 'Now we await the visit of the German Emperor to the Holy Land … But maybe what we will have is the privilege of welcoming Jesus, Who has promised that He would come again … Many signs are multiplying around us, announcing the Coming in a very brief time.'[5] Herzl was not unaware that Hechler's mind was running in this direction. Indeed, he had encouraged Hechler to put all of this in writing for the readers of the very first issue of his Zionist journal, *Die Welt*:

> Children of Abraham, awake!
> God himself, the Heavenly Father, calls you back to your ancient fatherland and wants to be your God, as He promised of old through his prophets …
> As a Christian, I believe as well as you in what is called the Zionist Movement, for according to the Bible and its ancient prophets a Jewish state must be raised in Palestine. I am convinced by the signs of our own time that the Jews will soon recover their beloved homeland … I am certain that the establishment of a Jewish state, with the support of the Princes of Europe, will inaugurate the salvation forecast by Isaiah, Micah, and Zechariah.[6]

Hechler was behind the series of articles on the Ark of the Covenant which appeared in *Die Welt* during 1898. These articles Hechler had used to convince the Grand Duke, who in turn evidently convinced the Kaiser and some in the Kaiser's circle, that discovery of the actual Ark was imminent. During the interview with Eulenburg back in September, the Count had told Herzl and Hechler that the Kaiser intended to ask the Sultan for his permission to conduct a search for the Ark. Hechler had written that the recent discovery of the Moabite stele at Mesha was a sign that other documents would swiftly appear in mint condition in this same area. 'No doubt [the archeologist] will also find [on Mount Nebo, in the Dead Sea area] the manuscripts of the five books of Moses, written by his own hand, and hidden away in the Ark. All of this will prove how deranged are those theologians of our day when they tell us that Moses wrote nothing!'[7]

Thus, two remarkable and entirely unanticipated circumstances have come together, creating the preconditions for the Messiah's sudden return. First, there was the re-appearance out of the long-neglected soil of the Holy Land of evidences of the historical reliability of scripture – and, by moral and logical extension, of the reliability of its prophecies. Second, there was the coming-together of the scattered Jewish people in a movement which committed them to reclaiming their Holy Land, the creation of a Jewish state.

The Second Zionist Congress at Basle, demonstrates once more how the Jews are accomplishing the prophecies of God, without even knowing it ... [The Zionists are pursuing their goal] every bit as unaware as were their fathers when the Saviour came the first time to Jerusalem ... We theologians find every detail of this totally engaging, seeing ourselves as the watchmen on the spiritual walls of Zion ... observing that raising of the dead bones in the valley forecast by Ezekiel.[8]

The rendezvous between Herzl and Hechler took place at Jaffa on 27 October. As always, Herzl found himself simultaneously exhilarated and exasperated by Hechler's behaviour. There were reports that Hechler was going about proclaiming the imminent Coming of the Lord, and that some were taking this to mean that Herzl was the Messiah, while others were taking it to mean that Herzl had undertaken to convert the Jews of Palestine to Protestantism.

The Kaiser entered the city of Jerusalem, on horseback, on 19 October 1898 (one of the most photographed public events of the age). Wearing one of his famously splendid costumes – a white ceremonial uniform with a helmet topped by a gold eagle – he passed through the opened wall, then through two specially built ceremonial arches, one the gift of the Turks, the other the gift of the local Jews. Then he set about visiting all the Holy Places at the head of long processions. He later described his reaction in a personal letter to Czar Nicholas: 'The thought that His feet trod the same ground is most stirring to one's heart, and makes it beat faster and more fervently.' However the Czar's mother took a jaundiced view of the scene: 'Revolting. All done out of sheer vanity, so as to be talked about! ... perfectly ridiculous! ... no trace of religious feeling!'[9]

Between 17 October, when Herzl met the Kaiser in Istanbul, and 2 November, when they met by prearrangement in Jerusalem, something went wrong. The scholars tell us that there is no reliable documentation for the meeting between the Kaiser and the Sultan in October, but they are agreed that the former failed to persuade the latter of the value of the Protectorate. Whether because he believed this to be only a temporary setback, or whether because he simply lacked the courage to speak the truth, he did not deal candidly with Herzl when they met in Palestine.

Arriving in Jerusalem on 29 October, Herzl found that many obstacles had appeared to hinder the agreed official audience with the Kaiser. The local rabbis had apparently received some kind of warning from highly placed persons in Istanbul that they should not appear to be allied with Herzl and the Zionists. Fearful that the wrath of the Ottoman authorities towards the Zionists would fall on them once the Kaiser left, they virtually put Herzl under house arrest.

Now came the moment when Hechler compensated Herzl for all the embarrassment he had caused him over the previous few days, as Herzl summoned Hechler to prove again his ability to gain access to the Kaiser's entourage. This Hechler did – to find that, indeed, some were working to derail the meeting; whereupon, he went directly to the Kaiser. There is every reason to believe that this intervention saved the day.

The meeting did take place, in the Kaiser's magnificent tent at his splendid encampment outside the walls. Herzl read his Address of the Zionist Deputation. The tone of the meeting was genial. The Kaiser spoke of being favorably impressed by the agricultural colonies of the Jews. They talked of irrigation, sanitary conditions, eye diseases, etc. 'He then assured us of his constant interest', but Herzl sensed that the Kaiser's attitude had changed. 'He was less obliging than at Constantinople, from which I inferred that our stock was lower … Evidently a lot has been happening behind the scenes.' It was perhaps significant that von Bülow spoke more at this meeting and seemed more forward. Something, Herzl was sure, had gone wrong at Istanbul.

In his memoirs, von Bülow brazenly denied that the meeting with Herzl had even taken place. However, a German wire service report under the date 2 November 1898, makes sufficient record that the meeting was not a figment of the imagination of the five men of the Zionist delegation. Here the Kaiser is quoted as telling 'the Jewish delegation' that 'any such endeavors could count on his benevolent interest to the extent to which they aimed at furthering agriculture in Palestine and promoting the welfare of the Turkish empire, while scrupulously respecting the sovereignty of the Sultan' – language that seems to signal the Kaiser's intention to back away from the larger pledge to the Zionist leaders.[10]

AFTERMATH

William Hechler did not play a leading role in the history of Zionism after the great adventure of 1898. Herzl continued to rely on Hechler's advice about the proper ways of approaching Christian statesmen, but no further advance was made in Herzl's few remaining years down the path of power in Germany. Hechler does seem to have assisted in establishing the contacts with British ecclesiastical and political leaders that eventually made possible Theodor Herzl's entrée into British Government circles; but others played more important roles here.

The best proof we have of their continuing friendship is that Hechler was the last visitor not of Herzl's immediate family to have been allowed to come to his bedside during his last illness. On 2 July 1904 (the day before Herzl died) Hechler spent considerable time recalling with his friend their visit to Palestine. Taking to heart the encouraging diagnosis of Herzl's doctor, Hechler sought to cheer Herzl with the promise that they would return together to the Holy Land, 'But', Hechler recalled, 'he seems to have known that there was no hope for him. He placed his right hand on his heart, and holding my right hand in his left hand he said: "*Grüssen Sie Alle von mir, und sagen Sie ihnen, ich habe mein Herz-Blut für mein Volk gegeben*" [Greet all of them for me, and let them know that I gave all my life for my People].'[11]

In 1910, Hechler retired from his chaplaincy in Vienna, and returned to England for the final time. His biblical studies now occupied him almost entirely, but he maintained his friendship with his Zionist comrades, most directly with those of the Zionist Organization Office in London, which honoured a request of Herzl in his last days by granting him a small pension.

In March 1914, convinced that a great war was imminent, he made one last effort to get an interview with the Kaiser on the matter of the Jews and Palestine, but was rebuffed. In that same month of March 1914, he said to Martin Buber: 'Dr Buber, your homeland shall soon be given to you, for a grave crisis is about to break out, whose deepest purpose is to break off from messianic Jerusalem the yoke of the Pagans. We are heading for a *Weltkrieg*.'[12]

After the war broke out, he became convinced that he had been mistaken in courting Germany on behalf of Israel. He reread Ezekiel, and now saw clearly that 'the ships of Tarshish', which would bring the Jews to Palestine were the ships of England.

We know that on 22 July 1922, he was present in Parliament when the British Government accepted the Palestine Mandate. In the years that remained he was often dejected because the Jews of the world did not rise *en masse* to the challenge of emigration to Palestine – which failure, of course, was the primary cause of Britain's loss of confidence in the years that followed in the viability of the Balfour proposal. David Pileggi tells us of the distress of his last years:

> He repeatedly warned his Jewish friends that there would be an extensive massacre of Jews in Europe. It would make the Crusades and Spanish Inquisition look like 'child's play' he predicted. His forewarnings grew into an obsession and he made them with increasing frequency until his death in 1931. Tragically, Hechler's predictions were politely dismissed by everyone.[13]

PART TWO

THE CYRUS CONNECTION

4

The Restorationist Tradition in Britain

*Seldom, indeed, has a coming event
cast so obvious a shadow before it
as the intervention of Britain on
behalf of Jewish Palestine.*

Israel Zangwill[1]

ROOTS OF BRITISH RESTORATIONISM

Of the English Jews whom Herzl met in his visits to England few could trace their roots in that country past the time of Cromwell. It was Cromwell who had welcomed the Jews back to England, putting an end to the official ban against them which could be traced back to the time of Edward I (1290). Cromwell was stirred by the talk of Restoration of the Jews to Palestine. In opening the 'Barebones' Parliament, he had said to the members: 'Indeed I do think something is at the door: we are at the threshold, you are at the edge of the promises and prophecies ... and [invoking Isaiah 60] it may be as some think, God will bring the Jews home to their station from the isles of the sea, and answer their expectations from the depths of the sea.'[2]

The historian Cecil Roth identifies three fundamental forces at work in the story of the successful incorporation of the Jews into English life that followed – namely: 'a sympathy for Hebraic idealism as expressed in the Bible, the fundamental religious document both of Christian and Jew; an intense sympathy and even shame for Jewish sufferings, both past and present; and a fervid hope for the fulfilment of the prophecy in the restoration of the Jews to Palestine, and of Palestine to the Jews.'[3]

Yet enthusiasm for Jewish Restoration was by no means confined to Puritans like Cromwell. Anglicans of all types and sub-types and even many notable rationalists shared the elements of the faith. John Locke, in his *Commentaries on St Paul's Epistles* wrote: 'God is able to collect them into one Body ... and set them in flourishing condition in their own land.'[4] Isaac Newton gave over the best of his energies in the latter years of his life not to his work in celestial mechanics, but to preparation of an enormous speculative work on End Times, for which he prepared himself by learning the languages (Hebrew and Aramaic) of the Old Testament prophets.

Brooding on the same texts which, a century and a half later, inspired William Hechler's confident predictions and led him to the door of Theodor Herzl, Newton, in his *Observations upon the Prophecies of Daniel and the Apocalypse of St John*, concluded that 'the "commandment to return [Daniel 9:25]" may perhaps come forth not from the Jews themselves but from some other kingdom friendly to them'.[5]

For all British millennialists, Isaiah 60:9–12 was the key passage:

> Surely the isles shall wait for Me;
>   And the ships of Tarshish first,
>   To bring your sons from afar,
>   Their silver and their gold with them,
>   To the name of the LORD your God,
>   And to the Holy One of Israel,
>   Because He has glorified you.
>
> And the sons of strangers shall build up your walls.
>   And their kings shall minister to you;
>   For in My wrath, I struck you,
>   But in My favor I have had mercy on you.
>
> Therefore your gates shall be open continually;
>   They shall not be shut day or night,
>   That men may bring to you the wealth of the Gentiles,
>   And their kings in procession.
>
> For the nation and kingdom which will not
>   serve you shall perish,
>   And those nations shall be utterly ruined.

If, as biblical scholars usually claimed, 'Tarshish' stood for the islands and coasts of the Mediterranean, these passages must speak of the flight of the Jews from Spain and her possessions; and the 'isles' that 'wait for Me', and the people who 'bring your sons from afar' were obviously the British of Oliver Cromwell's time. It is the British who, 'in time to come, shall build up your walls', and whose 'kings shall minister to you'.

NINETEENTH-CENTURY RESTORATIONISM

For British millennialists, the deepest implications of the French Revolutionary Wars were laid bare during those months in 1799 when Napoleon was in the East. His goal was to force the British to their knees by cutting them off from their Empire; to do this, he must conquer Egypt, then seize Palestine and Syria from the Ottomans, establishing an empire for France athwart the paths that led to Britain's Empire in India and beyond. After the dramatically successful Battle of the Pyramids, Napoleon began the march into Palestine (January 1799), pursuing the dream of recreating the Empire of Alexander, from Egypt to India, with himself the new Alexander. This prompted Prime Minister Pitt to conclude a treaty with the Turks, guaranteeing the integrity of the Ottoman empire. After victories at many places memorable in biblical history – notably Mount Tabor, where he defeated a Turkish Army (16 April 1799) – Napoleon issued proclamations to all the subject nationalities of the Empire, inviting them to join him in overthrowing the Turkish yoke. Amongst these was a proclamation to all the Jews of Asia and Africa:

> Israelites arise! Ye exiled, arise! Hasten! Now is the moment, which may not return for thousands of years, to claim the restoration of civic rights among the population of the universe which have shamefully been witheld from you for thousands of years, to claim your political existence as a nation among nations, and the unlimited natural right to worship Jehovah in accordance with your faith, publicly and most probably forever.[6]

Nineteenth and twentieth-century Zionists were often brought back to this moment during their reflections on the past, present, and future of their cause. How ironical it was that it should be Napoleon who had opened the door for the British into Palestine! Indeed, he had done something even more dramatic: he had proposed the restoration of the Jews to their Holy Land; he had told them it was their right; he had told the Christian world that it was its duty, and that in this context Turkey had no countervailing right. This was precisely what British Restorationists believed! Theology, of course, played no part in Napoleon's consideration: he was a complete unbeliever. Yet, millennarians saw the deeper significance of the moment. It made sense that in the last hours of human history Antichrist would mimic the Truth – that is, the Eternal Truth about the Jews and their Land and the responsibilities of the nations towards both. British Restorationists were soon insisting that now was the time to simply take Palestine from the Turks and give it to the Jews, to whom it belonged.

SHAFTESBURY AND PALMERSTON: CHRISTIAN RESTORATIONISM AND BRITISH IMPERIAL STRATEGY

Yet rolling up the Ottoman empire was not to be the policy of the British political leaders of the nineteenth century. There were many times during the middle and late decades of the nineteenth century when circumstances tempted the statesmen of Europe to dismantle the Ottoman empire forever. No one doubted that such action was well within the strength of the European Powers acting together, and would be extremely popular everywhere in Europe, as public opinion had always been profoundly disdainful of the Turks and their Empire, but the statesmen, always and everywhere confident that issues could not be as simple as the public believed, were loath to see the Ottoman tyranny overthrown, until they had a clearer idea of what would replace it.

The crisis caused by Mehemet Ali's revolt in the 1830s brought to everyone's attention 'the Eastern Question'. As we have seen, Lord Shaftesbury, constantly alert for 'signs of the times', had seized this moment of popular interest to promote the idea of a British Protectorate of 'Syria'. The first fruit was the protestant bishopric, but that was only the beginning. Shaftesbury's article, 'The State and Prospects of the Jews', appeared in the *Quarterly Review*, January–March 1839, marking, notes Kobler, 'the first time a distinguished magazine had treated the problem of Restoration in all its aspects – religious, political, historical, philosophical'.[7] Suddenly, articles, pamphlets, and books on this theme were everywhere. In August 1840, *The Times* told its readers that there was a plan being promoted by Anthony, Lord Ashley, 'to plant the Jewish people in the land of their fathers' under the protection of Great Britain.[8]

As Shaftesbury himself put it, Palmerston 'did not know Moses from Sir Sydney Smith', but that did not matter: God was turning to none other than his own stepfather-in-law to be the Cyrus *redivivus*. What won the day was Shaftesbury's ability to state the argument for British presence in the area in terms that appealed to Palmerson's own true creed: British empire.

During negotiations leading to the Treaty of London, July 1841, Lord Palmerston wrote instructions to Lord John Ponsonby, the British ambassador at Constantinople which echo the motifs of the missives he had been receiving from Shaftesbury:

> There exists at the present time among the Jews dispersed over Europe, a strong notion that the time is approaching when their nation is to return to Palestine ... It would be of manifest importance to the Sultan to encourage the Jews to return and to settle in Palestine because the wealth which they would bring with them would increase the resources of the Sultan's dominions; and the Jewish people, if returning under the sanction and protection and at the invitation of the Sultan, would be a check upon any future evil designs of Mehemet Ali or his successor ... I have to instruct Your Excellency strongly to recommend [the Turkish government] to hold out every just encouragement to the Jews of Europe to return to Palestine.[9]

MISSIONS TO THE JEWS

Like William Hechler, then, Shaftesbury was a Christian Zionist. Like Hechler, he championed the use of the government of his Christian state to bring about a Jewish state in Palestine. Like Hechler, he was absolutely persuaded of the good results that would follow from this for all the people of the Ottoman empire, and that the project should not wait upon the Sultan's coming to that conclusion unassisted : it should be the publicly declared policy of Her Majesty's Government. Unlike William Hechler, however, Lord Shaftesbury looked to the conversion of the Jews as part of the process that would bring on the Restoration.

Shaftesbury was a leading force behind the Society for Promoting Christianity Amongst the Jews – the 'London Jews Society', or 'LJS' for short, founded in 1808. Among the most broadly supported of all the evangelical societies of the day, it had, without doubt, the least to show – that is, in terms of its stated purpose of converting Jews to Christian faith. Perhaps six or seven converts a year were won at home in England. The victories abroad were of the same order.

As we have seen, events in the Ottoman empire in 1838 created the opportunity for the appointment by Great Britain of the first European diplomat to the biblical part of the Ottoman empire. This, in turn, created the conditions for extension of the program of the British conversionists to the Holy Land. Palmerston's choice as first vice-consul at Jerusalem was William Young, a zealous supporter of the Jews Society recommended to him by Shaftesbury. In his diary, Shaftesbury takes note of the departure of Young for the Holy Land: 'Took leave this morning of Young, who has just been appointed her Majesty's Vice-Consul at Jerusalem! What a wonderful event it is! The ancient city of the people of God is about to resume its place among the nations, and England is the first of the Gentile kingdoms that ceases "to tread her down".'[10]

Young pursued vigorously the instruction about providing British protection to the Jews, and so often rescued individual Jews and indeed the whole Jewish community from the arbitrary actions of Ottoman authorities that the Jewish leaders could be in no doubt that their future peace depended on continuing friendly relations with the British representative. This consideration served to temper their hostility to the English missionaries. Nonetheless, the missionary results were embarrassingly small – given that most of the Society's supporters, including Shaftesbury, were convinced that the conditions of the times had made the Jews sensitive at last to the case for Jesus of Nazareth being the Messiah.

COLLAPSE OF THE DREAM OF A JOINT GERMAN/BRITISH ROLE IN THE RESTORATION OF THE JEWS

In a previous chapter we told the story of the joint Anglo-Prussian Protestant bishopric in Jerusalem. After Germany walked away from this project, the British and German Protestant communities had gone their separate ways – the situation in the Holy City now mirroring the new realities in world affairs. The now-separate German congregation (the Church of the Redeemer) lost interest in the work among Palestine's Jews – and, for that matter, among Palestine's Arabs. The Anglicans at Christ Church continued to seek the conversion and the restoration of the Jews. Later on, however, another Anglican Church (St George's Cathedral Church), built outside the Old City's walls, would establish a mixed congregation of English expatriates and Arabs, a cockpit of anti-Zionism, then and now.

Had it ever been in the cards that Great Britain and Imperial Germany might have been the co-sponsors of the Restoration of the Jews, sharing the office and the dignity of Cyrus *redivivus*?

Certainly it made excellent good sense. Their combined pressures on the Ottoman ruler would have been irresistible. Likewise, their combined pressure on the Czar, to encourage emigration of the Jews to Palestine, would have been irresistible.

Hechler's original project (Israel as the Middle Eastern Belgium, living under guarantees jointly made by Britain and Germany) was eminently reasonable (as, for that matter, were the guarantees to Belgium itself, which were the inspiration for Hechler's proposal.) There should be no underestimating the contributions that this arrangement might have made both to European and Middle Eastern stability, but all of this was wrecked by German militarist imperialism – the same force that led to the tearing-up of the piece of paper which recorded the pledges to Belgium. The only agent of sufficient authority who might have restrained these militaristic ambitions was the German Monarch.

The legacy of Frederick William was squandered by Kaiser William. Though he was heir to the same religious legacy that shaped the visionary diplomacy of Frederick William, he was, in contrast to Frederick William, a weak man, who lived in constant fear that his Christian faith might be judged simplistic by learned philosophers and theologians, and who therefore did not dare to risk opportunities for aggrandizement of German strength upon visionary projects – like the Jerusalem bishopric, or Herzl's project of a homeland for the Jews. By the end of the decade of the 1890s, jealousy of Britain's empire had led him to naval rivalry, to reckless provocations of Britain in such matters as encouragement of the Boers, the search for African and Southeast Asian Empire, and opportunistic gestures in the Far East.

Long before his visit to the Ottoman realms in 1898 Kaiser William had abandoned the notion of co-operation with Britain. Precisely, 1898 is the moment when he decided to leave behind forever Hechler's vision of a restored Israel under European auspices – the Belgium of the Middle East.

Thereafter, the Kaiser began to move toward German Imperial diplomatic and economic domination of the Ottoman empire. Until the actual eve of the First World War, Germany's alliance with Austria-Hungary prevented the Kaiser from being too fulsome in his embrace of the Ottoman Empire, but already before the end of the 1890s he had come to believe that there was no future in co-operation with Britain in this area – or anywhere else.

5

Germany Declines the Mantle of Cyrus, and Britain Takes It Up

In the aftermath, it all made sense: that Britain, with her attachment to the idea of the Restoration of the Jews, with her record of toleration towards her own Jewish population, and with her leadership in democratic and liberal institutions, should be Zion's champion, against the decrepit and illiberal Turks and the autocratic Central Powers. British missionary and diplomatic presence in Jerusalem had been the largest factor in creating the conditions which made possible the growth of Jewish population there.

Still, virtually down to the eve of the Balfour Declaration, many Zionists throughout the world believed that Germany was more obviously being prepared by History (or Providence, or God, according to philosophical taste) to be Zion's champion. Zionists in Germany worked hard, privately and publicly to persuade their Government to take the initiative in announcing their support for a Jewish homeland in Palestine – which, they insisted, would give to Germany commanding influence in a newly ordered Near East. However, the fact was that by the time that the Great War broke out in August, 1914, the German-speaking elite of the World Zionist Organization had probably lost the confidence of the masses of Central and East European Jews, among whom 'Zion' stood for a real hope of escape from tyrants, not a theoretical solution to a philosophical problem. These people had been enraged in 1903 to learn that their German-speaking champions could confuse the sacred earth with Uganda! Increasingly their voice was being expressed by young Eastern European Jews like Chaim Weizmann.

It is this same Chaim Weizmann, only recently emigrated to England, but already the undoubted leader of the Zionists of England, who, over the first three years of the War, almost single-handedly (using Herzl's metaphor) 'moved the fulcrum of Zionism to its new Archimedean point': the government of Great Britain.

CHAIM WEIZMANN (1874–1952)

Chaim Weizmann was born 27 November 1874, in the *shtetl* called Motel, near Pinsk, 'White Russia' (Belarus), deep in the Russian Empire's 'Pale of Settlement'. Chaim was one of the fifteen children of a timber merchant, a prosperous man by the standards of this area of great poverty, but Chaim's father was not only a man of business: he was an intellectual – a *maskil*, that is, an 'enlightened man', familiar with secular learning, including contemporary literature, but also religiously observant however and pious – a man of prayer, esteemed as a *Chazan*, or prayer leader. Hebrew and Yiddish were spoken at home; Russian in the world outside the *shtetl*.

In some ways, Chaim Weizmann is the *wunderkind* of Zionism. His precocious devotion to the dream of Restoration is illustrated in a letter, written in 1885, at the age of eleven, as he was heading off to board with relatives while attending the *gymnasium* in Pinsk. Addressed to one of his teachers, it is a sort of a farewell address to the childhood scene:

> [Do] not imagine that when I attend the *gymnasium* I shall throw off the garb of Judaism. No! On no account. I have determined in my heart to observe Judaism and I shall oppose the opinion of those who say that one becomes a doctor because he casts off his faith.
>
> I am sending you one of my ideas ... AND THAT CONCERNS HEVRAT HOVEVEI ZION AND JERUSALEM WHICH IS IN OUR LAND ... Let us carry our banner TO ZION AND RETURN TO OUR FIRST MOTHER UPON WHOSE KNEES WE WERE BORN. – For why should we look to the kings of Europe for compassion that they should take pity upon us and give us a resting place? In vain! All have decided: THE JEWS MUST DIE, but England will nevertheless have mercy upon us. In conclusion to Zion! – Jews – to Zion! let us go.[1]

This is the first of Weizmann's surviving letters, collected in twenty-three volumes – the letter of an eleven year old. And there is the meaning of his life, as the world came to pronounce it at his death, some sixty-odd years later: the declaration of his intention to be a leader in the Restoration of the Jews to Palestine; a pointed summary of the vision of history that made it all necessary and possible; and then the key to his own entirely unique contribution to its historical realization:

All have decided: THE JEWS MUST DIE, but England will nevertheless have mercy upon us!

In striking contrast to the story of Herzl, there is for Chaim Weizmann no moment of conversion to Zionism. He was reared in an atmosphere of popular faith in the Return to Palestine, invigorated recently by the pogroms which took place during the years of his childhood. In his school years, he was drawn into '*Bilu*', the youth wing of *Hoveve Zion*.

In 1893 Weizmann went to Germany, in search of a university education in chemistry – something effectively closed to him as a Jew in the Czarist empire. At school, first in Pfungstadt, near Darmstadt, and then at the University of Berlin, Weizmann found 'the assimilated Jews of Germany, then in the high summer of their illusory security, and mightily proud of it'.[2] Though he recognized the narrowness of the life of the Yiddish communities, and though he gave up orthodox observance, he did not despise these, as the German intellectuals did. In Berlin, Weizmann belonged to a circle of *emigré* Russian Jews, the *Russisch-Juedischer Wissenschaftlicher Verein*, which he liked to think of as 'the cradle of the modern Zionist movement'.[3]

Weizmann was still a student in Berlin when Herzl's *Der Judenstaat* appeared. He was annoyed to find that Herzl showed no awareness of the precursors of Zionism, whose books and ideas had long fueled discussion in Eastern Europe. 'Herzl did not know of the existence of Chibat Zion; he did not mention Palestine; he ignored the Hebrew language ... Fundamentally, *the Jewish state* contained not a single new idea for us',[4] but like all his contemporaries in the movement Weizmann saw in Herzl the man of action, with the connections in high places, who could give practical expression to their visions, and so he strove mightily for and won the privilege of attending the Second Congress, at Geneva in 1898, as a delegate from Pinsk.

MAKING A 'NEW START IN ENGLAND'

Even before he had undergone the disappointment which followed from his encounter with the Kaiser in Jerusalem in 1898, Theodor Herzl had often spoken of England as the key to the Zionist program. For example, in a letter of 28 February 1898, to the Chairman of the Jewish Conference in London he affirmed: 'From the first moment I entered the Movement, my eyes were directed towards England, because I saw that by reason of the general situation of things there it was the Archimedean point where the lever could be applied.'[5] However, as we have already seen, Herzl's strategy had always been exceedingly flexible, and we should not take these sorts of statements at their apparent value. Herzl was not especially disposed towards the British system of political and social life, and seems to have had a genuinely patriotic preference for the German system. We should assume that up to his dying day he would have quickly realigned his hopes and his movement with Germany, had the Kaiser given him the least encouragement to do so.

The case is quite different with Chaim Weizmann. Though bitterly opposed to the Uganda scheme, he was equally convinced that the affair had proved the genuine willingness of the British public and their

Government to find a solution to the Jewish problem – and, furthermore, that this friendly disposition was just one expression of the peculiar virtue of the British political system and way of life, and, more especially, of the basically philo-Semitic disposition of the British people.

Weizmann had first visited England in 1903. His purpose in going at that time was to rally opposition to the Uganda proposal in advance of the Zionist Congress. After the congress (and after the death of Herzl) he decided to move to England, where he would take up a teaching position in chemistry at the University of Manchester.

Living and working in England strengthened Weizmann's disposition to trust the British and to believe that their Government would prove to be the lasting friend of Zionism. 'My hatred of the Russian regime grew as I contrasted life in Russia with life in England.'[6] He quickly became involved in the Manchester Zionist Society.

As it happened, there was a large concentration of Jews in Manchester, and several of their number were prominent figures in the commercial and political life of the nation. Politicians were becoming more alert to what in American terms would be called 'the Jewish vote'. English Zionists had learned that it was well worthwhile to cultivate the goodwill of the *Manchester Guardian*, then one of England's most influential journals. In any case, Manchester's Jewish leaders tended to see eye to eye with the *Manchester Guardian*'s left-of-center liberalism, particularly on the need for government to enlarge the area of its responsibility for problems of social and economic need.

Before Weizmann had settled into his new life in England, and while he was still struggling to learn the new language, he was brought to meet Arthur Balfour. The General Election of 1905/6 was on, and Balfour was the local candidate for the Conservative Party. Balfour had not forgotten the excitement of the Uganda Affair back in 1903, when he was Prime Minister, Joseph Chamberlain was Colonial Secretary, and Lord Landsdowne was Foreign Secretary. He had then been struck by the tenacity of the opposition to the Uganda 'solution'; something about the way that passion and sentiment and ideas had got all stirred up together in everybody's arguments appealed to the philosopher-statesman. He wanted to hear Weizmann's story.

> He asked me why some Jews, Zionists, were so bitterly opposed to the Uganda offer. The British Government was really anxious to do something to relieve the misery of the Jews; and the problem was a practical one, calling for a practical approach. In reply I plunged into what I recall as a long harangue on the meaning of the Zionist movement. I dwelt on the spiritual side of Zionism. I pointed out that nothing but a deep religious conviction expressed in modern political terms could keep the movement alive, and that this

conviction had to be based on Palestine and on Palestine alone. Any deflection from Palestine was – well, a form of idolatry. I added that if Moses had come into the sixth Zionist Congress when it was adopting the resolution in favor of the Commission for Uganda, he would surely have broken the tablets once again ... Then suddenly I said: 'Mr Balfour, supposing I were to offer you Paris instead of London, would you take it?'

He sat up, looked at me, and answered: 'But Dr Weizmann, we have London.'

'That is true', I said, 'but we had Jerusalem when London was a marsh.'[7]

Weizmann was drawn more and more deeply into Zionist activity in the months following the interview with Lord Balfour. While he was greatly encouraged by expressions of interest from the British politicians, and would indeed become more and more confident that England would emerge as Zion's champion, he was by and large disappointed by the English Jewish community. At the heart of all their failings as Jews was, ironically, the very fact of their success in English commercial, social and political life – their prosperity, in short. That prosperity would never have come about except for the historically unparalleled general goodwill of the gentiles among whom they lived. Consequently, English Jews had lost the capacity to imagine what life was like for most Jews in the world – who had neither prosperity nor the goodwill of their neighbours and their governments. Indeed, were it not for the immigration of waves of Central European Jews into England of recent years, English Jews would be virtually without insight into the larger reality of the life that most Jews elsewhere lived, and this new knowledge clearly embarrassed them. It was as though they feared that by being forward in the defense of the cause of Zionism they would cause their government and their gentile neighbours suddenly to see the likeness between their well-scrubbed selves and the recent newcomers from Central Europe – 'real Jews', meeting the outward description of the Jews of English literature, the Shylocks and the Fagans.

WINNING THE GOODWILL OF BRITAIN'S POLITICAL LEADERS: TOWARDS THE BALFOUR DECLARATION

As we have seen, the German and Austrian régimes were not without assets in the contest with Great Britain and France for the goodwill of the Zionists, and, even had these assets been much fewer, the liabilities of the Russian régime, allied to Britain and France, would have sufficed to make most Zionists pro-German at the outset of the Great War. Thus, it would have been premature, during at least the first half of the war, to write off the possibility of a compact between the Zionists and Germany. However, somewhere during 1916 or 1917 there is a watershed, when it began to be clear to German policymakers themselves that they valued their continuing alliance with the Turks too highly to go on letting the Turks see them dealing with Zionists. Yet while the German Zionists saw it happening – because there came a moment when no one in authority would answer their calls – the British, of course, could not discern the truth for a long while thereafter. Indeed, in the spring of 1917, the most powerful of British statesmen believed that German Zionists were making inroads into the decision-making of the Central Powers. Lord Balfour, the Foreign Secretary, told the War Cabinet on 4 October 1917 that a decision had to be taken soon, since the German government was making great efforts to gain the support of the Zionist movement.

So completely did circumstance vindicate Chaim Weizmann's argument that Great Britain must be the sponsor of Jewish Restoration to Palestine that afterwards everyone – Zionists and non-Zionists, Jews and non-Jews – would quickly forget how eccentric this belief seemed at the start of the war. At the outset of the war, most Zionists joined with most Jews everywhere in hoping for victory of the Central Powers. So long as Czarist Russia was on the other side, the best interests of the Jews of Central Europe seemed to require the defeat of Czarist Russia, their immemorial persecutor.

For the duration of the war, the World Zionist Organization ceased to function. Though its letterhead stated that its headquarters was now in Copenhagen, most of the prewar leaders were behind the lines of the Central Powers; their writ ran nowhere on the other side. The irony was that, although (in Weizmann's words) 'Our enemies in England did not hesitate to point out, during the First World War, that we were a German organization', the European Zionists in fact 'discouraged my first tentative steps to get in touch with the British statesmen'.[8] There were, however, no sanctions they could apply against him, and Weizmann was confident where all this must lead.

Balfour's Conservatives had not come back to office in that election of 1905/6 when Balfour had introduced himself to Weizmann – nor, for that matter, had Balfour retained his own seat. When war broke out in 1914, it was a Liberal government under Asquith. Soon Weizmann acquired entrée to this government and had begun to brag: 'I am convinced that I have achieved more than Herzl with all his diplomacy.' Of great tactical significance were his interviews with C.P. Scott, editor of the *Manchester Guardian*, who not only became a powerful champion of Zionism, but also led him to the seats of the mighty – to meet David Lloyd George (Chancellor of the Exchequer, and later Prime Minister of the wartime coalition government, 1916–18) and other Cabinet and Foreign Office figures. As a result of these various interviews, a memorandum on the subject of a Jewish state under British auspices was circulating in the Cabinet by the end of December 1914.

Of crucial importance in this story was the support of David Lloyd George, whose Nonconformist Welsh parents had passed on to him the Cromwellian legacy of biblically based philo-Semitism and Restorationism. He recalled: 'When Dr Weizmann was talking of Palestine he kept bringing up place names which were more familiar to me than those on the Western Front.'[9]

Of no less importance was the support of Arthur James Balfour – now back in government as First Lord of the Admiralty and later as Foreign Secretary. When Weizmann and Balfour met again for the first time since 1906, Balfour said: 'You know, I was thinking of that conversation of yours, and I believe that when the guns stop firing you may get your Jerusalem.'[10]

Weizmann's influence upon the policymakers was increased exponentially when the government became aware that his professional work as a chemist had potential applications to the war effort. When all the world's supplies of acetone produced by the hitherto known methods began to dwindle, the race was on for substitutes – and there was Dr Weizmann of Manchester, the world's foremost authority on synthetic acetone, already well known in the highest circles. He was recruited by Winston Churchill, then First Lord of the Admiralty. Churchill, in turn, was recruited as one of the most fervid champions for the Zionist cause.

The greatest burden which Weizmann bore in those days was the opposition to the Zionist program from the upper ranks of England's Jews. Their most effective leader was Lucien Wolf, an eminent historian of the time, with abundant, long-established contacts in the Foreign Office. Weizmann recalled:

> Zionism was in his view a purely East European movement, with a certain following in the East End of London, and beneath the notice of respectable British Jews. It was still harder, in fact, impossible, for him to understand that English non-Jews did not look upon his anti-Zionism as the hallmark of a superior loyalty. It was never borne in on him that men like Balfour, Churchill, Lloyd George, were deeply religious, and believed in the Bible, that to them the return of the Jewish people to Palestine was a reality, so that we Zionists represented to them a great tradition for which they had enormous respect.[11]

Chaim Weizmann is perhaps the only well-informed observer of those times who got the impression that Winston Churchill was a 'deeply religious man'. It would be more accurate to say that he was attracted to the mystical side of Zionism. Like others of his class and upbringing, he had been immersed as a child in public school Anglicanism and carried about with him a substantial repertoire of memorized Bible passages, fondly remembered hymns, and a good knowledge of Biblical history. An ancestor, Colonel Charles Henry Churchill, had promoted the idea of a British

Protectorate of the Jews, back in the days of the Mehemet Ali insurrection, and thereafter in a book published in 1853.

In the autobiography which he completed during 1948–49, the last year of his life, Stephen Wise reflected on the record we have just considered – the story of British Restorationism and the part it played in the decision of British statesmen in favor of the Balfour promise. He recalled that, when the Balfour Declaration was announced, he had stood before a mass audience in New York and said: 'The Balfour Declaration is not and never will be regarded as a scrap of paper [as Bethmann-Hollweg had said of the Treaty guaranteeing the neutrality of Belgium]. It is written not in German but in English, the language of freedom and of freemen. It will always be honored in the observance, not the breach', but by the time Wise came to write his autobiography, it had become clear to him that, while he had correctly judged the generation of Balfour and Lloyd George, he had been wrong with regard to his expectations of the generation that succeeded them. 'I was wrong', he confessed, 'and I quote that sentence [of November, 1917] the more readily because of the bitter tension today [1948–49] between the British government and the Jewish people.' This later generation's abandonment of the Balfour pledge Wise attributed to the attenuation, in the thirty years intervening, of the grip of the legacy of British Restorationism:

> Whatever may happen today, the fact uncancelable remains that it was England which, in the Cromwellian tradition and by the Balfour Declaration, was the first nation after more than eighteen hundred years, since the year 70 AD, to recognize 'the Jewish people' and to undertake 'to use their best endeavors to facilitate the establishment of a national home for the Jewish people'. What the British government failed to do in 1947 must dishonor all those who have shared in the betrayal of the Balfour Declaration, but it does not diminish nor detract from the grandeur of British action in 1917.[12]

Chaim Weizmann offers, in his autobiography, written at precisely the same moment of time, a strikingly similar judgement on the political morality of the two generations:

> The deeper meaning of Zionism must not be lost sight of in the record of practical steps, of day-to-day strategic adjustments, which led up to the granting of the Balfour Declaration, and which accompanied future developments. I am reverting now to the common accusation that Zionism was nothing but a British imperialistic scheme, the Balfour Declaration a *quid pro quo*, or rather payment in advance, for Jewish service to the Empire. The truth is that British statesmen were by no means anxious for such a bargain ... England felt she had no business in Palestine except as part of

the plan for the creation of the Jewish Homeland ... They understood as a reality the concept of the Return. It appealed to their tradition and their faith.[13]

Thus, at the very outset of the War, Weizmann had become persuaded that Great Britain was about to emerge as Zion's champion. Britain's very best instincts, rooted in history, disposed it to play this role. Nonetheless, he foresaw three possible obstacles. One was opposition to the Zionist program expressed by dominant voices of the Jewish establishment. The second was the concern of British authorities not to alienate the Russians, who took a very dim view of the British Government's open dealings with Jews; but this concern was suddenly made moot in February of 1917, when the régime of the Czar was overthrown. The third was American opinion.

Here, again, it was Chaim Weizmann who found the way to victory.

BRINGING IN THE NEW WORLD

From the outset, Weizmann saw the Great War as a contest between the values embodied in the history of Great Britain and those embodied in the history of the Central Powers. His view of the war was, in short, fundamentally ideological. He had long believed and argued out loud that what he called 'the deeper meaning of Zionism' could not safely be entrusted to German auspices, but could be safely entrusted to British auspices. Jewish values thrived under liberal and democratic auspices, while under authoritarian régimes they withered away. This point – that British soil was congenial to Jewish life – was proved, he felt, by the experience of the immigrant Jews in Britain.

Yet if this general principle was true, would one not expect to find it illustrated *a fortiori* in America?

The outbreak of the war accelerated in his thinking a tendency to associate the destiny of the Jews of Europe with the performance of the Jews of America. As he studied the American scene, he learned that through the American Jewish community there ran the same fundamental line of division that he had found in Britain. Jews who had been there longest were much further along the road towards assimilation than were the newcomers. In the American case, 'a long time' was much less than a century – as (apart from a numerically insignificant, widely scattered and almost totally assimilated 'Sephardic' remnant), the most established Jews in America descended from German-language immigrants of the 1840s. Immigration of East European Jews to the United States had begun in the 1880s, and had been on a vastly greater scale than that to Great Britain. Alert observers were already predicting that the Americans would soon be the largest community of Jews outside Poland. As in Britain, Zionism, while still only a minority enthusiasm, was proportionately much stronger among the Eastern Europeans – the Yiddish Jews. Given the arithmetic of the recent immigrant trends, prospects for ultimate victory of the Zionists over the non-Zionists was greater, therefore, in the US than in Britain.

6

The Restorationist Tradition in the United States

PURITAN ORIGINS

English Puritans expected to be blessed by their welcoming of the Jews to England in Cromwell's day. They believed that the End of the Times of the Gentiles could not be far off; and when those days came, the people would collectively play the role of Cyrus *redivivus*, giving the command for the restoration of the Jews to Israel, thus setting in train the events of the final 'week' before the millennium. In the meantime, God would weigh the fortunes of the nations according to the rule found in Genesis 12:3: 'I will bless those who bless you [Abram], and I will curse him who curses you; and in you all the families of the earth shall be blessed.'

The Puritans who went to America took all this even further.

It is often said that the Puritans saw their own experience of 'fleeing into the Wilderness' from doomed Europe as a parallel to the experience of the Jews, led from Egypt by Moses, but it was much more than just a parallel. They believed that their experience was truly a living-out of the Exodus experience. They interpreted their experience as a reliving of the history that formed the ancient People of God. By way of illustration, Cotton Mather, looking back on the life of the founder of the Bay Colony, John Winthrop, found it to be shaped by all the forces that had shaped Moses:

> Accordingly when the noble design of carrying a colony of chosen people into an American wilderness, was by some eminent persons undertaken, this eminent person was, by the consent of all, chosen for the Moses, who must be the leader of so great an undertaking; and indeed nothing but a Mosaic spirit could have carried him through the temptations to which either his farewell to his own land or his travel in a strange land must needs expose a gentleman of his education.

And when Governor Winthrop died, there was inscribed on his tombstone a lengthy memorial which picks up the biblical theme:

> But let his mourning flock be comforted,
> Though Moses be, yet Joshua is not dead;
> I mean renowned Norton; worthy he Successor to
> our Moses is to be,
> O Happy Israel in America,
> In such a Moses, such a Joshua.[1]

No doubt there was much delusion in this notion that seventeenth-century Englishmen could simply reach into the experience and practice of the People of God and apply whatever they found there to themselves in the American wilderness. What matters here, however, is that they saw themselves in that role: that it nurtured a profound philo-Semitism in them (admittedly, in the absence of any live Jews to test it on!), which had incalculable long-range effects; and – most important for our purpose – that it disposed them to identify their own destiny with that of the Jews, which they understood to be spelled out in literal perfection in the Scriptures, which were the rule for their own lives.

Once aroused, American enthusiasm for the Restoration of the Jews to Israel would prove more powerful, because more vital and more broadly based, than English Restorationism. To the English conviction of a special responsibility for rescue of the scattered Jews the American version adds the conviction that America herself has been molded in that experience from her beginnings, and that her destiny is embraced by that of Israel.

Yet, unless their whole 'experiment' as the 'City set upon a hill' was a satanic delusion, would it not follow that there is prefigured in biblical prophecy a role for America, separate from that prefigured for England, and of no lesser dignity?

But where, in prophetic Scripture do we find 'the United States'?

'THE LAND SHADOWING WITH WINGS'

During the early years of the New Nation, an enormous number of books, pamphlets, sermons and public addresses were written to answer this question. We will pause, however, over one very influential item, published in 1814, which carries its message in its extended title: *A New Translation of Isaiah, Chapter XVIII, with Notes Critical and Explanatory, A Remarkable Prophecy, Respecting the Restoration of the Jews, Aided by the American Nation; with a Universal Summons to the Battle of Armageddon, and a Description of that Solemn Scene*, by John McDonald.[2]

Caught up in the powerful wave of American patriotism that swept the nation in the days of the conflict against Great Britain (the War of 1812–15), McDonald had searched the Scriptures in that same spirit of literalism that moved the earliest Puritans and found what (he claims) no previous biblical scholar had managed to find: a clear-cut allusion to the United States of America – and found this, furthermore, couched in a central part of the prophecy of the greatest of the prophets, in language of the most explicit instruction.

McDonald's entire case turns on an interpretation of one unusually brief Old Testament chapter: Isaiah 18. This speaks of 'the land shadowing with wings, which is beyond the rivers of Ethiopia, that sendeth ambassadors by the sea, even in vessels of bulrushes upon the waters, saying, Go, ye swift messengers to a nation scattered and peeled, to a people terrible from their beginning hitherto; a nation meted out and trodden down, whose land the rivers have spoiled'. McDonald was familiar with what the English Restorationists said about the role that England was to play in rescuing the scattered Jews, but this goes further. In McDonald's scenario, there are 'ambassadors' – literally understood as the diplomatic agents of a nation – whose work will be literally to seek out and bring back the 'scattered' Jews to Zion, back 'to the place of the name of the Lord of Hosts, the mount Zion'.

Whose 'ambassadors' match the description given by Isaiah? In fact, only those of the United States!

> Every other nation, ancient or modern with whose history or manners we are acquainted could, and actually did, send their ambassadors by land ... America is the only nation on earth, which cannot send her ambassadors to any civilized, or commercial nation, or state, but by sea.

The land which provides the 'ambassadors' is described with certain realistic traits which could apply only to the United States. To speak of it as 'beyond Ethiopia', is to say that it as far as possible beyond the furthest lands known to the Jews of the time . Certainly, this must be beyond Europe, including Britain. But most telling of all is the reference to the 'shadowing wings', a clear-cut allusion to the eagle, the national symbol of the United States, appearing on all of its insignia, and evoking (not incidentally) the role of Cyrus the King of Persia – of whom the same Isaiah says (Isaiah 46:10, 11) that God would 'call ... a bird of prey from the east, the man who executes my counsel from a far country', and who did indeed appear, and did indeed restore the Jews to Jerusalem – the first time.

JEWS AND THE HOLY LAND

McDonald's book is one of an enormous number which were firing American interest in the future of the Jews in the Holy Land. At the same time, the Holy Land itself was taking on clearer form in their imaginations, as the first generation of scientific archeologists reported their discoveries back to the world.

Dominating the first chapter of modern 'biblical archeology' is the figure of Edward Robinson, who, beginning in 1837, undertook the first comprehensive survey of the topography, the extant buildings, and the archeological remains of Jerusalem and its vicinity. His book, *Biblical Researches in Palestine, Mount Sinai, and Arabia Petraea* (1841) created the first rush of interest in biblical archeology. Before long, a full-blooded contest was under way among the archeologists of the various European nations – notably British, American, French and German. The work of scientific archeology had applications to other fields: the work of map-making and surveying of natural features and natural resources was found to be of interest to the statesman, and soon was being subsidized from military budgets, including that of the United States.

The first American missionaries to the Jews of Palestine were sent out by the American Board of Commissioners for Foreign Missions (the principal inter-denominational missionary authority) in 1819, taking with them a pledge of full protection from Secretary of State John Quincy Adams. They and their successors had no greater success than did their British colleagues – and eventually they would turn their attentions more to the Arab populations. Yet during the middle decades of the nineteenth century their colorful stories, told and retold to Sunday School children, kept alive the dream of the Restoration of the Jews of Europe to the Holy Land and their conversion there *en masse* by American missionary effort.

Thus, the Holy Land bulked larger and larger in the public imagination from the 1840s onward. And most Americans found it impossible to think of the Holy Land without also thinking of the Jews and their undoubted future possession of it.

BEGINNINGS OF OFFICIAL AMERICAN INTEREST IN THE JEWISH QUESTION

American public attention was for the first time sharply focussed on the issue of the future of the Jews by the 'Damascus Affair' of 1840. In that year, riots broke out against the Jews of that city. Behind the riots was a sudden resurgence of the ancient 'blood libel' (deliberately fomented, it was later said, by French agents in Syria, seeking to create a pretext for the intervention of France as protector of the Christians). The Ottoman authorities looked the other way, but US consuls in Alexandria and Constantinople were instructed 'to interpose [their] good offices in behalf of the oppressed and persecuted race of the Jews'. This action of President Martin Van Buren and Secretary of state John Forsyth was thereafter invoked as precedent for many future declarations of American 'interest' in the welfare of the Jewish residents of the decadent house of the Ottomans.

During the 1880s, the United States found itself increasingly involved in the destinies of the Jews of the world as a result of the worsening of the situation of the Jews of the Russian Empire. The combined effects of the pogroms and severe crop failures in the Russian empire drove millions of Jews to seek to emigrate. Hundreds of thousands eventually made their way to the United States, but among many millions more there was a growing passion for emigration to Zion. In the face of this, Turkish authorities decided that now was the time to close down legal immigration of the Jews into their Empire.

As floods of Jews from the Russian empire poured towards the United States, Congress, in August, 1890, asked Secretary of State Blaine for information on the situation, and Blaine in turn instructed his Ambassador to Russia to raise all of these matters with the Russian Foreign Minister, stressing the American view that 'each [Government] should use its power with due regard for the results which its exercise produces on the rest of the world'. President Harrison reported the results of this exchange to Congress in his Annual Message of 1891: 'This Government has found occasion to express, in a friendly spirit, but with much earnestness, to the government of the Czar, its serious concern because of the harsh measures now being enforced against the Hebrews in Russia.'[3]

7

William Blackstone and the Blackstone Memorial

William Eugene Blackstone, born in Adams, Jefferson County, New York, was told by his family that he was a descendant of the great eighteenth-century legal scholar, William Blackstone. If so, nothing in his family's circumstances reflected this distinguished legacy. His father was a tinsmith, and the boyhood home was, in William's recollection, 'humble'. Adams was the town where Charles Grandison Finney was converted, left his legal practice, and set about pioneering the methods and the theology of Revivalism that have shaped Evangelical Protestantism ever since. Revival meetings were still going on at scarcely reduced pace when the ten-year-old William was 'saved' at one such meeting. Though he never attended a college or seminary and was never ordained as a minister, he served all his life as a lay Bible teacher and preacher. Sometime after William's marriage to Sarah Louise Smith in 1866, his father-in-law died, leaving a large estate, with instruction that it be administered by William in support of evangelical and missionary work. The Blackstones settled in Rockford, Illinois, where he was successful as an insurance agent, and grew prosperous through wise real-estate investment. Eventually, he left the business life to enter into full-time work as an evangelist. His judiciously invested personal wealth, added to the funds entrusted to him by his father-in-law, financed his travels and the printing and distribution of his books and pamphlets.

Somewhere during these early years as an evangelist, he was won over to the school of biblical interpretation called 'dispensationalism'.

There is much that is anomalous about the legacy of William E. Blackstone. After he died on 7 November 1935, he received no obituary in the *New York Times*, nor did any of his activities ever receive mention in the *New York Times*, so far as the *New York Times Index* shows, apart from the brief item the day he presented his Memorial to President Harrison (5 March 1891). His only biography is a slim booklet, published and circulated by a little-known missionary society. His name appears nowhere, so far as I can discover, in any general historical account of American political, intellectual, cultural or religious history. In scholarly books on 'American Fundamentalism' he is sometimes given a few paragraphs, but nothing approaching the attention which he deserves. For William Blackstone was one of the most influential and admired religious figures of his generation: a writer, lecturer, preacher, active missionary, and the author of one of the most widely-read books of his time, while, with regard to our concern in this book, he is one of a handful of the most influential American actors in the story leading to the achievement of the state of Israel in 1948.

Certainly, he is not forgotten in Israel, where one can see at the Herzl Museum the bible (with many significant prophetic passages marked for his attention) which Blackstone sent to the Founder, and where one can visit the Blackstone Forest. Among scholars of the history of political Zionism his large role is generally conceded. In this respect he has fared better than William Hechler.

In its official bulletin, 'Fact and Comment', of 14 March 1941, the Emergency Committee for Zionist Affairs took note of the fiftieth anniversary of the 'Blackstone Memorial', and recommended that Zionists go to that document to review 'the three Zionist postulates that need emphasis today[:]'

>
> [F]irst, that the Zionist solution must be commensurate with the magnitude of the Jewish problem; second, that the establishment of Palestine as a Jewish commonwealth must seek its accomplishment through international political action; and third, that the project commands a vast fund of sympathy that is deeply imbedded in the consciousness of the American people ... [Blackstone's Memorial] offers, in fact, essentially the same solution as the *Judenstaat*. Blackstone is entitled to rank as an important precursor of political Zionism.[1]

On the seventy-fifth anniversary of the day (5 March 1891) that William Blackstone presented his 'Memorial' to President Benjamin Harrison, a group of religious leaders met in New York to honour his memory. Their press release (not noted by the *New York Times*) was signed by 16 religious leaders, Christians and Jews, including Cardinal Spellman and the Director of the Protestant Council of New York. The signatories noted that, while Blackstone did not live to see the founding of the state, he would have 'joyously pointed to the host of Bible passages that read today as though they had been written specifically for our time'.[2]

In his own lifetime, Blackstone was honored by official Zionists more than any other American Christian friend. In correspondence with Blackstone, Justice Brandeis gave it as his opinion 'that you [Blackstone] are the Father of Zionism, as your work antedates Herzl'.[3] This sentiment was expressed with equal force publicly at the meeting of the Provisional Committee Conference in Philadelphia, 2 July 1916. On that occasion, Brandeis introduced, as the meeting's special guest – 'a most important ally which Zionism has in America outside the Jewish rank, Rev William E. Blackstone'.

> Those of you who have read with care the petition presented twenty-five years ago by Mr Blackstone and [to] the president of the US, asking that the president of the US use his influence to consider Jewish problems with a view to the giving of Palestine to the Jews; those of you who have read that petition with care, and I hope it includes you all, must have been struck with the extraordinary coincidence that the arguments which Mr Blackstone used in that petition were in large part the arguments which the great Herzl presented five years later in setting forth to the world the needs and the hopes of the Jewish people. That coincidence, the arguments presented in America, arguments later presented by Herzl without knowledge of the fact of what had been done in America, show how clearly and strongly founded they are. They come to all men who will regard in a clear and statesmanlike way the problems of the Jewish people.[4]

Again, Blackstone was publicly honored at a large Zionist meeting held in Los Angeles, 27 January 1918. It is an extraordinary testimony to the respect that Blackstone's name and work had won among the Zionists that the assembly on that occasion sat courteously before him while he delivered a passionate sermon, calling for their repentance and conversion. Describing the source of his Zionist conviction, he told them,

> I am and for over thirty years have been an ardent advocate of Zionism. This is because I believe that true Zionism is founded on the plan, purpose, and fiat of the everlasting and omnipotent God, as prophetically recorded in His Holy Word, the Bible ... [There are] only three courses open to every Jew ... The first is to become a true Christian, accepting Jesus as Lord and Savior, which brings not only forgiveness and regeneration, but ensures escape from the unequaled time of tribulation which is coming upon all the earth ... Second – become a true Zionist and thus hold fast to the ancient hopes of the fathers, and the assured deliverance of Israel, through the coming of their Messiah, and complete national restoration and permanent settlement in the land which God has given them. It is true that this leads through unequaled sorrows, as prophesied notably by Jeremiah ... [Third – there is the way of] the assimilants. They are the Jews who will not be either Christians or Zionists. They wish to remain in the various nations enjoying their social, political, and commercial advantages ... Oh, my Jewish friends, which of these paths shall be yours? ... God says that you are dear unto Him ... He has put an overwhelming love in my heart for you all, and therefore I have spoken thus plainly. Study this wonderful Word of God ... and see how plainly God Himself has revealed Israel's pathway unto the perfect day.[5]

'DISPENSATIONALISM'

Although most of the elements which make up what is called 'Dispensationalism' had already appeared over the centuries, the nineteenth century 'Dispensationalists' are a distinct school of interpreters who derive from a specific teacher, John Nelson Darby (1800–82), and an elaborate schema that he worked out, whereby the entire history of mankind since Adam is understood as a succession of 'dispensations', during each of which God deals with mankind according to a different 'covenant'. Leaving out all the hard parts: the present 'dispensation' is the last, before Christ's return. During this period, mankind is being sifted, and a remnant of true Christians is being prepared by God for 'Rapture' – that is, to be suddenly and without warning removed from the sphere of history in the moment before the Tribulation (the time of Jacob's troubles), which in turn precedes the Second Coming of Christ. A crucial element of doctrine binding all the subgroups of 'Dispensationalism' is this: that the Rapture of the true Church leaves the Jewish Nation in place, facing the last Chapter (Seven Weeks) of History, culminating in the Return of Jesus Christ.

From our present point of view: the distinctive element in the Dispensationalist understanding is this rigid, axiomatic, distinction between church history (how it has been proceeding since Pentecost, and how it will end), and the history of the Jews (how that has been proceeding since the Destruction of the Second Temple, and how that will end). Hence, this order: the 'Rapture', then the countdown of the events immediately preceding Christ's return (Daniel's 'seven weeks'), then Christ's return, and then the inauguration of the Millennium. All these events await the Restoration of the Jews to their State of Israel.

Above all, we must note the fact that these dogmatic convictions give a constancy to the Fundamentalist's enthusiasm for the Jewish people (and, after that is achieved, for their state) that is rarely found among Christians of more 'liberal' or 'rational' theology. Right at the beginning of their dealings with the Fundamentalists, the Herzlian Zionists noticed that the allegiance of the latter does not follow from arguments of abstract justice or considerations of global power politics; nor is their allegiance dependent upon arguments about what Christendom might owe to the Jews by way of redressing the injustices of the past.

It is true that one does not need the authority of Dispensationalism for concluding what Darby and his followers concluded about Israel and its future. We should note, for example, that William Hechler came to his convictions apparently without the benefit of Dispensationalism. On the other hand, Hechler's writings never became authoritative for a broad-based school of interpretation, as did Darby's, which gave focus to the daily bible reading and the daily prayers of millions of Americans.

Following upon a series of extended visits of John N. Darby to the United States from 1862 forward, the Dispensationalist form of Premillennial teaching took hold at the centre of the religious constituency that kept alive the Puritan legacy: that is, revivalist, or 'evangelical' Protestantism. A powerful element in that story is the success of the *Scofield Reference Bible*, which first appeared in 1909 – not only the most influential vehicle of the Dispensationalist world-view, but undoubtedly the most widely disseminated tool for popular religious instruction in the History of the United States.[6] In part because of 'Scofield's Bible', Dispensationalist Premillennialism was, by the eve of World War One, the interpretation favored by Protestants who were 'conservative' in theology and 'revivalist' (or 'evangelical') in practice, and the one book most responsible for disseminating this interpretation by that time was *Jesus Is Coming* by William E. Blackstone.

JESUS IS COMING

As originally published in 1878, *Jesus is Coming*, was a 96-page paperbound tract, whose author was identified only as 'W.E.B.'. The work was subsequently revised and expanded twice before the year 1916. Well over a million copies of that edition (expanded to 250 pages) were eventually distributed. It has been translated into at least 43 languages, including Hebrew. In it, the Dispensationalist argument is developed deliberately, assisted at every step by a massive apparatus of scriptural references.

What interests us here is the section (beginning at page 161) where Blackstone addresses the present situation of the Jews and explicitly the Zionist movement of the day. Here, Blackstone draws our attention to the unique history of the Jews – the miracle of their persistence to this day:

> Said Frederick the Great to his chaplain: 'Doctor, if your religion is a true one, it ought to be capable of very brief and simple proof. Will you give me evidence of its truth in ONE WORD ?' The good man answered, 'Israel'.
>
> Other nations come and go, but Israel remains. God says of her, 'For a small moment have I forsaken thee; but with great mercies will I gather thee. In a little wrath I hid my face from thee for a moment; but with everlasting kindness will I have mercy on thee, saith the Lord, thy Redeemer.' Isaiah 54:7–8 ...
>
> In the first restoration only those who were MINDED came back from Babylon (Ezra 7:13), while many remained both there, and in Egypt and elsewhere, but in the future, or second restoration, not one will be left out. [He cites Isaiah 43:5–7; Ezekiel 34:11–13, and 39:28–29] ...
>
> In the first restoration it was only Jews who returned.
>
> In the second, or future restoration, it will be both Judah (the two tribes) and Israel (the ten tribes). [Jeremiah 3:18; Ezekiel 36:10, 37:15–22] ...

> At the first restoration they returned to be overthrown and driven out
> again, but in the second, they shall return to remain, no more to go out. They
> shall be exalted and dwell safely, and the Gentile nations shall flow unto them.
> [Amos 9:15, Ezekiel 34:28 and 36:11–12, Isaiah 60:15–16] ...
>   The detail of the manner of their restoration, and of their repentance and
> acceptance of Christ, is not so important to us. For those who are of the
> Church are to be taken away first, in the Rapture, and escape all these things
> through which Israel must pass.[7]

Those who have studied Dispensationalism from the outside will know
what follows: that in immediate contradiction of this disclaimer of concern
about the 'detail' of the scenario leading to End Times, the author will now
display the evidence of his very considerable preoccupation with the 'signs'
which he has found in the daily newspaper.

In a section evidently written a few years prior to the outbreak of World
War One, he writes:

> We believe, if we can rightly read the signs of the times, that the godless, law-
> less trio of communism[,] nihilism, and anarchy, so alarmingly permeating
> the nations today, are unclean spirits preparing the way for the Antichrist.[8]

The history of Israel, Blackstone says, is 'God's sundial'.

> If we want to know our place in chronology, our position in the march of
> events, look at Israel. [T]he Jews are, even now, returning to Jerusalem ...
> [T]he entire Jewish population of Palestine is said to be more than 80,000,
> so that a greater number have already returned than the 49,697 who went up
> with Zerubbabel from Babylon. Ezra 2:64–65.
>   The anti-Semitic agitations in Germany, Austria and France, and the fierce
> persecutions in Russia and Romania, have stirred up the Jews of the world
> as the eagle doth her nest. Deut. 32:11.
>   National hopes and aspirations have found vent in the organization of
> *Chovevi Zion* (Lovers of Zion) societies and *Shova Zion* (colonization)
> societies throughout Europe and America. Land is being purchased and
> funds raised, on instalment plans, to send back the members by lot ... The
> Turkish hold upon the country is continually weakening, and there is
> considerable talk of a Jewish state. May we not conclude that the Lord is
> even now setting 'His hand again the second time for the restoration of His
> people?' [citing Isaiah 11:11] ...
>   This brings us to speak of Zionism, the present movement of the Jews to
> return to the land of their fathers.[9]

Blackstone discovers within contemporary Zionism a variety of motives
and inspirations, extending from the religious beliefs of the Orthodox, to
the visions of the secularists.

> The orthodox Jews who have enlisted under the Zionist banner, are animated
> by the most devout religious motives ... [T]he Reform Jews or Neologists

have rapidly thrown away their faith in the inspiration of the Scriptures. They have flung to the wind all national and Messianic hopes. Their Rabbis preach rapturously about the mission of Judaism, while joining with the most radical higher critics in the destruction of its very basis, the inspiration of the Word of God. Some have gone clear over into agnosticism.

Strange to say, from these agnostics now comes the other wing of the Zionist party, and not only have they joined this party, but they furnished the leaders, namely, Dr Max Nordau of Paris, and Dr Theodore Herzl of Vienna ... [These agnostics] aver that this is not a religious movement at all. It is purely economic and nationalistic. Dr Herzl, its founder and principal leader, espoused it as a *dernier ressort*, to escape the persecutions of anti-Semitism, which has taken such a firm hold of the masses of the Austrian people. He conceived the idea that if the Jews could regain Palestine and establish a government, even under the suzerainty of the Sultan, it would give them a national standing which would expunge anti-Semitism from the other nations of the world, and make it possible for all Jews to live comfortably in any nation they may desire ...

The call, issued by Dr Herzl, for the Zionist Congress held in Basle, Switzerland, in 1897 met with severe opposition from the German Rabbis and also a large portion of the Jewish press, as well as the mass of rich reformed Jews. Nevertheless, over 200 delegates, from all over Europe and the orient and some from the United States, met, and carried through the program of the congress with tremendous enthusiasm ... It is significant that this first Zionist congress assembled just 1,260 years after the capture of Jerusalem by the Mohammedans in AD 637. Dan. 12:7.[10]

WILLIAM BLACKSTONE AND THE ZIONISTS

On 4 November 1887, Blackstone and his friends founded the Chicago Committee for Hebrew Christian Work (later incorporated as the Chicago Hebrew Mission [1891], and later still [1953] renamed the American Messianic Fellowship). Blackstone's zeal for practical missionary work among the Jews remained unabated to the end of his life.

From its beginnings, the Chicago Hebrew Mission experienced much greater success than did any of the British or American missions among the Jews of Palestine. As partial explanation for this success, Yaakov Ariel writes:

Dispensationalist missions, including Blackstone's Chicago Hebrew Mission, took an innovative approach. Formerly, Jewish converts to Christianity were supposed to gentilize as well as christianize. They were expected to turn their backs on their Jewish heritage and abandon all ties with the Jewish community. Their Jewish background was often regarded as a shameful disability that had to be overcome.

This 'difference of approach' followed from a distinctive difference of theology. 'The dispensationalists', notes Ariel, in contrast to other

Protestant missionaries, 'emphasized the importance of the Jewish nation
in the great events that would precede the establishment of the millennial
kingdom and its leading role in the millennial kingdom itself'.[11] Thus,
paradoxically, despite the extraordinary zeal for conversion of the Jews
which moved the Blackstone organization – certainly equal to the zeal of
other missionaries to the Jews anywhere – they did not envision the complete
conversion of the Jews.

Many Orthodox Jews, it seems, saw Blackstone as a kindred spirit in the
warfare against loss of Jewish identity. The risk in opening the door to
Blackstone and his missionaries was obvious to them, but temptations to
lose one's Jewish soul were all around one in America. Here was a man and
a movement which, in one key point at least was an ally: namely in his zeal
to redirect the attention of Jews to their Scripture and to the messianic
future.

Not all dispensationalists were Christian Zionists. Among the best
known of the dispensationalist preachers was Arno C. Gabelein who
consistently warned against alliance with the Zionists.

> Zionism is not the divinely promised restoration of Israel ... [and] is not the
> fulfillment of the large number of predictions found in the Old Testament
> Scriptures, which relate to Israel's return to the land. Indeed, Zionism has
> very little use for arguments from the Word of God. It is rather a political
> and philanthropic undertaking. Instead of coming together before God,
> calling upon His name, trusting Him, that He is able to perform what He
> has so often promised, they speak about their riches, their influence, their
> Colonial Bank, and court the favor of the Sultan. The great movement is one
> of unbelief and confidence in themselves instead of God's eternal purposes.[12]

The difference between Blackstone and Gabelein on this matter had
nothing to do with what we would today call 'racial attitudes'. Both were
strongly philo-Semitic. The line that divided them was a theological line.
It is, in fact, the same line that ran then and still runs through Orthodox
Judaism, dividing those who felt that God required them to assist the
coming of his Kingdom, and those who said that it was impious to try to
speed the arrival of the Messiah through political work.

As for the secular, the Herzlian, Zionists, they soon discovered (as we
shall see) that Blackstone was an invaluable ally – a propagandist of genius
and a man having great influence within the Christian community, who was
accomplishing in a democratic setting essentially what Herzl hoped that
Hechler was accomplishing in the authoritarian setting of Old Europe:
leading the way to the Princes.

Blackstone proved a constant friend of the Jews in all of the controversies
that threatened them. He was a champion for rescue of the Russian Jews,
and of Jewish immigration to America. He consistently brought his great

personal influence to bear against any and all evidences of anti-Semitism
around him. He denounced the *Protocols of the Elders of Zion* when it
appeared after 1905. To be as forthright as Blackstone was in this was no
small matter, when we recall, for example, how widespread was belief in
their authenticity in the highest circles at the time of the First World War
and how important the document thereafter became to populist movements
in the United States in the 1920s. Sometime in the 1920s, Blackstone wrote
to the editor of Henry Ford's influential paper, the *Dearborn Independent*:

> I do not believe for a moment that the Jews have any organization for securing
> control of the government of the world, neither do I believe that they were
> instrumental in the production or propagation of the so-called protocols,
> and it is amazing to me that such anti-Semitic propaganda could be
> established in this country as well as in England.[13]

And (as is developed later in this text) he eventually established the friendli-
est of relationships with the Zionist leaders in the years of the hegemony
of Louis D. Brandeis – few of whom were Orthodox, and none a likely
candidate for conversion to Christianity.

A few months after launching the Chicago Hebrew Mission, Blackstone
made his first visit to the Holy Land, where he was particularly struck by
the pace at which the Jews were reclaiming the land; this he took as a proof
of the blessings that Jewish immigration would bring to the Ottoman
Empire. It was also a clue that 'the times' were further along than he had
so far guessed.

A few months after his return from the Holy Land, Blackstone organized
the first conference between Christians and Jews in Chicago: The
Conference on the Past, Present and Future of Israel, 24–25 November, at
the First Methodist Episcopal Church in Chicago. Among the participants
were three Reform rabbis, and a number of Christian clergy and teachers,
representing a considerable theological and institutional range. When the
matter of Restoration was raised, the Reform rabbis proved not to be
enthusiastic. One said:

> We modern Jews do not wish to be restored to Palestine. We have given up
> hope in the coming of a political personal Messiah. We say, 'the country
> wherein we live is our Palestine, and the city wherein we dwell is our
> Jerusalem'. We will not go back ... to form again a nationality of our own.

Warm unanimity was achieved, however, on a resolution to be forwarded
to the authorities in Russia, expressing 'disapprobation of all discrimination
against the Jews', and pleading that 'they stay the hand of cruelty from this
time-honored people, which have given them as well as us our bible, our
religion, and our knowledge of God', and further, it was 'resolved, that we
call upon the rulers and statesmen of our own country to use their influence

and good offices with the authorities of all lands to accomplish this humane and righteous end'.[14] These initiatives played their part in encouraging the concern for this issue shown by the Harrison Administration.

THE BLACKSTONE MEMORIAL (1891)

Encouraged by all of this, Blackstone now set about the project for which he is honored in Israel today, the Blackstone Memorial. This was, simply, a petition, addressed to the President of the United States, Benjamin Harrison, and the Secretary of State, James G. Blaine, to 'use their good offices and influence with the governments of the European world' (which are then named, one by one) 'to secure the holding at an early date of an international conference to consider the condition of the Israelites and their claims to Palestine as their ancient home, and to promote, in all other just and proper ways , the alleviation of their suffering'. Its opening line is in the form of a question – the question that dominated the proceedings at Blackstone's Chicago Conference: 'What shall be done for the Russian Jews?' The answer comes in the form of another question: 'Why not give Palestine back to them again?' Evoking the example of the Congress of Berlin of 1878, the Memorial calls upon the powers to meet again and give Palestine back to the Jews, as in 1878 it gave Bulgaria to the Bulgarians and Serbia to the Serbians and Cyprus to Great Britain. 'Whatever vested rights by possession may have accrued to Turkey can be easily compensated, possibly by the Jews assuming an equitable portion of the national debt.' In short, it is Herzl's program, presented to the rulers of the world five years before *Der Judenstaat*, and six years before the First Zionist congress.

The argument of the Memorial depends throughout upon appeal to 'sympathy, justice, and humanity'. Explicit theological language occurs only in one sentence, where, speaking of Palestine, the Memorial says, 'Why not give Palestine back to them? According to God's distribution of nations it is their home – an inalienable possession from which they were expelled by force.'

In the letter accompanying the Memorial, signed only by himself, Blackstone does briefly address the higher logic of Christian eschatology, in the penultimate paragraph:

> [T]here seem to be many evidences to show that we have reached the period in the great roll of centuries, when the everlasting God of Abraham, Isaac and Jacob, is lifting up His hand to the Gentiles (Isaiah 49:22) to bring His sons and his daughters from far, that he may plant them again in their own land, Ezekiel 34, etc. Not for twenty-four centuries, since the days of Cyrus, King of Persia, has there been offered to any mortal such a privileged opportunity to further the purposes of God concerning His ancient people.

The most remarkable thing about the Memorial is the list of signatures appended. Four hundred and thirteen prominent Americans signed, including the Chief Justice of the United States, the Speaker of the House of Representatives, the Chairman of the House Foreign Relations Committee, and several other Members of Congress, several of the greatest industrialists of the day (including Rockefeller, Morgan, and McCormick) famous clergymen, Christian and Jewish, writers, journalists, and the editors of several of the great newspapers of the day.

It is a matter of record that President Harrison received the Blackstone Memorial on 5 March 1891, and that he 'promised to give it careful attention', and we have evidence of the considerable stir that it made on public opinion. We know that Secretary Blaine sought the advice of the government's representatives in the Ottoman lands about the notion – and that all of them recommended not approaching the Ottoman Government about it.[15]

It is true that the government of the day never rose to the challenge of calling an international congress of the powers for the purpose of establishing a Jewish homeland. In fact, no reference to the Memorial or any related documentation appears in the volumes of *Foreign Relations of the United States* for the period, and the principal biographies of President Harrison make no mention at all of this story, yet the Memorial had very great effects in the long run. The notion of American sponsorship of a Jewish return to Palestine was firmly planted in many minds.

Almost exactly one-quarter of a century later, the story of the Memorial came to the attention of the leader of American Zionism, Louis Brandeis – with very great consequences, which we shall discover in due course (Chapter nine). Brandeis was so intrigued by the story, that he made enquiries in the State Department. Incredibly, the Department reported back that their researchers had failed to find any trace of the original petition. This seems extremely unlikely. Probably, they were simply resisting giving support to the embarrassing notion that a President of the United States – or , worse still, the State Department! – was in the habit of giving the time of day to End Times pamphleteers. Left to his own resources, Brandeis tracked down newspaper stories about Blackstone's presentation of the original Memorial, and searched the papers and magazines of the day for editorial comment.[16]

Some 47 pages of handwritten notes in the Brandeis Papers record this research. Brandeis notes a wide range of Jewish reactions. On the favorable side, *The Menorah* notes that 'there is evidently in this movement no proselytizing scheme ... [T]hose who are moving in this direction are entitled to our appreciation and gratitude.' The *Jewish Exponent* called the

Memorial 'a great conception, one worthy of exciting the enthusiasm of the greatest Christian and Jewish minds – certainly not a proposition to be met with derision and scorn'. The *Reform Advocate* of Chicago had mixed feelings: 'We are grateful for the effort made but deplore that so much money has been expended on what, to calm minds, cannot but be seen as a "fool's errand".' On the other side, the *American Israelite*, noting that the publishers of the *Chicago Tribune* were among the signatories, insisted that 'Nations are not made in the manner suggested by the Tribune and the Rev Mr Blackstone ... Let those who are able to help [the Russian Jews] do so, in a practical manner, and not waste energy and money on a barren ideality.' The *Jewish Messenger* was not at all grateful to Blackstone: 'The Jew apparently has a double persecution to undergo, from his friends as well as his enemies ... This [Memorial] brings two evils: (1) it revives anti-Semitism ... (2) it makes the Jews the subject of newspaper comment.' The *Jewish Messenger* affected alarm: 'This petition will recoil against the Jews of Turkey ... Mr Blackstone's ultimate aim is the evangelization of the Jews. His personality is charming, his zeal praiseworthy, but let him evangelize the Czar and his counsellors.' Perhaps the sanest response from the Jewish side was that of the editor of *Ha Pisga*, the only Hebrew-language journal of the day. Speaking of the matter of the well-known theology of its author, Wolf Schur wrote:

> It is not their intention to bring us under the wings of Christianity in our time ... but rather in the days to come when peace returns and each of us sits under his fig tree and vine, and after the battle of Gog and Magog. Let the Christians do whatever they can to help us in the resettlement in Palestine. As to the question of our faith, let that rest until Elijah comes and then we shall see whether or not their dream materializes.[17]

LIFE AFTER THE BLACKSTONE MEMORIAL

To reinforce the propaganda value of the Memorial, Blackstone wrote that same year a widely read article entitled, 'May the United States intercede for the Jews?' It begins: 'The pitiful condition of Jewish refugees is attracting universal attention', then turns to a review of the efforts of the Jews and the governments of the world to deal with this crisis. Quickly, he gets to the solution, a home for the Jews in Israel:

> There is room there for two or three millions more people, and the ancient scriptural limits of the country would largely increase its capacity. The rains are returning, agriculture is improving, its location promises great commercial possibilities, and only an independent, enlightened, and progressive government is needed to afford a home for all of Israel who wish to return ... Especially should they have possession and control of the *Haram*,

or ancient temple enclosure. The possibility of rebuilding their Temple under Divine direction would fire every Orthodox Jew with religious enthusiasm, and furnish an irresistible stimulant for a world-wide rally to their father-land.[18]

Yet Blackstone reaches beyond the constituency of like-minded Dispensationalists to meet the questions of statesmen and laymen. Here, as in the *Memorial*, the Congress of Berlin of 1878 provides the precedent for action by the Great Powers. Especially fascinating is the section where he addresses arguments about legal title to the area under consideration – questions which have not gone away. Whereas in *Jesus is Coming* he sweeps away modern doubt with the thought that, 'the title deed to Palestine is recorded, not in the Mohammedan Serai of Jerusalem nor the Serglio [sic] of Constantinople, but in hundreds of millions of Bibles now extant in more than three hundred languages of the earth',[19] – here he takes on the scholars of international law, calmly presenting his case in terms of the judicial concepts of 'prescription', 'usucaption', and 'dereliction of the proprietor' – a case so subtly presented that it might well have come from the pen of his famous eighteenth-century namesake.

In the decade and a half following his presentation of the Memorial to President Harrison, Blackstone never ceased reminding the politicians that it was there to be read, and that it reflected the powerful appeal of the idea of Restoration to the American people. He resubmitted the Memorial to President Theodore Roosevelt, in 1903. More tracts were written and published, elaborating his premillennial theology, and describing the present state of the process of the reclamation of Palestine by the Jews. He pursued his missionary efforts on an expanded front. To the fund entrusted to him by his father-in-law, other wealthy friends had added other funds, so that he was now responsible for distributing millions of dollars in support of missions and evangelical literature. One of his children became a missionary to China, and William Blackstone, now a widower, followed him there (1908–14) to serve in the field, and to distribute the Chinese version of his famous book. He became an avid world traveller, always studying to make the best of his opportunities, and contracting translations of his book to meet the needs of the countries he visited. His fundamentalist-dispensationalist reading of the past, the present and the future was never changed by anything that he encountered in his travels: indeed, he was always discovering new evidences for the most literal readings of scriptural history and prophecy. For example, on a visit to Mesapotamia (then under British occupation) in 1921, he wrote: 'I want to see the site of ancient Babylon, which I verily believe will soon suddenly spring up as the head and center of all commercialism. See Rev. 13 and 18.' Of the European Empires, he wrote, following his wide travels through the Mideast and Far

East: 'Gentile dominion is culminating in such a manifestation of hate and savagery that … there is no hope except in the predicted sudden conversion of Israel … and the re-establishment of theocratic government for the oppressed peoples of the earth'[20] – that is, the earthly reign of the Messiah.

The outbreak of the War inspired speculation about End Times everywhere, and on an unprecedented scale.[21] By 1916, there was added to the rumours of war rumours of the dealings between Zionist leaders and the Great Powers. Among Fundamentalist Christians, all this prompted even greater interest in Blackstone's book – which he therefore revised and enlarged.

DECLINING ENTHUSIASM FOR THE CAUSE OF THE JEWS AFTER THE 1890s

Earlier, we noted certain initiatives taken by President Harrison and Secretary of State Blaine on behalf of the Jews of Russia which gave encouragement to those who believed that the Restoration of the Jews to their land would come about under American sponsorship. These initiatives proved popular. Henceforward, the American public understood that there was what a later Secretary of State would have called 'linkage' between the general question of American relations with the Ottoman empire and the question of the destiny of the Jews.

At the same time, in the ranks of those responsible for the actual carrying-out of the policy – the diplomats in the field and the State Department personnel – a certain amount of foot-dragging can be detected. We find no Dispensationalists of record in the upper ranks of American policymakers in these prewar years – no policymaker that we know of was seized by the conviction that this was the hour to realize the role outlined for the United States by Scripture, nor do we find any known Dispensationalists in the ranks of the Presidents of this period. The United States' resident agents advised against the Blackstone policy from the beginning. Selah Merrill, the US consul at Jerusalem during most of the thirty years following 1882 reported that 'Palestine is not ready for the Jews, and the Jews are not ready for Palestine'. On the Blackstone Memorial, his comment to the State Department was that,

> To pour into this impoverished country tens of thousands of Jews would be an unspeakable calamity both for the country and for the Jews themselves. When and where have they learned the art of self-government? The quickest way to annihilate them would be to place them in Palestine with no restrictions or influences from any civilized government, and allow them to govern themselves; they would very soon destroy each other.[22]

Yet Presidents, unlike State Department mandarins, are required to be elected by the whole public, and are thus capable of being made aware, under the right circumstances, of the political weight of such populist forces as Christian Restorationism. So long as the President and Secretary of State were bearing down on them, the mandarins carried out the policy. Up to a point, the conviction that the United States was involved in the rescue of the helpless appealed to the philanthropic instinct of the mandarins, but this instinct is notoriously unstable, and so we find by the turn of the century a note of weariness appearing in State Department communications on these related matters. By the time Theodore Roosevelt came into the Presidency (1901–9), those in the permanent ranks of foreign-policy makers were finding ways to work together against the premises of the policy which came into place in the days of Harrison and Cleveland. Throughout the whole upper tier of foreign policy making, the Blackstone Memorial, if it was thought of at all, was remembered as an embarrassment.

It is not at all difficult to document the old fashioned gentlemen's anti-Semitism pervasive in these ranks, and this factor should not be discounted. Much more effective however in the long-run against any policy turning upon 'visions of grandeur in the Jewish destiny' was another kind of prejudice, the contempt of the well-educated for the unsophisticated, especially the theologically unsophisticated. In the Episcopalian, Congregational, Unitarian, and occasionally Presbyterian circles in which the policymaking elite were reared, nothing was so vigorously despised as 'Fundamentalism', and to this mind the very type of the worst fruit of Fundamentalism was (and still is) the End Times pamphleteer. So long as the only constant champions of 'Jewish destiny' were Fundamentalist pamphleteers, there was no need to give Zionism the time of day. Simple, old-fashioned, country-club anti-Semitism is as nothing in this equation, compared to the fear and loathing of Fundamentalism among properly educated Protestants.

Re-enforcing this anti-Zionist drift among policymaking elites was another long-term trend dating from this period, the growing influence of Protestant missionaries in the making of American foreign policy. In the United States as in Britain, zeal for the conversion of the Jews of Palestine had accompanied the first expressions of Christian Restorationism, but well before the time of Blackstone's Memorial it was evident to all that the missionary effort among the Jews was bringing very little result. Missionaries to the Jews became few and far between, and many ended their work in disillusionment. By the late nineteenth century missionary efforts in the lands of the Ottoman Empire were redirected towards the Arab population – which was to be numbered in countless millions, as compared to the roughly 80,000 Jews of the area. Now the missionaries were reporting rates of conversion vastly better than anything that anyone had ever been able to show for the efforts among the Jews.

Increasingly, therefore, the missionaries were reporting from the field to their churches in a manner sympathetic to their Arab clients. It is now something of a cliché – and like most clichés, more true than people guess – that Arab nationalism, the ultimate adversary of Zionism, was a product of the missionary movement, in that the latter provided the opportunities for literacy, and inadvertently the indoctrination in European concepts of nationalism that nurtured the 'Arab awakening'. In this connection, Robert College in Constantinople and the Syrian Protestant College (later, American University) in Beirut played the key roles. Thus, within the State Department, an 'Arabist' point of view was emerging well before the Great War. Even when one was well disposed to the cause of the Jews, one had now to admit that bringing the Jews in their hundreds of thousands, let alone their millions, and settling them in Palestine was, to put it mildly, a much more complicated matter than it had seemed in the days of President Harrison.

In summary: an original outburst of concern for Jews at the outset of the period of Russian pogroms triggered an authentic, though apparently short-lived, popular enthusiasm for Restoration of the Jews. After the issue faded, the professionals could safely pursue what they knew was a better, because a more realistic, policy: appeasement of the Turks and the Russians.

8

Louis Brandeis and Woodrow Wilson

A COUP IN THE HOUSE OF ZIONISM: AUGUST 1914

As we have seen, when war broke out in Europe in the August of 1914 the World Zionist movement was in effect decapitated. Jews who were citizens of Allied nations – Britain, France, later Italy, and above all the masses of Russia – would not take advice or instruction from the official leadership, most of whom were citizens of one or other of the Central Powers. In this situation, who would now represent the Jewish people before the princes of the world? Who would provide for those Jews, in particular, whose lives were now at greatest possible risk: those who lived in the Ottoman Empire (which, in November 1914, joined the Central Powers), those who lived in all parts of the Russian Empire (in recent years racked by cycles of officially inspired pogroms); and those in Central Europe, who stood in the paths of the armies which fought the very first major battles of this war?

As it happened, at the outbreak of the European war Shmaryahu Levin of the Actions Committee of the WZO was stranded in the United States where he had been on a speaking tour. Immediately he joined Louis Lipsky, executive director of the Federation of American Zionists, and Jacob de Haas to review the situation and devise an emergency plan. Within days a telegram arrived at the office of Louis Brandeis:

> Zionist headquarters Berlin disorganized. Actions Committee scattered. European organization disabled through military service of Zionists in armies. Extraordinary conference American Zionist representatives with Schmaryahu Levin very urgent to consider political administrative economical situation and save Palestine institutions. Make every sacrifice to attend Hotel Marseilles New York August thirty wire.[1]

Off the record, Jacob de Haas told Brandeis that he intended to offer Brandeis' name for the chairmanship of the Committee.

Needless to say, Levin had received no mandate for what he was doing from the European Zionist executive – a rump of which met a little later in Copenhagen, but was effectively ignored thereafter. In plain words: it was a coup.

However, as we have seen, one European member of the Zionist leadership, Chaim Weizmann, heartily approved of the American initiative. Discouraged by the Copenhagen organization's insistence on 'neutrality', and believing, as he later put it, 'that our destiny lay with the Western democracies', Weizmann simply broke with the European leadership, and acknowledged the leadership of American Jewry, which 'perhaps bears within itself the seed of "eternity"'.

Thus, in August 1914, leadership of World Zionism was settled for an uncertain term upon a small and inexperienced coterie of American Jews, under the leadership of Louis D. Brandeis.

ZIONISM COMES TO AMERICA

It needed great optimism to argue in 1914 that Zionism's future lay with its American branch. At that time, American Jewry numbered about three million. At the Annual Convention of the Federation of American Zionists held in Rochester in June, 1914, it was reported that there was a membership of a little over 14,000. A budget of $12,500 was proposed, which would exceed anticipated revenues by $2,600.

Before the massive immigration of European Jews began in the early 1880s, American Jewry was a small community of about 250,000 all told. Most of these spoke German as their first language but were now fluent in English; most were Reform in religion (90 per cent of American synagogues were Reform), and thought of themselves as belonging to 'perhaps the happiest community in the long history of the Dispersion'. This unprecedented 'happiness' was put in jeopardy by the arrival between 1882 and 1914 of nearly two million Jews, nearly all from Central Europe, nearly all Yiddish-speaking and mostly Orthodox.

'Zionism', a complete mystery to America's German Jews (*Yahudim*), came in the baggage of a minority of the new immigrants. The subject first came to Gentile notice in the mid-1890s, when major articles appeared in *Harper's Weekly* and the *Literary Digest*, the latter noting that 'two aims of the Zionists were the revival of Hebrew and the colonization of Palestine'.[2] The history of Herzlian Zionism in the United States begins formally with the founding of the Federation of New York Zionists in November, 1897. Some months later, a loose alliance of some 100 Zionist groups met in New York to form a Federation of American Zionists, whose first president was Professor Richard Gottheil of Columbia University, and whose first secretary was Stephen Wise, a young Reform Rabbi. By 1905, there was a 'paper membership' of 25,000, enough barely to support a small staff and a monthly journal, the *Maccabean*.

Very early on, the habit of schism in the ranks of the American Zionists had been brought to the attention of Theodor Herzl. In 1901 he had despatched Jacob de Haas, a British Jew of Dutch Sephardic origin, to America to try to win unity in Zionist ranks. By 1905 the membership was built up to 25,000, but thereafter it slumped again, to about half that figure. The American Zionist movement was still essentially a mission province of Herzlian Zionism. Unable to finance its own activities, how could it be expected to carry the work of the worldwide movement?

LOUIS DEMBITZ BRANDEIS (1856–1941)

In 1849, 23 members of three interrelated families, Brandeis, Wehle and Dembitz, came together to America. They were Jewish merchants from the vicinity of Prague, sympathizers with the liberal cause that briefly triumphed, and then was suppressed throughout the Austrian Empire during the turbulent months of 1848–49. In search of promising new settings for the various merchant enterprises they had in mind, the families moved to settled parts of the frontier, first to Ohio, then to Indiana, then to Louisville, Kentucky.

Louis David Brandeis was born in Louisville, 13 November 1856. His father was Adolf Brandeis, a merchant, who, after many ups and downs, eventually owned the successful retail firm called A. Brandeis and Son (the 'Son' being Louis' brother Alfred). Louis was raised in material comfort, and had the privilege of wide travel and education.

The intellectual side of the legacy was somewhat stronger on the side of Louis' mother, Frederika Dembitz Brandeis. Her brother, Lewis Naphtali Dembitz, was a scholar of wide-ranging interests, notably in languages, philosophy, history and the law, but also in the sciences. He was a scholar-specialist in law, author of the authoritative *Kentucky Jurisprudence*. A dedicated abolitionist, he had helped found the Republican Party of Kentucky, and had been a delegate to the Convention which chose Abraham Lincoln for the Presidency. Alone, in the midst of this non-observant, assimilated family of German-speaking Jews, he had sought out Orthodox Judaism in his teens, and become a pious observer. He wrote learned works on Judaism, and was vice-president of the Orthodox Jewish Congregational Union of America.

The sabbath was not observed in Louis Brandeis' home. Already in Europe, the family as a whole had advanced a long way towards assimilation. In America, the advance continued. Yet, as so often happens when one's parents have voted against the religious legacy of the grandparents, Louis found himself drawn to the example of his observant uncle. In later years he recalled 'the joy and awe with which my uncle, Lewis Dembitz, welcomed the arrival of the [Sabbath] day and the piety with which he observed it'.[3] It is significant that in his teens Louis formally changed his middle name to Dembitz to honor his uncle. On the other hand, as an adult he followed the example of non-observance laid down by his parents. It is said that Louis Brandeis only set foot in the synagogue twice: once, during a Zionist convention in Pittsburg in 1916, the other time when he visited the synagogue at Zichron Yaakov in Rehovot, Palestine, in 1919.[4]

Louis Brandeis received his undergraduate education at the University of Dresden, Germany, before returning home to study at Harvard Law School. His brilliant record there brought him patrons among the professors and leading lawyers, including Professor Oliver Wendell Holmes, Jr. This in turn gave him an entrée into Boston's intellectual circles, which, in those days, were still dominated by descendants of Puritans, 'the Brahmins of Boston', as they were called – mostly unchurched by now, but still notably 'Puritan' in their moral preoccupation. Louis had no trouble establishing a successful law firm (Warren and Brandeis) in partnership with socially prominent Sam Warren, nor in gaining membership in the exclusive clubs of Boston, including the Union and the Exchange. It is not strictly true that he 'ceased to be a Jew', as some have overstated it. Rather, although he 'used his German-Jewish connections in Boston as a source of business ... he did not feel impelled to ... socialize with his German-Jewish clients ... He played no role in Boston Jewish society, and the Jewish Encyclopedia did not even mention his name.'[5]

By 1910, he was a millionaire. He found outlet for his Progressive idealism by becoming a 'people's lawyer', working without fee to defend the public interest in cases involving transportation franchises, savings banks, regulation of hours and wages, and many other causes. Well before 1912, he was nationally famous as the champion of what came to be called the 'New Freedom' wing of Progressivism.

During the presidential term of William Howard Taft (1909–13), the Republican Party was torn apart. With all necessary allowances for differences of personality and personal grudges, what was principally at stake was a difference of political philosophy which separated 'Conservatives' from 'Progressives'. In this conflict, Brandeis was clearly associated with the Progressive side, and closely allied with its longest-standing national champion, Robert La Follette, formerly Governor and now Senator from Wisconsin. He supported La Follette's National Progressive Republican League, founded in December, 1910, as a vehicle for La Follette's bid for the Presidency. Through 1910 and 1911, he undertook a speaking tour on behalf of La Follette through several states, but by early 1912 Theodore

Roosevelt had entered the ring, and La Follette's support among Republicans was dwindling. Though courted by TR, Brandeis remained loyal to La Follette, a close personal friend as well as a political ally, even after it had become clear that La Follette's own Progressive Party intended to abandon him in order to nominate the colorful ex-President. From that moment, the substantial political asset that attached to Brandeis' reputation came within the sights of the Democratic nominee, Woodrow Wilson.

WOODROW WILSON (1856–1924)

The ancestors of Thomas Woodrow Wilson came from Scotland, on one side directly, on the other by way of Northern Ireland. His paternal grandfather, James Wilson, left County Down in 1807, coming first to Pennsylvania, then to Ohio, where for a while he served in the Ohio State Legislature. On his mother's side, Woodrow Wilson descended from a long line of scholars and Presbyterian preachers in Scotland.

The future President's father was Thomas Ruggles Wilson, a broadly educated man, who combined a career as a teacher in various fields, including the sciences, with the Presbyterian ministry, into which he was ordained in 1849. By the time that Thomas Woodrow Wilson was born, on 28 December 1856, his father was the full-time minister of the Presbyterian church at Staunton, Virginia. Two years later, the family moved to Augusta, Georgia, where Thomas Wilson continued his ministry at the First Presbyterian Church. Then in 1870, when Woodrow was fourteen, they moved to Columbia, South Carolina, where his father became professor of pastoral theology at the Presbyterian seminary.

Woodrow Wilson frequently asserted that the key to understanding him was that he was 'a son of the manse'. He was raised in a pious home which was also a bookish one. There was much reading aloud and discussion about books and learning – the old learning of theology, moral philosophy, literature, and the new learning of the sciences. By the time that Woodrow was ready to go off to college, the family was living in substantial comfort, though they certainly were not rich.

Another powerful shaping force in Woodrow Wilson's life was his recollection of the Civil War. His father, though born in the North, followed the Southern branch of the Presbyterian church when it divided in 1861, and served as a chaplain in the Confederate army. Thus, although Woodrow Wilson's career after 1883 was lived out almost entirely in the North, his essential moral and political character remained Southern.

Woodrow Wilson attended Davidson College, near Charlotte, South Carolina, (1873–74), then Princeton (1874–79). After attending Princeton, he studied law at the University of Virginia, and followed this with a distinctly unsuccessful stint at practice of the law in Atlanta, Georgia. In 1883 he returned to the academic world, where he remained until his political career began in his fifties. At Johns Hopkins University, Baltimore, he studied history and political economy. Teaching jobs at small colleges followed the completion of his PhD, and then in 1890 he went back to Princeton as Professor of Jurisprudence and Politics.

He was a great success as a teacher, and drew steadily growing, eventually very large, lecture classes. At the same time, he won substantial fame and income as a writer of a standard University-level textbook in American History, as an essayist, and as an after-dinner orator, speaking all across the country on a wide range of themes: literature, moral philosophy, politics, and the role of the universities.

All the authorities on his life agree that he was powerfully devoted to the religion in which he was raised. He read the Bible daily, and was active in the work of his church. In a letter to a friend he says: '*My* life would not be worth living if it were not for the driving power of religion, for *faith*, pure and simple. I have seen all my life the arguments against it without ever having been moved by them ... There are people who *believe* only so far as they *understand* – that seems to me preposterous and sets their understanding as the standard of the universe ... I am very sorry for such people.'[6]

In 1902, the Board of Governors of Princeton University chose him to be the University's president. Committed as ever to his lifelong vision of higher learning grounded upon confidence in God as Creator and Sustainer, he set an example for students and faculty by regular attendance at chapel, and, indeed, normally led the services himself twice a week. At the same time, he was determined that Princeton should stand clearly at the forefront of modern learning in all its departments. With respect to theology, this meant working successfully to reduce the strength of the conservatives in the theological faculty (some of them among the most respected voices on the 'Fundamentalist' side of the theological wars) and their allies on the Board of Governors. He succeeded in getting appointments for the first Jew and the first Roman Catholic to the Faculty of Theology, and in 1906 persuaded the Board to formally resolve that Princeton was a non-sectarian institution.

Wilson's speech-making on the theme of the University as the training ground of leaders for Democracy struck a responsive chord. The American public of the Progressive Era was already accustomed to the idea of scholars in politics as champions of democratic causes. There was more than sufficient precedent, therefore, for political leaders in the State of New Jersey to begin to think of President Wilson as a notable political property. Early in 1910, Wilson was approached by Jim Smith, boss of the New Jersey

Democratic machine, and offered its support (tantamount to nomination) as Democratic candidate for Governor of New Jersey.

After his election, he stubbornly refused to take the machine's direction, refusing, for example, to endorse its nominee for the US Senate. He succeeded in establishing irresistible leverage over the legislature through his generation of popular support for key measures of his legislative program. Most of these were in line with the progressive agenda of his day: a primary and elections law, a corrupt practices act, workmen's compensation, utilities' regulation, and more.

As one of a very small number of Democratic Governors of a large Northern state in the North, he was thus an attractive candidate for the Party's Presidential nomination in 1912. Meanwhile, the division in national Republican ranks meant that for the first time since 1896, the Democratic nomination was a prize to be coveted.

WILSON AND BRANDEIS

Wilson's task in 1912 was to stake out a position on the progressive side of public issues, distinguishing a Democratic or 'Jeffersonian' approach from that of men who had been in public life much longer than he, and who seemed to have better title to the name of 'progressive'. It made sense, therefore, that he should send an emissary to sound out Louis Brandeis more directly on how he might serve in Wilson's campaign.

The emissary proved to be none other than Jacob de Haas – the same Jacob de Haas whom Herzl had sent to America back in 1902 on a mission to shape up American Zionism, and the same Jacob de Haas, who would approach the same Louis Brandeis almost exactly two years later with the request from the European Zionists to take charge of the provisional Executive. While continuing since 1902 as secretary of the Federation of American Zionists, de Haas had gone on to become the editor of the *Boston Jewish Advocate*. That summer of 1912, he had been hired by the Democratic National Committee to help in fund-raising, and 'to work among the nationalized citizens in the interest of the Democratic candidates'.[7] A few weeks later, after a direct face-to-face interview between the principals (28 August 1912), Brandeis agreed to undertake a speaking tour on Wilson's behalf.

After Wilson's election, informed observers speculated about the possibility of Wilson's choosing Brandeis as his Attorney-General; but Wilson, though greatly tempted, concluded that Brandeis was perceived as too anti-business. Brandeis did, however, play an influential role as an advisor to Wilson, helping, notably, in drafting anti-trust legislation and other matters. Indeed, in the opinion of the doyen of Wilson scholars, Arthur Link, he became 'the chief architect of the New Freedom'.

The knowledge of this close relationship was of course a considerable factor in the decision of de Haas and Levin to offer to Brandeis the leadership of the provisional Executive in August, 1914.

LOUIS BRANDEIS AND ZIONISM

When, on that August day in 1912, Jacob de Haas set out on behalf of the Democratic National Committee to speak to Louis Brandeis, he had in mind a second purpose which he did not reveal to the Committee – certainly not to the Campaign's finance chairman, Henry Morgenthau. As Louis Brandeis told the story in letters to friends over the next few days, it was after they had finished their discussion on the campaign and as he was driving de Haas back to the train station that the conversation took an apparently but not really fortuitous turn. De Haas asked Louis Dembitz Brandeis whether he was related to Lewis Dembitz, who had died in 1907 – 'a noble Jew', with whom he was well acquainted through their shared Zionist involvements. Evidently, Brandeis was so taken by this reference to his admired uncle, that he simply turned the car around and brought de Haas back to the cottage, where they spent the rest of the day listening to him tell the story of Theodor Herzl, the Basle Convention, and de Haas' own adventures as the emissary of Herzl in America. This was the first of many conversations between Brandeis and de Haas over the next two years. Thereafter, Brandeis spoke of being 'eternally grateful' to de Haas, whom he considered 'the maker of American Zionism'.[8]

In the course of the previous decade, Louis Brandeis had been consciously and conscientiously studying the life and the beliefs of American Jews, deliberately closing the gap of knowledge and experience which had kept his public and private life apart from theirs. The key to understanding Brandeis' Zionism is that in effect it came to him as a newly discovered corollary to his fundamental Progressive faith. In February, 1911, in a letter to Bernard Gerson Richards, editor of the *Maccabean*, he wrote: 'My sympathy with the Zionist movement rests primarily upon the noble idealism which underlies it, and the conviction that a great people, stirred by enthusiasm for such an ideal, must bear an important part in the betterment of the world.'[9]

On 17 April 1913, Louis Brandeis formally joined the Zionist Association of Boston, and during the summer of 1914 Brandeis embarked on a program of intensive reading in Zionist theory and philosophy. In 1915, in a speech entitled, 'Zionism as Patriotism', he declared:

During most of my life my contact with Jews and Judaism was slight. I gave little thought to their problems, save in asking myself from time to time, whether we were showing by our lives due appreciation of the opportunities which this hospitable country affords. My approach to Zionism was through Americanism. In time practical experience and observation convinced me that Jews were by reason of their traditions and their character peculiarly fitted for the attainment of American ideals. Gradually it became clear to me that to be good Americans, we must be better Jews, and to be better Jews, we must become Zionists.[10]

9

'A Son of the Manse'

In turning to Brandeis, the official Zionists were passing over an entire generation of faithful Zionists – under whose direction American Zionism had been declining steadily for the previous decade – to prefer a recent convert. Fully sensitive to this situation, Brandeis, before accepting the chair at the meeting of August, 1914, spoke of his 'disqualification for this task': 'I have been to a great extent separated from Jews ... I am very ignorant in things Jewish.' This said for record, he set to work.

A resolution was quickly adopted, committing the new Committee to collect a sum of $100,000 for Palestine – about seven times the size of any annual collection previously made. Brandeis' practical leadership began immediately with the circulation of a letter, which went out in hundreds of copies in Yiddish and English, announcing the formation of the Provisional Executive Committee (PEC) and the start of Louis Brandeis' leadership within the movement:

> To Zionists of America
> 31 August 1914, New York, NY
> The war in Europe has brought a crisis upon the Zionist organization ... At an Extraordinary Conference of American Zionists held at New York on 30 August 1914, a Provisional Executive Committee for General Zionist Affairs was formed, to act until such time when the Actions Committee shall reassemble ... Zionists, the duty of the hour is supreme. Strain every nerve to obtain at once the One Hundred Thousand Dollar fund that is essential to the welfare of our movement. Put the machinery of all your organizations into motion without delay ... Who knows but that our tried people everywhere, hearing the message of Zionism ring above the din and clash of battle, will strive, united with us, for permanent justice, peace, and liberty for the Jewish people in the Jewish land.[1]

In an effort to bring the Zionist issue to the forefront of public discussion Brandeis undertook a cross-country lecture tour. At the same time, he recruited his friend Norman Hapgood, editor of *Harper's Weekly*, to write an article, 'Zionism's Crisis', which appeared in the magazine on 26 September 1914. Many other articles followed in the next few months, all conforming to Brandeis' representation of Zionism as part of the cause of globalizing American progressivism. Under Brandeis' leadership, membership grew from 20,000 in 1914 to nearly 200,000 in 1918.

Perhaps the most enduring part of the legacy of these months was Brandeis' recruitment of a generation of young professionals and intellectuals, many from his own circle at Harvard, others from the ranks of graduate students, youthful lawyers, academics, and rabbis. These included Felix Frankfurter, Benjamin V. Cohen, Julian Mack, Emanuel Neumann and Stephen Wise.

STEPHEN S. WISE (1874–1949)

Aaron Weisz, born in Hungary and descended from a line of scholarly Orthodox rabbis in Hungary, emigrated to the United States in 1874, shortly after the birth of his son, who is remembered as Stephen Wise. There he worked for a while as a laborer, before receiving the call to serve as the rabbi in a synagogue in Brooklyn; thereupon, he called for his family to join him in America. Though his father was zealously Orthodox, Aaron Weisz in America moved towards the theology and practice of Reform, which, he concluded, was better adapted to American life. He was in the moderate wing of the reformers who founded the Jewish Theological Seminary, which in turn became the source of the movement called Conservative Judaism.

Stephen was educated in New York public schools, but the better part of his education took place at home, in German and English literature. His education in Judaism came in private classes at the feet of scholars of the Jewish Theological Seminary, friends of his father. He attended City College of New York, then moved to Columbia University, where he studied Semitic Languages and Literature under an eminent scholar and a zealous Zionist, Richard J.H. Gottheil. After a year of study in Vienna, he returned to be ordained as a Rabbi, immediately taking up his first post as an assistant Rabbi in New York city in 1893 at the age of 19!

After serving this congregation briefly, Wise took a pulpit at the other end of the nation, in Portland, Oregon, where a small Jewish community sustained itself by effort of will on the margins of Protestant society. As it happened, certain of the leading Protestant clergy of Portland were active in aspects of the work and preaching of 'Social Gospel', and Rabbi Wise was able to make good use of his own social activism as a bridge to friendship with these men. Becoming quickly active in local progressive circles, he was among the guests at a dinner meeting honouring President Theodore

Roosevelt in 1903, and he seized the moment to speak to the President about the recent Kishinev pogrom.

In 1907, Wise returned to New York city to serve a new, denominationally independent congregation formally organized on 19 April 1907. Henry Morgenthau was the first President of the Congregation, and other prominent Uptown Jews were conspicuous in its leadership in its beginnings. Wise served the Free Synagogue until his death in 1949, after which it took the name, the Stephen S. Wise Free Synagogue. His practice of pulpit-exchange with like-minded Protestant clergy drew complaints from the Orthodox rabbis, so that all his life he was thought of as something of a disturber of the religious peace of New York Jewry.

In New York, he continued the progressive involvements he had begun in Oregon. He was a vocal champion of labour, and he was among the founders of the National Association for the Advancement of the Colored People (NAACP). Soon he was speaking out on the New York political scene, attacking corruption, and loudly supporting reform candidates against the party candidates in local elections. In the White House of William Howard Taft he was consulted regarding appointments and for advice on immigration and on those foreign policy issues which were of special interest to the Jewish community.

Few Reform Jews were Zionists. Rabbi Wise, in this as in so much else, was an exception. He was active in the early organization of American Zionist groups, he represented American Zionists in Basle at the Second Zionist Congress (1898), reporting on the session to the *New York Journal*. There he met Herzl, whom he worshiped thereafter. All his life, Stephen Wise remembered Herzl, at the last Zionist meeting that Herzl attended (April 1904), saying to him, 'I shall not live to see the Jewish State, but you, Wise, are a young man. You will live to see the Jewish State.'[2] He did, in truth, live to see the day when the state was created – but died in 1949, before he could visit it.

THE BRANDEIS/WISE/DE HAAS CONNECTION

Stephen Wise's dealings with Woodrow Wilson went back to early 1911, when the latter had come at Rabbi Wise's invitation to address the Free Synagogue on the subject, 'Politics and Morals'. Wise introduced Henry Morgenthau to Wilson early in 1911, 'in the hope that he would be impressed with him and become one of his supporters for the Presidency'. Indeed he did. He became one of a very small group who funded Wilson's bid for the Presidential nomination, and after the convention, the Chairman of the campaign's Financial Committee. (Later still, President Wilson appointed Morgenthau his Ambassador to Turkey.)[3] By May 1912, before either

Convention had met, Wise was ready to support Wilson openly for the Presidency.

On 28 January 1916, President Wilson nominated Louis Brandeis for the Supreme Court. Senate hearings on this nomination then followed. These proved to be unprecedentedly long and heated, owing (most scholars believe) not to Brandeis' Jewish 'belonging' nor to his Zionism, but rather to what many regarded as his antibusiness views. Not until 24 May 1916 did the Senate confirm him, voting 10–8, along party lines. After Brandeis' nomination editorials appeared in influential papers contending that it would be inappropriate for Louis Brandeis to continue in his role as leader of the American Zionist movement. Brandeis, who privately attributed the entire editorial campaign to 'a traitorous, anti-Zionist, assimilationist cabal centred around the publishers of the *New York Times*', resisted the clamour as long as possible, but eventually yielded. At a convention held in Philadelphia in July 1916, he handed over the Chairmanship to Stephen Wise, who assured the assembly that 'my appointment is in some degree, wholly I devoutly hope, a nominal and technical one'.[4]

There is abundant documentation in the Brandeis archives to prove that Brandeis remained the active, unchallenged chief of American Zionists until the day of his death in 1941, but Stephen Wise was for now the active, visible conduit between the Zionists and the President. He seems, indeed, to have had easy access to President Wilson through the latter's entire term, bringing up matters of appointments to office, and matters of greatest concern to the Jewish community.

At Wise's side was Jacob de Haas, who continued his service to Woodrow Wilson as liaison to the important 'ethnic blocs'. Among other duties, early in the 1916 electoral season he prepared a confidential memo for the President, entitled, 'The Political Situation and the Jewish Voters'. Its principal conclusion was that for Jewish voters 'the Jewish question eclipses all other considerations, and the sentiment prevails that Wilson can best bring about its solution'. Appended to the memo is a list naming every town in the United States in which there are Jewish voters – 40,000 of them, the memo claims. Given the very close electoral result of 1916, de Haas, if so minded, could have claimed to have contributed a substantial part of the margin of victory.[5]

WINNING WILSON FOR THE BALFOUR DECLARATION

With Wilson narrowly re-elected in 1916, the American Zionists' undivided attention could now be given to the task of getting Wilson aligned behind the efforts, under the leadership of Chaim Weizmann, to secure a public pledge by the British government in favor of the 'homeland for the Jews' –

what became the Balfour Declaration of 2 November 1917. Zionists wanted to believe that the extraordinary access that their chiefs, Brandeis and Wise, had to the President guaranteed American endorsement of the Zionist program, but realistically, the auguries were mixed. It was well known that Woodrow Wilson was closer to the missionaries than any of his predecessors – and that these were overwhelmingly hostile to Zionism.

The American Zionists' formal approach to the Administration began with a meeting with Edward House, the President's confidential advisor on foreign policy matters in late January 1917, even before the American entry into the war. Wise brought a memo which he, Brandeis, and Felix Frankfurter had prepared, arguing for American endorsement of some kind of British protectorate of Palestine, with guarantees to the Jews (the essentials of the eventual Balfour Declaration.) House gave the impression of being persuaded; but years later, when the documents were opened, it became clear that he was far from friendly in reality – and that the same was true, in greater or lesser degree, of most of Wilson's official advisers.

By the late spring of 1917, it had become clear that the proponents of the Balfour plan would have to find some way to get past the anti-Zionism so well entrenched in Wilson's official family. The strategy that won the day for the Zionists was conceived by Chaim Weizmann, and involved taking advantage of Lord Balfour's declared interest in getting to meet the famous jurist, Justice Brandeis, and the latter's established entrée to the President. Arrangements were made for Lord Balfour to meet quietly with Justice Brandeis in April 1917, while the former was on a visit to Washington. It was clearly understood that Brandeis spoke to Balfour in his capacity as the chief of the American Zionists. Each had greatly admired the other at a distance; and now their personal bond became a powerful factor in bringing Woodrow Wilson around to commiting himself to the position that came to be expressed in the Balfour Declaration (2 November 1917).

THE BRANDEIS–BLACKSTONE CONNECTION

Historians of our present theme – how Woodrow Wilson was won to the Zionist cause – occupy themselves almost entirely with this story of the comings and goings of the diplomats and the courtiers, which we have sought to recapitulate in the three previous paragraphs. Yet there is another element in this story which, though almost totally ignored by most of the historians, was taken with the greatest of seriousness by the Zionist principals at the time – and that is Wilson's religious motivation. Indeed, both Louis Brandeis and Stephen Wise later said, for record, that what guaranteed the victory for the Zionists was not their greater skill in playing

the political and diplomatic game, but their success in appealing to Woodrow
Wilson's biblically based Christian faith.

Both Wise and Brandeis, we know, directly appealed to Wilson's self-consciousness as 'a son of the manse', his sense of awe at the possibility that he had being divinely prepared to fulfill possibilities that were inherent in the position of President of the United States, but which could not be seen except with the eye of faith, disposed by long training in scripture. Yet Brandeis and Wise did not simply leave Wilson alone to brood on these things. They set to work to mobilize the Cyrus connection.

As we have already noted, early in 1916, almost exactly one quarter-century after President Harrison's receipt of the Blackstone Memorial, the story of the Memorial was brought to Louis Brandeis' attention. The Brandeis Papers contain the correspondence which documents Brandeis' unsuccessful efforts to recruit the State Department's help in his research. Undaunted, Justice Brandeis researched the matter on his own, and eventually produced some forty-seven pages of handwritten notes – most of them consisting of excerpts from newspapers of 1891–12. Then, Nathan Straus, at Brandeis' behest, wrote to Blackstone, 8 May 1916:

> Mr Brandeis is perfectly infatuated with the work that you have done along the lines of Zionism. It would have done your heart good to have heard him assert what a valuable contribution to the cause your document is. In fact he agrees with me that you are the Father of Zionism, as your work antedates Herzl.[6]

Immediately, William Blackstone and Justice Brandeis started up a correspondence which continued until the death of the former in 1934.

A little later, Straus wrote Blackstone again, suggesting that now was the time to resuscitate his Memorial.[7] Sensing that time was short if the United States was to get to the head of the line of powers who were already dealing with the Zionists, Blackstone did not attempt to match in number the signatures appended to his original petition to President Harrison, settling instead for eighty-two. As he wrote to President Wilson, 'It would have been possible to have secured any number of signatures of the most representative character to the Memorial, but this was so evident that it was not necessary. The endorsement of the Presbyterian General Assembly, the Ministers' Meetings of the Methodists and the Baptists, and many representative individuals and officials, evidence the General approval which the Memorial receives from our entire population.'

The situation in 1916–18 was strikingly different from that in 1891. Rather than standing alone as a pioneer expression of public support for a novel idea – the creation by fiat of the Great Powers of a Jewish homeland – this 'Second Memorial' was one of many items pouring upon Wilson's head at the time, under many auspices, urging him to act in support of a proposal now on the active Great Power agenda. It is for this very reason impossible to isolate and weigh the impact of this second Memorial. No trace of it appears in the published Wilson Papers, but the great stir it was causing in church circles must have had some effect on Wilson.

Blackstone's Second Memorial was ready by May of 1916, but Justice Brandeis now wrote to Blackstone to say that he believed the impact of the Memorial would be greater if its formal presentation were postponed 'until such times as ... he [Wilson] will be free to give his mind to this special cause'. It was not until May 1917 that Brandeis sent this instruction to de Haas: 'Talk with Wise, as to whether this would be a good time to get the Blackstone crowd to cheer.' Stephen Wise was entrusted by Blackstone with the Memorial and with Blackstone's covering letter, which he took to the President on 30 June 1917. 'In God's Providence', Blackstone had written,

> it has been my privilege to secure a remarkable endorsement of the Memorial in behalf of the Jews, which is presented herewith ... believing that the progress of events augurs the imminence of the psychological moment for benign action in behalf of the Jews, similar to that exhibited by Cyrus of Persia, and assured of your sympathy and willingness to aid the Jewish people in their present tragic sufferings, and praying that you may seize the opportunity of securing to yourself and our nation the blessing promised by God to Abraham and his seed, by showing loving kindness to Israel.

However, the Zionist leaders again proposed to delay the President's public endorsement of the Memorial. According to Wise's report to Blackstone, the President and Justice Brandeis agreed to wait for 'the most favoring hour' in which to make public the President's receipt of the Memorial. Blackstone was not impressed with the argument for delay. Immediately, he wrote to Wise: 'I have a firm conviction that the most solemn and unprecedented events in human history are impending, and I shall not be surprised if from such delay these events occur before the Memorial is presented.' In view of the impending 'fearful destruction of nations', Blackstone urged Rabbi Wise to impress upon the President the importance of having the United States publicly declared on behalf of Israel before Christ's imminent return.

But the 'favoring hour' never came. The clue to these tergiversations is in a letter which Brandeis wrote to Jacob de Haas in May 1917, in which he reveals that, 'My inclination is against presenting Blackstone's petition now, because of its suggesting of international guarantees'.[8] By the summer of 1917, there was the real prospect that Britain would take upon herself the task of establishing the Homeland for the Jews. In the light of this new situation, the Blackstone idea, because of its emphasis on international auspices for the Jewish state, could cause embarrassment. Anticipating

Wilson's warm response to the document's theology and to the testimonies to widespread support within the churches, Brandeis and Wise were keen that Wilson should privately be made aware of the Memorial. Brandeis described the situation to James de Rothschild:

> As to the non-Jewish sentiment, we have every assurance, apart from the Administration attitude, which is also favourable, that the vast mass of Christian opinion in this country, particularly of course the Protestant Churches, supports our idea. A petition has been prepared on that head, signed by very many distinguished Christians, and which will be presented to the President at the right moment, which emphasizes this favourable attitude.[9]

Wilson's response fully justified their expectations., but the three (Brandeis, Wise and Wilson) apparently recognized that to publish the Memorial now would seem to commit the United States to the original political conception – which, we recall, was for the calling of an open conference of the world powers, resulting in collective international action. The solution currently being proposed to Wilson from the British side was for either a joint US/British régime in Palestine (which Wilson believed the American public would not accept) or for a British régime. So long as Wilson knew about the Memorial and was moved by its arguments, the Zionists would have its full benefits, without causing complications to their negotiations with the British – which, indeed culminated in November 1917, in the Balfour Declaration.

Needless to say, none of these political considerations would have moved Blackstone, and therefore no hint of these matters was offered to him. Blackstone's Restorationist faith took no notice of political calculations of this kind. In the light of all that would follow – the eventual abandonment by Britain of her Balfour pledge – we might well conclude that Brandeis and Wise calculated wrongly in the summer of 1917, when, having encouraged Blackstone to crank up his Memorial campaign again, they then, in effect, conspired with Woodrow Wilson to deprive it of public notice. Perhaps the future of the Jews would have been better served had the President of the United States publicly received – and, better still, publicly endorsed, the Memorial which was, in effect, quietly suppressed on the advice of the Zionist leaders in the summer of 1917.

Thus, in the end, the Zionists won Wilson. In June of 1917, Wilson said to Wise: 'Whenever the time comes, and you and Justice Brandeis feel that the time is ripe for me to speak and act, I shall be ready.' Five agonizing months followed, during which Wilson still hesitated to give the British an unambiguous declaration of American support, but finally, on 13 October 1917, Brandeis was permitted to convey to Lord Balfour and the British cabinet the President's 'entire sympathy' with the proposed Homeland for the Jews. Without that declaration, most scholars agree, the British Cabinet would never have adopted the Balfour Declaration.

AFTERMATH

The Zionist leaders – at least those of Brandeis' circle – maintained their friendly connections with Blackstone until his death in 1935. Brandeis' enthusiasm for the work of Blackstone was clearly genuine, and Blackstone's enthusiasm for Zionism was equally genuine and undiminished. Over the following years, Blackstone sent Brandeis very large sums of money for support of Zionist work. Though their dealings appear to have been conducted strictly by correspondence, it is not far-fetched to say that their relationship had something of the character of the relationship between Herzl and Hechler. Like Herzl and Hechler, Brandeis and Blackstone presented the strongest possible contrast in background and moral philosophy. Brandeis, like Herzl, considered himself a humanist, and was, if anything, even less patient with religion. Yet his dealings with Blackstone opened to his eyes and his heart the universe of pious faith.

As one striking example, we learn that Blackstone (who, we recall, had responsibility for disbursing millions of dollars entrusted to him for missionary and evangelical work) wrote one day to explain to Justice Brandeis that he had made plans to deposit these funds in a safe place, so that in the event of his own death preceding the Rapture, they would be secure until the Rapture. Now he was requesting that, 'if the Rapture does come and you are not among those who participate in it', Justice Brandeis would assume responsibility for disbursing these funds after the Rapture as needed for the relief of Jews who would thereafter be converted to Christ, and would then face the burden of evangelism throughout the world. Somewhat anticlimactically, he noted that 'there are apparently no human laws which provide for any such event as this'.[10]

If the Herzlian Zionists sometimes had trouble taking the Christian Zionists whole, they always valued their constancy; and most, it seemed, retained great respect and even affection for them. To turn the coin over, the Christian Zionists were equally embarrassed to find themselves aiding and abetting the work of secularists, deniers of God, in the political arena. As we have seen, Blackstone did not mince words in his castigation of Herzl and his contemporaries for their faithlessness to the God of Israel. In *Jesus Is Coming*, he wrote:

> [T]he Zionists have seized the reins and eschewing the help of Abraham's God they have accepted agnostics as leaders and are plunging madly into this scheme for the erection of a godless state.
> But the Bible student will surely say, this godless national gathering of

> Israel is not the fulfilment of all the glorious restoration, so glowingly
> described by the prophets.
> No, indeed! ...

Blackstone's understanding was that the official Zionists were those foreseen by Zephaniah:

> Gather yourselves together, yea, gather together, O nation that hath no
> longing, before the decree bring forth, before the day pass as the chaff, before
> the fierce anger of the Lord come upon you.

Could this prophecy be more literally fulfilled than by this present Zionist movement, Blackstone asked.[11] As Zephaniah foresaw, it was 'the nation that hath no longing' – that is, those Jews who had no longing for God; that is, having no religious motive in their political behaviour, who were in fact accomplishing the Return. Regardless of their infidelity, their work is a work appointed by the God of Israel – a necessary work, being carried out with unworthy motives, but which must be assisted, out of the worthiest motives, by pious Christians. Just as open-minded Zionists, like Herzl himself, were drawn to the Christian zealots by fascination with the road not taken in their own lives – the road of pious faith – so, it is safe to say, the Christian zealots were drawn to the Zionists, as their counterparts today are drawn to Israeli politicians, by fascination with the road not taken in their own lives: the road of political action in the secular realm.

It is probably true to say that Woodrow Wilson was the last President of the United States who was disposed to be persuaded by the arguments of the Blackstone Memorial. The Presidents of the 1920s were not men of the same intellectual and mental and moral type. Furthermore, the 1920s was the decade when the public mind turned away – so far as we know, forever – from the fundamentalist convictions which made the Blackstone Memorial such a popular and powerful document in the days of its invention. The 1920s was the decade when the hegemony of American Protestantism was finally broken up – in the realms of thought and learning and in the realm of politics, and within the increasingly beleaguered house of Protestantism itself, Fundamentalism, though it won many battles, finally lost the war for control of thought and policy in all the major denominations.

Yet, while it would be reckless to claim that we can trace a clear line of cause and effect from Blackstone's Memorial of 1891 to the Creation of the State of Israel in 1948, it is not at all far-fetched to say that the Memorial is the place to go to find the clearest expression of the motivation that won President Woodrow Wilson, and which would continue to be the surest, the most constant source of American Christian Zionism. Despite the dissolution of the Evangelical-Protestant matrix in the years following 1916, and despite the decline of the intellectual prestige of 'Fundamentalism', there were still individuals for whom Blackstone's ideas had powerful appeal. 'Blackstone', Peter Grose recalls, 'had tried to persuade the President of the United States [Benjamin Harrison] by recalling the Persian monarch, Cyrus, who permitted the Jewish nation to return from Babylon and build their Second Commonwealth in Jerusalem ... Harrison himself was unmoved, but no one could then know the impact which the Bible story of Cyrus and the restoration of the Jews would have upon a later holder of presidential office, then a seven-year-old farm boy in Missouri.'[12]

PART THREE

RALLYING THE CHRISTIAN ZIONISTS

10

Working on Public Opinion

THE PALESTINE QUESTION IN THE REPUBLICAN ERA

In June 1918, the Zionist Organization of America published the results of its survey of editorial opinion in the United States with respect to the Balfour Declaration. 'There is no opposition to the movement, as such', they found, 'in the minds of secular editors. No editorials were excluded from this pamphlet for that reason. There simply aren't any.'[1]

Public opinion continued favorable through the remaining years of the Wilson Presidency – and through the years of the three Republican Presidents who succeeded him.

Before the end of Wilson's term, the Senate of the United States repudiated the package of treaties which Wilson had brought home from Versailles; these consisted of the multilateral Treaties imposing peace terms upon the defeated powers and defining the new boundaries of Europe, and the agreement (Article X) by which the United States would enter the League. This verdict of the Senate of the United States against multilateral involvement was then effectively ratified by the election of the Republican Warren Harding to the Presidency in 1920.

While there is a textbook cliché to the effect that the Republican presidents (1921–33) were practitioners of a policy of 'isolationism', this is a misconception. The policy pursued by Harding and Coolidge and Hoover might better be called 'unilateral internationalism': it was characterized by refusal to participate in the League, or in any other collaborative responsibility, together with a fairly aggressive unilateral diplomacy designed to open economic opportunities for the United States throughout the world.

American attitudes in these years greatly tried the patience of the Europeans, notably the British. Notwithstanding its refusal to enter the League and its policy of settling for separate bilateral peace treaties with each of the defeated powers of the War, the United States still insisted that it had a right to be consulted by Britain or France or the League in any actions which seemed to the United States to involve the interests of the United States. The issue of the Palestine Mandate was tailor-made for this purpose: here was the one area of the world where Great Britain was actually implementing a policy to which the United States had pledged itself, in her endorsement of the Balfour Declaration of 1917. The American Government knew that popular support for the Zionist goal was still extraordinarily high, but Great Britain, unlike the United States, was actually entrusted with implementing it, and there was much to criticize in her performance.

We ought to pause at this point to recall that in 1919 the United States had walked away from the opportunity to share with Britain jurisdiction over Palestine. There was, indeed, a moment when the British Government was proposing that the Americans take responsibility for the Mandate, but President Wilson knew (or thought he knew) that this was far too advanced an idea for the American public.

Distrust of Britain's motives ran high from left to right of the American political spectrum in the 1920s and early 1930s. The special appeal of the issue of the Jews and their future was that it was designed by God to demonstrate the fundamental moral superiority of Americans to Brits. Needless to say, American declarations on the subject of Palestine greatly irritated the British, who bore the heat of the day.

THE LODGE–FISH RESOLUTION, 1922

In 1922, the League of Nations formally assigned the mandate for Palestine to Great Britain. The United States, as just noted, was not a member of the League; but she was determined that nothing done by the League should be in violation of American interest nor in contradiction of principles to which the United States was pledged. Accordingly, a Resolution was introduced into the US Congress reaffirming the commitment of the United States to the Balfour Declaration, and calling upon Britain to work towards completion of the goal envisaged in that Declaration.

Yet the inspiration for the Congressional Resolution did not come full-blown from the brow of the Congressmen. In truth, its beginnings are to be found in the work of a lobby of relatively junior Zionist activists led by an Assistant US Attorney from Boston, Elihu Stone, and including Emanuel Neumann. In his autobiography, Neumann speaks of this as the first political victory of a new generation of Jewish lobbyists: it was achieved by what he calls 'our people', 'the "immigrant" Jews of humble origin, without any help from the prestigious leaders who had headed the organization [the ZOA]'.

EMANUEL NEUMANN (1893–1980)

Of all the official Zionists, Emanuel Neumann seems to have been the most constant in his belief that there was such a thing as a Christian conscience, and he certainly made the most conscientious efforts to study and understand it, so that he could recruit it on behalf of the cause of Zionism.

Born in 1893 in Liban, Latvia, Emanuel Neumann was brought to America by his parents only a few weeks after his birth. He was raised in a zealously Zionist family, in which the two strains of pious and secular Zionism flowed together. His father was a Talmudic scholar and a *Hohev Zion*, a believer that the Restoration of the Jews was God's plan, commanding the active co-operation of Jews everywhere. At the same time, he was a follower of *Haskalah* ('Enlightenment'), a champion of the use of Hebrew in all branches of literary and scientific life, and a devotee of Theodor Herzl. In the Williamsburg section of Brooklyn, Sundel Neumann founded a school for Jewish education in the Hebrew language. It was called *Shaare Zion* (Gates of Zion). Hebrew was the only language permitted in conversation in the Neumann family. Emanuel later carried this policy into his own household – as did his children into theirs.

Emanuel Neumann's life serves well to give us a realistic, human perspective on the time-frame with which we are dealing in this book. Born just three years before the publication of *Der Judenstaat*, he was active in Zionist youth groups during the years of doldrums for American Zionism immediately preceding the Great War. In a sense, he and American Zionism came of age together: it was in August 1914, just after he had turned twenty-one – and thus, by the more stringent definition of that time, became an adult – that he came into full-time service to Zionism as perhaps the youngest of that cohort of young people to whom Louis Brandeis turned for the full-time direction of the Provisional Executive Committee. Neumann then remained at the centre of Zionist action throughout most of the ensuing decades until his death in Tel Aviv in October, 1980. In the 1920s and 1930s, he played a crucial role in strengthening the American voice in the counsels of world Zionism. He was President of the American Zionist Organization in the *annus mirabilis*, 1947–48; and the last chapter of his life overlaps the first thirty years of the life of the State of Israel.

From Louis Brandeis and Stephen Wise, Neumann learned about the crucial importance of Christian conviction in Woodrow Wilson's decision to endorse the Balfour Declaration. Wise liked to tell the story of how he had reminded Wilson that King Cyrus, 'whatever else he was, had become enshrined in the pages of the bible as the Persian king who had enabled the exiled Jews of his land to return to Jerusalem and rebuild the land and Temple'. Whereupon Wilson soliloquized aloud, 'To think that I, a son of the manse, should be able to help restore the Holy Land to its people.'

Likewise, from Brandeis and Wise, Neumann had learned the story of the Blackstone Memorial. Many years later, when he was the Chairman of the Department of Public Relations and Political Action of the Emergency Committee for Zionist Affairs, Neumann composed the tribute to Blackstone, marking the fiftieth anniversary of the Blackstone Memorial (March 1941), which was noted earlier in chapter 7. His insider's knowledge of the Blackstone/Brandeis connection explains Neumann's appreciation of the possibilities of the Cyrus connection in general.

At the same time, Neumann had the sense to recognize that forces were at work that might draw Christian opinion in the opposite direction, if the opportunities of the moment were lost. The introduction of the Lodge–Fish Resolution (in Neumann's words)

> provoked a full-dress debate ... with pro-Arabs and anti-Zionist rabbis appearing [before the House Committee on Foreign Affairs] to give battle against us ... [The senior leadership of the WZO and ZOA] were uneasy about the whole affair ... fearing that the attempt to secure the official support of the Congress might well end in defeat and do the cause more harm than good ... [Nonetheless] the joint Congressional resolution favoring 'the establishment in Palestine of a National Home for the Jewish People' passed both Houses with flying colors and was eventually signed by President Harding.[2]

We can be quite sure that the majority of Senators and Congressmen who voted with the Lodge–Fish Resolution did so because they were persuaded that the cause was a popular one – which is how things ought to be in a democracy. Few Congressmen wished to be left out of the opportunity to declare support for the Balfour pledges – to be counted with the angels in the one 'international' issue of those days that most Americans felt they understood fully.

THE AMERICAN PALESTINE COMMITTEE, 1932

The Zionists' victory in the matter of the Lodge–Fish Resolution disclosed a great reservoir of support in Congress and the White House. Yet for many years thereafter no concerted effort was made by official Zionists to build something continuing upon the propaganda triumph of 1922. In the mid-1920s, a deceptive lull came over Jewish–Arab relations in Palestine – which broke dramatically with the Arab riots of 1929. To these the British responded with the first in what would turn out be a series of Royal Commissions of Inquiry into the Palestine situation, all issuing in official Government policy statements in one form and another, marking off the path of gradual but steady retreat from the Balfour commitment, and extending to the day of their abandonment of the Mandate (1947).

With the publication of the Passfield White Paper in 1930, the official Zionists sprang to life. In August 1931, Emanuel Neumann wrote to Selig Brodetsky, who was responsible at that time for the 'Political Affairs' portfolio within WZO:

> The political situation here [in the United States] presents a certain opportunity. The Republican Administration is in a cold sweat about the national elections in 1932. Because of the business depression there is a good chance that a Democrat may be elected. The outstanding possibilities are New Yorkers – Franklin D. Roosevelt and Owen D. Young. The former is distinctly friendly, having collaborated with Wilson in Paris during the Peace Conference. Because of our system of electoral votes, New York is of the greatest importance, and frequently of decisive importance in national elections. The State in turn cannot normally carry a Republican Presidential candidate without strong support in the City of New York where Jews constitute almost one-third of the electorate.
>
> Under these circumstances ... the Republican leaders would think twice before refusing us some reasonable requests. In the circumstances it may be advisable for me to endeavor to initiate political action in Washington with the help of our friends.

Despite the somewhat hard-boiled tone of those concluding remarks, we know that Neumann and his ally, Max Rhoade, had developed some respect for the Republican Administration, and rated very highly their good will. Among the best of the Christian friends of Zionism in those days was Herbert Hoover's Vice-President, Charles Curtis. He had played an active role in the business of the Joint Resolution back in 1922, and had frequently indicated readiness to help further the cause of the Jewish Homeland, notably by writing for the Zionist magazine, *New Palestine*.

Another good friend of Zionism was the arch-isolationist, Senator William E. Borah of Idaho. He first came into the viewfinder of the official Zionists when he took up the cause of Zionists being persecuted in the Soviet Union. His voice carried some weight in this matter, as he was one of the few serious proponents in those years of recognition of the Soviet Union. There is some evidence that it was the generous advocacy of Jewish causes by this Idaho politician – who owed nothing to any 'Jewish vote' – that turned the thoughts of Brandeis, Neumann, and Rhoade and others to the project that would issue in the American Palestine Committee in 1932. Secretary of the Interior Ray L. Wilbur, whom Neumann describes as 'Hoover's best friend in the Cabinet' was another valued contact, as was Assistant Secretary of State, James Grafton Rogers. Prominent Senators and Congressmen, many of them introduced to Neumann by Justice Brandeis and by Felix Frankfurter, were also showing great interest. To the Zionist Executive in London Neumann wrote a few weeks later:

'Fortunately the state of American politics is such that leaders of both Parties are likely to listen to us.'

On December 17, 1931, an exploratory meeting was held at the home of Justice Brandeis, attended by Neumann, Max Rhoade, Senator William H. King of Utah (a Mormon), Senator Robert La Follette, Jr, of Wisconsin, Representative Hamilton Fish, Assistant Secretary of State James Grafton Rogers, William Hard (a prominent journalist of the day), and William R. Hopkins. The last named, formerly City Manager of Cleveland, made a remark on that occasion which particularly struck Neumann:

> He explained his interest in Zionism by the fact that he was first of all of Welsh stock, and secondly, of a family of preachers and reared on the Scriptures ... It is Mr Hopkins' view that we are most likely to gain supporters among a certain type of Christians who have been brought up on the Scriptures, and who have a sentimental and emotional attitude toward the Holy Land, which makes them pre-disposed to favor the Zionist cause. He warns us against depending merely on politicians and liberals, who have no such background and sentimental attachment to Palestine.[3]

Neumann would have many opportunities over the next twenty years to experience the prophetic wisdom of those thoughts of William Hopkins.

The next step was a formal dinner meeting, held at the Mayflower Hotel in Washington, 17 January 1932, with the Vice-President of the United States presiding. A letter of endorsement came from President Hoover. Speeches were delivered by Emanuel Neumann, Felix Frankfurter, Senator King, and others, and at the end, the decision was made formally to launch the 'American Palestine Committee'. Those who joined on the spot included Senator King, Vice-President Curtis, Justice Harlan Stone of the Supreme Court, House Majority Leader Henry Rainey, Secretary of Agriculture Arthur M. Hyde, and both New York Senators, Robert Wagner and Royal Copeland. Generous coverage of the event appeared in the press.

Some weeks later, an organizational meeting was held, and the 'Statement of Aims and Principles of the American Palestine Committee' was circulated to the press. Its officers were: Robert F. Wagner, Chairman; Charles L. McNary, Co-Chairman; William Green, William H. King, John A. Ryan, Vice-Chairmen. Its intention was to serve as 'the vehicle for the expression of the sympathy and goodwill of Christian America for the movement to reestablish the Jewish National Home in Palestine.' Its philosophy and its programme echoed the Blackstone formula:

> The fulfillment of the millennial hope for the reunion of the Jewish people with the land of its ancient inheritance, a hope that accords with the spirit of biblical prophecy, has always commanded the sympathy of the liberal Christian world.

At once, Neumann prepared a report to the officers of the WZO, reflecting pride in the work so far, and sober realism about the task ahead. There must be a campaign of letter-writing to recruit new members, public meetings, and publications.

> It is essential of course that this and all other political work to be done in this country should be carried on in close contact with a committee representing the World Zionist Organization and the Jewish Agency for Palestine ... All this work will require funds ... There is much to be feared that, successful as our initial steps have been, the whole affair will be a futile gesture unless immediate steps are taken to continue the work properly. Not only that, but a most unfortunate and unfavorable reaction is bound to follow if such a group once formed is allowed to be quiescent or to dissolve. It will be impossible to revive it for years to come.

For the 1 February 1932 issue of the Zionist magazine, *Opinion*, Neumann wrote an article, 'Mobilizing American Opinion for Palestine', in which he reveals an extraordinary appreciation of the historical setting which we have been seeking to define in these pages:

> The genesis of American sympathy with the Zionist ideal has its roots in the cultural heritage of this country and the mentality of the people ... [We] recall the various American proposals for Jewish restoration in Palestine brought forward from time to time, both by Jews and Gentiles. Of these perhaps the most notable was that of the Reverend Dr Blackstone who in 1891, five years before the advent of Herzl, presented a memorial to the President of the United States, bearing the signatures of some of the most distinguished names in the Republic, and suggesting that America call an international conference to deal with the Jewish problem and to reestablish the Jewish Commonwealth in Palestine.

However, Neumann warned, there is the terrible possibility of the Zionists' losing the advantage of this 'restorationist' legacy, as the attitudes of American 'liberals' were being reshaped by 'a flood of powerful but subtle propaganda', which portrays Zionism as a front for British imperialism, and the Arabs of Palestine as their victims.

> In the end, we who were the victims of an organized and murderous assault [that is, the recent Arab riots], found ourselves depicted as the aggressors. To add to our distress, it was the liberals who took the lead in placing such a construction upon the situation. We were betrayed, as it were, in the house of our friends.

The goal of the new organization, then, was to exploit the 'great deal of latent sympathy for our cause in official circles', and 'to make our problems sufficiently clear'.

Louis Brandeis, whose role in all this was well known to the participants although never publicly discussed, had insisted from the beginning that there must be among official Zionists 'agreed priority in raising money', so that there could be 'a permanent office staff'. To accomplish this work, there must be a 'steering committee' of the most responsible figures in the Zionist Organization. The steering committee that emerged was drawn from the front ranks of Zionist executives: Julian Mack, Stephen Wise, Abram Magida (then the President of ZOA) and Max Sokolow of the WZO. It was agreed that Max Rhoade would handle the work of the APC in Washington, communicating regularly through Magida with ZOA and WZO authorities.

Complicating things from the beginning was the fact that Neumann himself had been assigned by the WZO Executive (of which he was now a member) to take up new duties in London early in 1932; and, as it developed, he served there only a few months before being sent even further from the scene, to Palestine. As Carl Voss later put it, it quickly became obvious that Neumann was 'its guiding spirit', and when he left America 'the APC, so well started, soon lapsed into desuetude'.

The financial situation of the ZOA had been desperate for some time now, and getting worse as the Great Depression advanced. Minutes of meetings of the Board of Directors of the ZOA, to which Neumann reported the progress of his APC efforts and proposed his budget for its operation, were entirely dominated by financial woes – statistics of falling membership, and the sad intelligence that only a minority of the remaining members were paying their dues. Highly placed Zionists were discussing the possibility of declaring bankruptcy, and disbanding.

What followed can only be called disgraceful. Long weeks after the inaugural dinner, the bills were still unpaid, and creditors were becoming nasty. We find Max Rhoade writing to the World Executive complaining of its failure to meet the budget agreed to.

> The situation has become a most embarrassing one both for myself personally and the Zionist Organization. Some of the Senators have been asking me when a meeting is to be held, and it has been difficult to think up a satisfactory excuse. A very wretched situation has been created, which I assure you, scarcely adds prestige to the ZO in the eyes of the personages whom we succeeded in interesting after so much effort and pains ... I am at a complete loss to know what to say to these people.

By May the APC had been orphaned. The Committee never formally disbanded, but rather it simply ceased to meet, and the public forgot about it.

So, the question arises: how could Neumann and Brandeis and Rhoade, thoroughly familiar with this larger picture, have persuaded themselves and others to launch this costly venture in 1932, only to watch it flounder and fall apart after only a few months of activity?

Making all possible allowance for the stringent financial situation of the time, we suspect that there was another factor at work in this story of the orphaning of the APC. This we find in the changing political situation between the moment when the project was first mooted (the fall of 1931) and the moment when a deathly hush seems to descend upon this theme in the correspondence of the official Zionists – that is, the late spring of 1932. In plain terms, there was by that later date virtually universal expectation that the Republicans would be defeated in the forthcoming Presidential elections. The thought must have occurred in many minds at once that there could be little profit for the Zionists in maintaining this bipartisan front, whose letter-head chiefs were incumbent Republicans. Surely the best policy was now to win a secure place with the winners.

By the late spring of 1932, most Zionists were aligned publicly with the campaign of Franklin Roosevelt. People with long memories were speaking of a return to the days of the Brandeis/Wise/Wilson axis – with Franklin Roosevelt now in the place of Woodrow Wilson. As most Zionists fancied themselves 'progressives', many were now embarrassed by the thought that so much time had been spent cultivating the captains of the old order. This hypothesis is not documentable, as it turns on the assumption that the principals were simply too embarrassed to put these thoughts into words.

The fact was, however, that the Zionists had done well by the Republicans' leadership, who had treated them with great and unalloyed courtesy. Many of them, as Rhoade reported, were at a loss to know why nobody was calling meetings any more, and must surely have wondered whether it was true that lack of funds was the only reason.

A few days after the election, Max Rhoade wrote to Stephen Wise:

> I know how delighted you must be over the prospects for Zionism as a result of the election – if for no other reason. The Hoover Administration was friendly of course, but the reappearance of the Wilson tradition, which you helped to mould, is bound to operate much in our favor ... All of us know that a number of our brethren are close to FDR and if someone could get on the 'in', it might help. Certainly if the new Secretary of State is friendly, we may be able to accomplish a great deal respecting the internal attitude of the Department.

Between the lines, we can read this thought: if the new Administration is indeed so thoroughly locked up for the Zionist cause, what purpose would it serve to keep alive the non-partisan American Palestine Committee?

And sure enough, almost at once everyone stopped mentioning it. Nowhere in the archives of this period do we find any formal expression of regret or apology from the Zionist Executive to the goodhearted public figures who lent their names and their enthusiasm to this effort.

The most extraordinary part of the whole episode is that when, nine years later, Emanuel Neumann came around to the statesmen with the proposal to launch another 'American Palestine Committee', most of the same figures came on board again! This second time around, however, as we shall see, the results were strikingly different.

In a memo, not dated, but apparently belonging to early January 1932, Emanuel Neumann reviewed for the ZOA Executive his plans for the APC, stressing (as we have seen) the urgent financial need. Then he notes: 'A further problem has arisen in the shape of a group known as the Pro-Palestine Federation of America.'

It is significant that this, the first reference to the Pro-Palestine Federation that we find in the official documents of ZOA is a throwaway – an aside, in which the organization appears as a 'problem'. The story of the Pro-Palestine Federation illustrates some of the best and some of the worst features of the history of dealings of the Herzlian Zionists with Christian friends of Zionism. When all is said and done, it is the latter which dominate in the story of this organization.

There is not very much documentation on the dealings of the official Zionists with this organization – and much of that (symptomatically) is misfiled under 'American Palestine Committee'. From the beginning, its principal fault in the eyes of the official Zionists was that it had not asked permission to begin life, and that it came into the world at the most awkward possible moment – when the best energies of the leadership were occupied with the founding of the American Palestine Committee. No reference to the Pro-Palestine Federation appears in the memoirs of Emanuel Neumann or of Stephen Wise, nor of any of the other principals who have left published autobiographical materials behind. Yet, as one works through the surviving unpublished documentation, the thought occurs that the Pro-Palestine Federation of America just might have had the makings of an effective vehicle for recruiting the full pro-Restorationist weight of American public opinion, had not the official Zionists been so disdainful of its unauthorized beginning and so sensitive about the failure of their own American Palestine Committee.

The Pro-Palestine Federation of America was founded by certain Christian leaders in the Chicago area who were interested in encouraging Jewish–Christian dialogue. A few meetings were held in which declarations were made in support of the cause of Zion, and some pamphlets were printed and distributed. The program of the 'Pro-Palestine Federation' was:

1. To promote and foster a spirit of goodwill and esteem between Jews and non-Jews.

2. To combat antagonistic attacks made by reactionary and prejudiced Gentiles intent upon raising religious and racial issues to the detriment of America and human progress.

3. To promote a better understanding of the historical problems of the Jewish people among the Gentiles.

4. To assist in the defense of the Balfour Declaration and insist on the Palestine Mandate being carried out by the Mandatory Power in letter and spirit.

These materials came to the attention of Chicago-area Zionists, notably Judge Julian W. Mack, a member of the executive of the ZOA, and currently its honorary chairman. Soon there came to the ZOA a request for $500, to help in financing a forthcoming conference, but up to the summer of 1931 the only contribution that we find coming from any branch of ZOA is some advice: namely, the suggestion from Judge Mack that the founders of PPF should prevail upon Charles Edward Russell to become its Chairman. This advice was evidently taken; and when regular correspondence then begins between the Pro-Palestine Federation and ZOA officials we find an entirely different set of officers than those appearing in the pamphlet of the original Chicago group. Charles Edward Russell now appears at the head of a list of well-known literary, academic and religious figures, including Norman Hapgood, William R. Hopkins, John Haynes Holmes, Pierre Van Paassen, and Carl Wittke (all considerable figures in the literary and academic life of the 1920s and 1930s); and A. Ben Elias now appears as Executive Secretary.

The suggestion of Charles Edward Russell as Chairman was an inspired one. Russell, nowadays long-forgotten, was then well known as a magazine journalist, in an age when magazine journalism was at its most influential. A prominent 'muckraker', an active Socialist, and one of the founders of the NAACP, he was the embodiment of the Progressive conscience. He broke with the Socialist Party following its Emergency Convention of April, 1917, when the Party passed, by a margin of four to one, a resolution denouncing the United States's declaration of war against Germany as 'a crime against the nations of the world'. Thereafter, he was put to good use by the Wilson administration's Information Committee, and soon became close to Wilson personally.

Russell's dealings with the official Zionists were cordial from beginning to end. He is a rather striking example of the liberal-Christian philo-Semite, whose support for Zionism stems primarily from conviction of the indebtedness of our civilization to the virtues and accomplishments of the Jewish people. In a first exchange of letters with Stephen Wise, Russell told the Rabbi that it was he who had 'converted me to Zionism':

> I doubt not you have forgotten the circumstance, but I remember it well. It was long ago, in either 1897 or 1898, when I was a managing editor on the old *New York Morning Journal*, you came in one day (it was the first time I had met you) and talked with me about Zion, talked so interestingly and so convincingly that from that day I was a Zionist, whereas before Zionism had meant to me scarcely more than a name. Years afterward, when I went to Palestine, I had you constantly in mind, recalling what you had said and wishing you were there to help to realize the fruition of your hopes. What I saw was an inexpressible joy to me. Palestine was no longer a dream but a reality... I owe to Jews such a debt of gratitude that I can't easily forego the opportunity to work with them in a cause like this [the Pro-Palestine Federation] ... There are many things in this world that I am ignorant of, but at least I know the Jewish spirit and Jewish heart.

In their further correspondence, Wise and Russell vied to see who could heap the most fulsome praise upon the other. Likewise, correspondence that we have between Russell and other Zionist leaders is always notably genial.

The same cannot be said, however, about any of the correspondence involving the Executive Secretary of the Pro-Palestine Federation, A. Ben Elias. Emanuel Neumann, for one, took a clear dislike to Ben Elias from their first communications by letter. Possibly there is more to this than appears in the documents. In any case, somehow Neumann had picked up the impression that the group initiating the PPF might be potential trouble for the official Zionists. In the memo (already cited) in which he makes his first mention of the group, he confesses some respect for the fact that, unlike the APC, they have so far been able to finance their own activities; but at the same time he seems to think this in itself is suspicious.

> It appears that the group is predominantly and almost exclusively of German-Americans, among them several who figured prominently during the war as pro-German and anti-British and who have been looked upon askance for that reason. Whatever their motives, some of them were apparently sufficiently interested to provide some funds with which to maintain a skeleton organization which was confined largely to Chicago and which was virtually quiescent for a year until my recent activity seemed to galvanize them into life once more. They seem to be clearly perturbed over the emergence of a new body [i.e. APC] which will not be part of their organization.

The hint about the abundance of German names among the founders is gratuitous – in fact, downright McCarthyite, and the notion that the group had sprung to life, as it were, out of envy or emulation of Neumann's labors in the vineyard of APC is not only unworthy but chronologically impossible. The best clue to all the headaches that are to come is in the next line: 'I am determined to bring this group and particularly its secretary under our supervision and control even if it involves a struggle which may be acrimonious but brief.'

In his first correspondence with the officers of PPF, Neumann, on behalf of ZOA, made unambiguous promises of financial support; but, by January 1932, embarked on 'the Washington project', he apparently regretted these pledges, and began working to channel financial and moral resources away from PPF and towards APC. PPF leaders then began writing to Stephen Wise, complaining that the APC project has drawn all the funds and all the goodwill that properly belonged to PPF.

There is an inexcusably cruel dimension to this. The official Zionists had simply lost their enthusiasm for volunteer gentile pro-Zionism and could not bring themselves to say so directly. Their imaginations swollen by their plans for 'the Washington project' and then by their intention to capture the Roosevelt Administration from the inside, they fell into 'despising the day of small things' (Zechariah 4:10). Clearly, they were looking for excuses to loosen their ties with PPF, and, one suspects, would have cut it adrift, had it not been for the admiration they all seemed to have had for the person of Charles Edward Russell.

During January and February of 1932, when Neumann was very distracted by the work of launching APC and also preparing for his transfer to London, he carried on a considerable correspondence with the PPF's three key figures: Charles Edward Russell, John Haynes Holmes, and A. Ben Elias. With the former two, all is smooth talk and clear sailing. With the latter, there is trouble at once.

Ben Elias is, in plain terms, a nuisance, as Neumann insists to Russell: he is constantly phoning and telegraphing (usually 'collect'), saying that we must all get together and talk.

Both Ben Elias and Russell had opposed the decision to launch APC, arguing instead that the official Zionists should throw the whole of such financial resources as they might have to encourage Christian support into an expanded PPF, but before long, Russell agreed to work out a plan for collaboration of the two groups, under ZOA auspices. Writing to Russell, Neumann spelled out the general lines of the understanding:

> The modus vivendi is simply this – that for the time being, the two groups will exist as separate bodies in the hope that sooner or later – I hope sooner ... they will consolidate and become one. In the meantime both of these groups are to keep in touch with each other, and above all, with a committee of the Zionist Organization, which will include Judge Mack and Dr Stephen Wise, so as to avoid duplication of effort or conflict.

But writing to fellow Zionist-officials, Neumann sounds a less genial tone:

> The agreement I reached with Dr Elias and also with Mr Charles Edward Russell was that their group should continue to exist until such time as it

may be deemed advisable by mutual agreement for the two organizations to consolidate. In the meantime our Chicago friends have agreed to be guided entirely by our views as to what they should do or refrain from doing ... I see no reason for writing to the districts at the moment about this, though it might be advisable to do so a little later. I think we should make full provision for the work of the American Palestine Committee first.

PPF's financial requests were modest, but even so it soon became obvious that the Zionist officials were not serious about meeting them. We have already noted the desperate financial situation within the ZOA in those darkest months of the Depression; but apart from the financial dilemma, there is something about the tone that the official Zionists adopt when they write to each other about this organization that suggests that the secret thought of their hearts was that PPF should not live forever.

It is difficult to make a fair judgement on this matter. Ben Elias never stops, from beginning to end, blaming the Zionist leaders with whom he corresponds for their underestimation of his organization. He is always the martyr and the prophet.

My great sacrifices of almost five years duration seem to be doomed to sterility ... Since the Federation was launched, I have contributed over $8500 for its maintenance – $4000, my own savings and the balance borrowed money on personal notes signed by me and which I, naturally, must reimburse. The Gentiles have also contributed over $3500, which in view of the small membership is quite right. From Zionist and other Jewish sources no more than $2000 came in in these four and a half years ... I, who have never made a penny through my hard toil for this cause, I had to leave my teacher's position, which is my livelihood, and get away from New York to Boston in order to secure some funds to save the situation.

I am asking myself questions which I cannot answer. Is it fair that *a whole nation's job should rest upon the shoulders of one lone individual?*

Elias did not blush to compare himself with the biblical prophets: in one of his letters he is 'a voice crying in the wilderness' (citing Isaiah 40:3). Elsewhere: 'Israel's fate is in the balance and I am calling for help! Like Jeremiah, I am in a quarrel with and for my people.' He is convinced that all of the Zionist officials have taken a strong personal dislike to him – which does indeed seem to be the painful truth of the matter.

Later on, the Zionist leadership would excuse its failure to use the PPF effectively with the rationalization that an organization claiming to speak for the Christian conscience could hardly be widely credible when it was known that it was being run by a Jew (namely, A. Ben Elias). This line is summed up in a letter which Ben Elias received in March of 1939 from Solomon Goldman, recently installed as President of the ZOA:

> I do not believe the Pro-Palestine Federation can be disguised as an organization of Christians as long as its Secretary and Director remains [*sic*] a Jew. Furthermore, I do not believe there is any need for disguising any effort made by Jews in behalf of Palestine.

Ben Elias, in riposte, insisted that his role was to serve as a link between the Christian leaders of this organization and the Jewish Zionists.

> The Pro-Palestine Federation of America is a truly Christian Organization. The fact that its secretary is a Jew does not mar or disguise the character of the organization. It is quite logical for a group of Christians, dedicated to a cause in which Jews are primarily interested, to entrust executive functions to a Jew, serving as a 'liaison-officer' between Jews and Gentiles ... It is a much needed partnership between Jews and enlightened Christians that the Federation is seeking to establish, a partnership that would greatly facilitate the quite difficult task of enlisting world-wide support for *Eretz Israel*.

In letters to Stephen Wise in the early years of the organization, Elias spelled out his conviction that this particular complaint against him and his work was a rationalization for the ZOA's own failure:

> If our good people would use vision and get behind this pro-Palestine group, we could wage a successful campaign enrolling thousands of Gentiles throughout the country. We could then organize an impressive action against any attempts to violate the Mandate and mobilize weighty and helpful support in favor of Zionist demands for an open-door policy and inclusion of Transjordania within the Jewish immigration and colonization sphere. We could also offer an effective antidote to the poisonous anti-Jewish propaganda so diligently dispensed by Hitler's henchmen in England and here in America.

Ben Elias' theory about the need for a Jew as 'liaison-officer', presiding over the daily activities of organizations of the Christian friends of Zion, makes a certain sense. In truth, the record shows that only when such a Jewish 'liaison-officer' was in place did such organizations succeed. This is notably the case in the matter of the later America Palestine Committee, during the years when its official leader was Senator Robert Wagner, while its practical day-to-day work was entirely carried out by Jewish executive officers.

It is clear, on the other hand, that dealing with A. Ben Elias must have required the forbearance of a saint. An example of A. Ben Elias at his most irresponsible is the story of the Charles Edward Russell luncheon. This was an occasion, sponsored by PPF in honor of its untiring chairman, held in the February of 1934. It was poorly attended – a great embarrassment for which Elias blames the hostility of the Zionist leaders to himself. It is only right, therefore, that they should assume responsibility for this embarrassment. To make this point, Elias simply forwards the unpaid hotel bills to Stephen Wise: 'Surely some collection could be taken up among your influential friends who have this great cause at heart, in order to save us from a fate that would gladden the hearts of the enemies of our people and of Zion.' A few months later, he adopts an even bolder tactic: he simply writes to Rabbi Wise advising him that he has paid the printing bills for his *Palestine Herald* with a cheque for which he has no funds, presuming that Wise will see his duty to advance him a short-term loan for that amount in time to beat the cheque to the bank. At this point, and for some while to follow, Ben Elias' correspondence to Rabbi Wise receives only curt and unforthcoming replies from the latter's secretary.

Eventually, it became necessary to be blunt with Elias about the effect of these tactics. In 1939, ZOA President Goldman wrote to him:

> I showed disinclination to see you because of the tactics you employed in order to get an interview. I am not moved by threats. To have someone phone me in the midst of the October emergency [planning to meet the forthcoming British announcement of their White Paper policy] to inform me that you are liable to arrest because of checks you have issued for which there is no money in the bank and to remind me that your arrest at such a time would reflect on the whole Zionist movement and the Jewish people – such tactics make it impossible for me to accept you as a co-worker.

Ben Elias, in reply, simply dismisses these charges as inventions. Yet anyone who has read the files will be quick to give Goldman the benefit of the doubt. Ben Elias seems to have operated from the premise that his own sacrificial service to the cause entitled him to impose responsibilities on others to come immediately to his financial rescue.

The Pro-Palestine Federation of America came into the world clamouring that it was the organization best equipped to rally the American Christian opinion for Zionism, and that all that it really needed was money.

Even allowing for inflation since then – let us, for purposes of argument, multiply the figure by twenty – the $500 which we find Ben Elias, at the beginning of this story, requesting of the ZOA in 1932 seems a bargain price for so great a boon. As the ZOA never came across with this sum – and in all the subsequent story never came up with more than a few token grants – we will never be able to say with confidence that Ben Elias was wrong, when he claimed that by withholding these small sums of money, the ZOA was failing to seize its God-given opportunity to command the support of the American Christian conscience.

Ben Elias was surely justified in complaining of lack of support from the Zionist leadership, but how seriously should we take his claims about the possibilities of his organization?

If he presumed to tell others their 'manifest duty'; if he did not hesitate to trick them into situations where they were forced to come to his rescue

– then, so did Theodor Herzl. Many passages from Ben Elias' letters to Stephen Wise or Solomon Goldman could, indeed, pass for excerpts from those letters which Herzl wrote (for example) to Baron Hirsch: there is the same presumption of the prophet's right to tell other people their duty to God and the cause. For example, to Stephen Wise he wrote in February 1938:

> An ocean of woes and misfortunes is engulfing our brethren across the Ocean. The scattered flock of Israel is looking up to God and to you for rescue and salvation. Your responsibility before God and history is unprecedented. I therefore appeal to you to set aside all prejudice against my work. The fate of millions of Jews is more important than the misguided views of petty Zionist officials. I need your support in this great task – please do not ignore my plea in this darkest hour for our people!

Melodramatic and megalomaniac he certainly was, but what right have we to say that about the substantial things he was wrong?

Yet again, how can we withhold sympathy from Rabbi Wise and others on the receiving end of such arrogance?

The question remains: what did the PPF actually accomplish?

Few of the press releases issued by the PPF were given space in the newspapers, if we can take the *New York Times Index* as best evidence. The highwater mark for the organization seems to have been in 1936. In May of that year, the organization brought a delegation of Christian clergymen, including the Episcopal Bishop of Washington, to help present a petition to the British Ambassador, for conveyance to the British Prime Minister, Stanley Baldwin. As in all of its public statements, the PPF claimed to speak for 'the consensus of enlightened Christian American opinion' – in this instance, to the effect 'that God has bestowed upon England one of the greatest missions in human history – the salvation of Israel and restoration to its ancient patrimony'. Then, in December of that same year the PPF sponsored an American Christian Conference on Palestine, held at the Hotel Astor in New York. Mayor LaGuardia was the honorary chairman on that occasion, and speakers included Methodist Bishop Francis J. McConnell, US Senator Royal Copeland, and William Green head of the AFL. 'More than 200 persons', reported the *New York Times*, 'including leaders in many denominations and several representatives of interested Jewish organizations', joined in passing a resolutions calling upon Great Britain 'to fulfill its convenental pledges'. After that, the FFP never again received mention in the *New York Times*.[4]

I have been unable to find record of the formal demise of PPF, but assume that it folded to make way for the new APC and the CCP (of which much more shortly.) Nor have I been able to find out what happened to A. Ben

Elias. His name is not in any of the standard biographical reference books. Nor is it in the *Encyclopedia of Zionism* – which it is not easy to excuse. Zionism owes a debt to this organization, and to this unlovely man, A. Ben Elias, for pioneering many of the methods later used by APC/CCP/ACPC, and indeed for originally recruiting many of the people (notably, John Haynes Holmes) who were stalwarts of later organizations. At least it outlasted the original APC, and this it did because it outlasted the shift in political tactics which, as I have argued, caused the ZOA leaders to skulk away from their commitments to APC.

THE RESTORATIONIST TRADITION IN POLITICAL ECLIPSE

During the 1920s, both the political and the cultural elites gave up, apparently forever, on the old Christian Restorationism. Well-educated churchmen soon followed suit.

Liberal Protestant spokesmen who had embraced the Balfour Declaration in the high Wilsonian spring of 1917–19, as an occasion for drawing political boundaries in ways that defended national identity, began to cool on Wilsonism and on Zionism at about the same time. It did not escape their notice that those whose zeal for the establishment of the Jewish homeland had not abated were those who spoke the language of classic Restorationism – who spoke with embarrassing dogmatism of 'God's Plan', of literal fulfillment of biblical promises: the despised 'Fundamentalists'.

As one works one's way through the literature put out by the various organizations of Christian friends of the Jewish cause in the three decades between the Balfour Declaration and the creation of the State in 1948, one finds a tendency to greater embarrassment about the argument from biblical prophecy – the bedrock of the original Christian Restorationist case, and the keystone of the argument of the Blackstone Memorial – and a corresponding tendency to prefer arguments based upon abstract justice, couched in current liberal assumptions about the rights of nationalities, the obsolesence of Empire, the march of civilization, and so on.

As the 1920s give way to the 1930s and the 1930s to the 1940s, one finds in these circles, increasing resort to secular arguments, decreasing use of explicitly theological vocabulary. As this happened, the Jewish cause lost its greatest political asset: its ability to evoke the ancient commitment of the American people to its Puritan faith in the inevitability of the Restoration of the Jews.

Zionist leaders of the 1920s through the 1940s made no effort to seek out and cultivate the support of the spokesmen of the Blackstone tradition, who remained constant in their commitments to Zionism, but who were also, as we have seen, held in disdain by the policy-making elites. The official

Zionists simply co-opted the judgement of liberal Christians – that Evangelicalism and Fundamentalism were marginal forces, intellectually irrelevant, politically insignificant.

The best mirror of opinion in the camp of liberal-ecumenical Protestantism for the entire period under review in this chapter may be found in the pages of the inter-denominational Protestant journal called *Christian Century*. Recognizing this, Hertzl Fishman conscientiously combed the pages of that journal for the entire period from the end of the World War until the early months of the Second World War, to document his story of Protestant attitudes to Zionism and to Israel. With the important *caveat* that these are the views not of Protestants in general, but of their most articulate elements, their clergy, we can register a few of Fishman's discoveries here as adequate for our present purpose.

Fishman finds little interest in the subject of Zion in the *Christian Century* through the early 1920s. This he attributes to the evident decline of pre-millennial enthusiasm in the post-war decade, and also to the mood of withdrawal from world affairs in the years of Harding and Coolidge.[5] An editorial in 1927 expresses regret for Britain's policy of encouraging 'aggressive Jews who claim the country as a "homeland" for their people', and advises that '... historically the Jew has never been in possession of Palestine'.[6] Beginning in 1929, when Arab riots draw the attention of concerned people back to the Holy Land, the *Christian Century* began to warn regularly of the impediment to clear thinking caused by fundamentalist talk about Restoration. 'It is the conviction of most modern biblical scholars', the editors pronounced, 'that the Old Testament contains no anticipation of the restoration of Israel to its ancient homeland which can apply to the Jewish people and to the present age.' By 29 October 1930, the *Christian Century* had concluded that the Balfour Declaration was 'a mischievous and ambiguous promise [which] could not be realized consistently with justice to other elements of the population'.[7]

The *Christian Century*'s attitude towards Zionism was strongly colored by its commitment to the concept of the American melting-pot:

> Can democracy suffer a hereditary minority to perpetuate itself as a permanent majority with its own distinctive culture, sanctioned by its own distinctive cult forms?... They have no right in a democracy to remove their faith from the normal influences of the democratic process by insulating it behind the walls of a racial and cultural solidarity. [9 June 1937] ... [Jesus] was crucified because he had a program for Israel which ran counter to the cherished nationalism of Israel's leaders – political and priestly. He opposed their nationalism with the universalism of God's love and God's Kingdom ... It was nationalism that crucified Jesus ... [He thwarted] their cherished ambition to make Israel and Israel's God the dominant power of the world [3 May 1933].

The anomaly with which we must deal in what follows is that though the constant champions of Christian Zionism were all on the theological right, the official Zionists leaders dealt, publicly at least, only with the theological left in the 1930s and 1940s. We should not doubt that the popular mind could still have been moved by the Restorationist arguments, but a generation of American Jews who were reading Sinclair Lewis was not about to reach out and pitch the Zionist tent in Popular Christianity.

A conscious determination was made to win the politicians and the opinion-makers to whom the politicians were believed to defer. From these elements were drawn the leaders of a sequence of organizations with which we have dealt or shortly will deal: the APC, the PPF, the revived APC, the CCP, and the ACPC. The official Zionists understood that there was no way of bringing the influential forces that they coveted into the same tent with the Fundamentalists. The support of Fundamentalists and Evangelicals could be taken for granted. It served no good purpose to draw the liberals' attention to it. Meanwhile, the support of Evangelical and Fundamentalist Christian Zionists was welcomed, but not celebrated out loud in the company of the liberals and not talked about in the pages of official Zionist journals.

Official Zionists were caught in a trap. They could not insult the Protestant establishment by turning for support to the despised 'Fundamentalists', whose theology made them the constant friends of Zion, but who were without political significance. It was best all around, therefore, not to stir up discussion about the Jewish cause in Christian theological circles, but rather to couch Zionist arguments in rhetoric of justice and political pragmatism. And best of all would be to get directly to a well-disposed and liberal-minded Administration, whose leaders were sober Christian gentlemen, but not disposed to expressing public purposes in religious talk.

11

Franklin D. Roosevelt, the Jews and the Zionists

The American Palestine Committee, founded in 1932, was designed to be a league of the most powerful politicians of both parties, their ranks rounded out with literary and intellectual figures and leading clergy, but a few months later, as we have seen, the Zionists withdrew their investments in this body, and took out stock instead in the Democratic team that swept the Presidential elections of 1932.

This was a tactical move, not a strategic one. The new tactic was, in fact, a revised version of the one that had won the Wilson Administration for the Balfour Declaration in the first place, working quietly from the inside of a well-disposed Administration, keeping public activities confined within bounds that were approved by that Administration. Since their game plan was now to win the ear of the establishment, it made sense for the Zionists to redirect their efforts to the new Roosevelt Administration – all the more since they knew that it had in its ranks an unprecedented number of Jews and countless friends of the Jewish community, as well (they believed) as a distinctly pro-Zionist disposition. The Roosevelt Government expected the Zionists to reciprocate by not making its life more difficult than it had to be: mass action was to be confined to occasions of exceptional outrage, but routine promotion of broadly based pro-Zionist propaganda was out of bounds.

The thesis of this and the following two chapters is that the switch in political strategy from bipartisanship to alliance with the Roosevelt Administration accomplished nothing, and in fact probably weakened the Zionists in the longer run by causing them to reduce their efforts at direct appeal to the whole American public, where the residual effects of Christian Restorationism were much stronger than they were in the narrower company of the elites from which FDR drew his Administration.

FRANKLIN D. ROOSEVELT (1882–45)

Franklin Roosevelt was raised in circumstances as closely resembling those of hereditary aristocracy as it would be possible to find in America. The families of both James Roosevelt and Sarah Delano had settled in earliest colonial times in the Hudson Valley of New York, where a quasi-feudal system of landholding, established by the Dutch in the days of New Amsterdam, was maintained down to the time of the 'Rent Wars' of the 1840s. Well into the twentieth century, outsiders commented on the entirely un-American deference shown by the local farming class to the gentry.

Franklin Delano Roosevelt, the only child of the marriage consummated in 1880 between the widower James Roosevelt (then aged 52) and Sara Delano (then aged 26), was greatly indulged as a child – by his parents, by his relatives, and by the tutors and governesses hired for his private instruction. He had the extraordinary privilege of some eight trips to Europe before the age of 15, each of several months' duration.

ROOSEVELT'S RELIGION

By his own testimony, the most enduring influence from his boyhood (apart from his beloved parents) was Endicott Peabody (1857–1944), the Founder and the Rector of Groton, the residential boys' school sedulously modeled on the great 'Public Schools', which Americans of the Roosevelts' standing liked to believe shaped the character of the ruling class of Great Britain. The regimen consisted of daily religious instruction, Episcopalian worship, classical learning, and vigorous exercise.

Likewise, by Roosevelt's own testimony, Peabody's daily sermons at the early morning Groton chapel and the instructions conveyed in his religious knowledge classes were the bedrock of his adult theological and moral reflections.

In contrast to his later mentor, Woodrow Wilson, Roosevelt did not make public confession of the specifics of his faith, and was not generally perceived to be 'a religious man', but he most certainly was, by any normal yardstick. Among those of Franklin Roosevelt's 'official family' who left memoirs, only two, namely, Rexford Tugwell and Frances Perkins, have given us any extended account of the matter of religion as a source of Roosevelt's motivation. It is striking that they describe the substance of Roosevelt's religious loyalty in nearly identical terms, while drawing nearly opposite conclusions about its impact upon his character and upon his work. Both comment on the relative regularity of his attendance at church, the frequent habit of recommending church attendance to others, the stress he placed on formal religious training as a support for domestic virtue and civic peace, the regularity of his doctrinal commitments, and his vagueness about the intellectual and philosophical dimensions of religious faith.

Tugwell sees Roosevelt as having 'an uncomplicated mind', and therefore an uncomplicated faith, which, in turn, issued in a self-assurance that could make him impervious to instruction. From this derives his characteristic 'deviousness', and instability of commitment in many large matters.

> There appeared later in his life the inevitable difficulties into which a non-self-examining mind may fall – he had trouble separating ends and means and sometimes used means he ought not to have used ... But that he felt justified or excused by a consciousness of having done his best, and having done it with divine approval, seems to me obvious.[1]

Perkins, in contrast, sees Franklin Roosevelt as a man of uncomplicated faith, and therefore of steady character.

> I remember saying to Mrs Roosevelt, 'You know, Franklin is really a very simple Christian.'
> She thought a moment and, with a quizzical lift of her eyebrows, said, 'Yes a very simple Christian.'
> I never developed the point further with her, but as I watched him and thought about him from time to time, I realized that his Christian faith was absolutely simple. As far as I can make out, he had no doubts ... It was a real relationship of man to God, and he felt as certain of it as of the reality of his life.[2]

ROOSEVELT THE POLITICIAN

After an undistinguished undergraduate career at Harvard, and an equally undistinguished year in Columbia Law School, Franklin Roosevelt entered politics, running successfully in 1910 to become the State Senator for his home constituency, Dutchess County, New York. An early supporter of the candidacy of Woodrow Wilson for the Presidency, he was rewarded, in March 1913, with an appointment just below the level of cabinet: Assistant Secretary of the Navy.

The outbreak of European war in 1914 made Roosevelt's job a crucial one; and by the time the war ended he was clearly at the head of the pack of young Wilsonian Democrats. As Vice-Presidential candidate (under James Cox, Governor of Ohio), Roosevelt impressed the public with his energetic campaigning, and when the dust settled, speculation began immediately about his chances for the Presidential nomination in 1924, but in the late summer of 1921 Franklin Roosevelt was struck with polio. Fully committed for the next several years to the heroic work of recovering his physical strength and rebuilding his personal life, Roosevelt built up quietly an enormous treasury of public admiration, while having the perfect excuse for standing aside from the election contests of the early 1920s – a season of Republican hegemony at all levels of Government, when Democrats were scraping the bottom of the barrel for candidates. He returned to public life in 1928, when he agreed to run for the Governorship of New York, being vacated by Al Smith, the Democratic candidate for President. His cliff-hanging victory in 1928, however, was followed, in 1930, by a sweeping re-election. His selection as the Democratic candidate for the Presidency in June 1932, guaranteed a sweeping Democratic victory in November of that year.

FDR AND THE AMERICAN JEWS

Right from the beginning, it was observed that a disproportionate number of Roosevelt's closest associates were Jews. In this matter he was distinctly out of step with his social circle. To go no further afield than his own household, we find, in a letter dating to the years of their early courtship, a letter in which Eleanor, his future wife, writes of a party she attended, at which Jews were present: '... the Jew party were appalling – I never wish to hear money, jewels, and sables mentioned again.' And, some years later, on first meeting Henry Morgenthau, Jr. '... an interesting little man, but very Jew.'[3] When he became Governor of New York, Franklin Roosevelt added to his own collection of Jewish friends, advisers, and political allies, a number of Jews who held positions of responsibility under Governor Al Smith. One of these, Herbert Lehman, served as his Lieutenant-Governor, then succeeded Roosevelt as Governor in 1933.

In the years of Roosevelt's Presidency, Jews who held important public office, or who were members of the informal 'Brain Trust', or who had steady access to him as labor leaders, policy advisors, or acknowledged leaders of Jewish opinion included Rose Schneiderman, Henry Morgenthau, Jr., Felix Frankfurter, Benjamin V. Cohen, Samuel I. Rosenman, Sidney Hillman, Bernard Baruch, David Lilienthal, Mordecai Ezekiel, Robert Nathan, and David K. Niles. Very early, some deep thinker hit upon the phrase: 'The Jew Deal.' Well-intentioned friends advised that there was no need to offer such easy bait to the bigots: perhaps he should curtail reference in public to these Jewish names; perhaps he should not have pictures taken with Jewish visitors, unless strictly necessary. When it came time to replace Louis Brandeis on the Supreme Court, Roosevelt relived Woodrow Wilson's experience when the latter was considering Brandeis' own nomination: a delegation of Jews urged him not to appoint a Jew (this time it was Felix Frankfurter) out of concern about 'anti-Semitism'. When his spirit was down, Roosevelt would react angrily to this weak-kneed advice

– as he did in the matter of the Frankfurter consideration. When (as more often) his mood was good, he reacted mischievously. Nahum Goldmann of the Jewish Agency tells the story of a weekend when he and Stephen Wise and Samuel Rosenman were brought to Hyde Park by Roosevelt to help him work out a statement on some matter: 'Imagine what Goebbels would pay for a photo of this scene', he suddenly remarked, '– the President of the United States taking his instructions from the three Elders of Zion!'[4]

Long before 1932 American Presidents had established the precedent of appointing Jews to Cabinet posts and one or two ambassadorial posts. These token appointments aside, the Government of the United States was still effectively run by the Protestant Establishment until Roosevelt deliberately set about rewarding the various hyphenate groups that had given their support to Al Smith in 1928 and to himself in 1932, with appointments at all levels more-or-less proportionate to their political weight. As for the Jews, although only 3 per cent of the population at the time, they made up 15 per cent of the most senior appointments made by President Roosevelt. In 1932, Jews voted for Roosevelt over Hoover 3.5 to 1; by 1940 and 1944, it was 9 to 1.[5]

STEPHEN WISE AND FDR

By the end of Franklin Roosevelt's first term as President, it was universally conceded that one man stood head-and-shoulders above all others as ambassador of the Jewish community to the Roosevelt administration – namely, Rabbi Stephen Wise. This is not how things stood at the beginning, however. In fact, throughout the election season of 1932, Stephen Wise had been publicly committed to Norman Thomas, the Socialist Party Candidate; and his name, by Inauguration Day 1933, was still on a short list of the least favorite people of Franklin Roosevelt.

After Wilson left the White House, Wise had lived in the hope of Wilson *redivivus*. In his letters to friends in the 1920s, Wise commends this one and that one as having been close to Wilson, or having been in or close to the Wilson Administration, or being a continuer of the Wilson legacy, or as having some Wilsonian quality about him. He never saw Franklin Roosevelt in that light until after his election as President in 1932.

Stephen Wise, like all progressives, had been made despondent by the turn that political life had taken in the 1920s – the celebration of business life and of 'normalcy', the materialism, the hedonism, the contempt for ideals, the alienation of the intellectuals from America's democratic tradition. In compensation for the loss of access to the seats of power, he returned to the political role he had played with such satisfaction before Wilson: the independent scourge of incumbent politicians.

The darkest chapter of Franklin Roosevelt's otherwise largely successful two-term tenure as Governor of New York was the Jimmy Walker Affair. This began for him on the night of 17 March 1931, when he returned home from a late celebration of St Patrick's Day (and also, incidentally, the twenty-sixth anniversary of his wedding to Eleanor) to find Rabbi Wise and Reverend John Haynes Holmes waiting in his study to present on behalf of the Civic Affairs Committee a petition bearing the signatures of several thousand New Yorkers demanding investigation into allegations of financial impropriety and influence-peddling by the Mayor of New York, Jimmy Walker. It was a most disagreeable encounter, according to all the principals. On the spot, FDR gave the two clergymen a severe dressing-down for meddling in politics. Afterward, Roosevelt tried to dispell the need for investigation, as the charges were 'too general', but it soon became clear that the public was persuaded differently; and so Roosevelt reluctantly appointed the Seabury Commission. In the months that followed until Governor Roosevelt finally secured Mayor Walker's resignation, on 1 September 1932, many carried about the impression that Franklin Roosevelt was too beholden to Democratic political machines to be entrusted with the Presidency of the United States. Franklin Roosevelt held Stephen Wise and John Haynes Holmes responsible for this. He said out loud: 'If they would serve their God as they seek to serve themselves, the people of the city of New York would be the gainers.'[6] In 1932, to friends, Wise wrote that Franklin Roosevelt 'had no deep-seated convictions, no bedrock in him. He is all clay and no granite.'

The first months of 1933, we recall, coincided with the first months of the régime of Adolf Hitler. The Administration of FDR, like all Governments of the day, agonized internally about the attitude it must adopt as the Hitler régime executed the first phases of its program of escalating terror against the Jews. Inside the Roosevelt Administration, the argument was for the most part carried by those who believed that Hitler could not last long, and that it would assist the moderates around him if outside Governments refrained from responding to his provocations of the Jews with equally provocative reactions.

Jews in the Administration or with *entrée* to it – those individuals whose influence was supposed by so many to guarantee a positive hearing for the cause of the Jews – proved unwilling to speak out about the plight of the European Jews. To the admonitions of Jewish leaders on the outside, those on the inside (Henry Morgenthau, Jr, Herbert Lehman, Bernard Baruch, Herbert Feis, James Warburg, Ben Cohen, Felix Frankfurter) all replied with the advice that 'the Boss' could accomplish much more if he did not appear to be responding to the appeals of a Jewish lobby. Afterward, the historians would find very little evidence of any ongoing effort by President Roosevelt to make the cause of the Jews his own in the diplomatic world.

During these first months of Roosevelt's presidency, while he was still an outsider, it was Stephen Wise who organized a mass meeting at Madison Square Garden, 27 March 1933 – when 25,000 persons inside and 30,000 outside, and unnumbered hundreds of thousands on a national radio hookup listened to speakers including Alfred E. Smith, Bishop William Manning, Bishop Francis McConnell, and Senator Robert F. Wagner. This was followed by a boycott campaign against Germany – in fact, a counter-boycott against Hitler's announced boycott of Jewish businesses and Jewish interests in Germany. All this he did despite the objections of the American Jewish Committee and *B'nai Brith*, who feared that such activities would have the effect of barring 'more constructive efforts'. To these objections, Wise's reply was: 'How can we ask our Christian friends to lift their voices in protest against the wrongs suffered by Jews if we keep silent?'[7] About this time he was describing the President as 'immovable, incurable and even inaccessible excepting to those of his Jewish friends whom he can safely trust not to trouble him with any Jewish problems', but his vanity conspired with his natural optimism to persuade him that all that was missing was the establishment of the personal link between himself and 'The Boss'.

Roosevelt, meanwhile was aware that Wise's prestige within the Jewish community had grown, as a result, mainly, of the courageous leadership he was showing in rallying public sentiment against the policies of the Hitler Government. Franklin Roosevelt, like Stephen Wise, was drawn nostalgi-cally to the Wilson days, and was sensible to the possibilities of renewing the equivalent of the Wilson/Brandeis/Wise alliance. In September 1935, Roosevelt took the initiative, by asking Stephen Wise to come to visit him. Given how inexhaustibly he had worked at getting *entrée* to the White House for nearly three years, Wise does not convince us when he writes in his auto-biography: 'It was not easy to go, for no man of importance in public life had ever attacked Holmes and myself as he had. Still, I could not permit personal rancor or resentment to stand in the way of giving my support to him.'[8]

After this meeting of reconciliation, Stephen Wise gave up his role as an organizer of public opinion outside the White House. From 1936 forward, he was universally acknowledged to be the American Jewish leader with greatest access to the President. Cynics said he had become FDR's 'court Jew'. Well ahead of election day, 1936, Stephen Wise issued his state-ment in support of Roosevelt:

> I give my whole-hearted support to President Roosevelt, not as a Jew but as an American. I never vote as a Jew ... Himself a member of one of the great Christian churches ... [FDR] is a good neighbour to all mankind.[9]

It is downright embarrassing to read some of Wise's letters and reports to FDR. As Disraeli said of himself in his dealings with Queen Victoria, he 'laid it on with a trowel'. Invariably, his letters open with the salutation: 'Dear Boss'. Returning from a trip to Europe, he reports 'about the faith of the European peoples in your leadership of the country, they rightly take it for granted that your re-election is a foregone conclusion. I am more eager than I can tell you to go through the country and add my voice to the chorus of understanding of a leadership which has averted great evil and given us so much that is good and promising for the future of our country.'[10] Never loath to display his influence at court, her turned out many 'Reports' like the following (to unnamed recipients, but presumably Zionist officials) of a 'Visit to President Franklin D. Roosevelt at Hyde Park, Monday 5 October 1936':

> STRICTLY CONFIDENTIAL
>
> 1. I expressed to the President at once, (who was cordiality itself) the deep appreciation of all of us at what he and Secretary Hull had done in the matter of intervention re Palestine. His face lighted up. He seemed well informed. I told him that my joy was shared by Justice Brandeis, Felix [Frankfurter] and Judge Mack, but he interrupted me to say, 'Grand men! You know, Stephen, we and the Inner Circle call him [i.e. Brandeis] "Isaiah"' ... [FDR then explained how he intended to bring the Chamberlain Government around on the matter of Palestine.] I need hardly add, in strictest confidence, (as everything herein is) that I told FDR that of course we could make no public use of this, excepting as of course there must necessarily be a certain amount of leakage; but wherever I go and to whomever I see I make clear that the Administration has rendered a supremely important service to us and that we have no right to forget it at such a critical time as this. 'Publicly, I dare not say more because of the reaction which might be hurtful and which might be used against you at this time by the other Party.'

FDR AND THE JEWS OF THE WORLD

Throughout the 1930s, the task before the Zionist leadership was to bring constant pressure upon the American Government to honour its never-rescinded commitments to the Jewish homeland, originating in Wilson's endorsement of the Balfour Declaration, re-stated in the Lodge Resolution of 1922, and again in the American–British Mandate Convention of 3 December 1924, and again in the State Department Statement of 13 October 1939. Franklin Roosevelt, no less than the Republican Presidents of the 1920s, went repeatedly on record with unqualified support of the Balfour pledges and expressing admiration of the Zionist cause, while in confidential conversations, he assured the Zionist leaders again and again that he was exploring every avenue, public and covert, to keep pressure on the British in the matters of immigration to Palestine and the future Jewish State. Yet the scholars who subsequently combed the record found very little evidence of the active stewardship of Jewish interests of which Franklin Roosevelt boasted to Stephen Wise at the time. Occasionally, Zionist lobbying resulted in the Government's issuing through diplomatic channels carefully worded reminders that the US considered itself entitled to have its views considered whenever Britain took action of the sort just taken (perhaps some new restriction on purchase of land by Jews in Palestine; some 'temporary' prohibition of Jewish immigration, pending the report of the latest inquiry; some particularly harsh steps taken against Palestinian-Jewish terrorists). In every instance, the British Government simply wore the Americans down over many months of diplomatic exchange, and nothing would change. Franklin Roosevelt, notwithstanding, accepted the thanks of the American Zionists for his valiant efforts, and moved on to other things.

We know that the British authorities were using all the contacts they had in Washington to probe the real mind of the American Administration; and we know that they were generally confident that the American Government would not persist beyond the margins of civilized remonstration. For instance, we have this memorandum, prepared for Cabinet by the Secretary of State for Foreign Affairs, Anthony Eden:

> For a long time there have been no public expressions of Jewish opinion which have been definite or important, and the Jews in America are so divided in opinion that a predominant Jewish attitude towards the Palestine question cannot be said to exist, but the following points may be regarded as common to the great majority:
>
> (a) All are in utmost distress over the sufferings of their race in other lands,
>
> (b) All are convinced that an area must be provided capable of affording refuge to those who need it, though there are wide differences of view as to what the political status of that area should be.
>
> (c) Practically all speak with gratitude of British efforts.

It is difficult to believe that honest research could have led the British Embassy to such a conclusion about American opinion.

By 1938, the situation of European Jews was desperate. Hitler boasted of his willingness to unload the whole Jewish population upon the democratic nations, confident that they did not want them. Steady pressure upon Franklin Roosevelt by Stephen Wise and Louis Brandeis resulted in the calling of an international conference on the refugee crisis at the French resort town of Evian, July 1938. Britain agreed to participate only if the matter of Palestine was excluded from discussion, and the thirty-three participating countries agreed. Many speeches were made deploring the circumstances which were creating the refugee crisis in Europe, but all of the countries, including the United States, declared that they were unable to accept any further refugees.

At this juncture, as we have seen, leaders of the Pro-Palestine Federation, with some modest assistance from the ZOA, responded with the formation of a 'Provisional Committee on Palestine'. Petitions came as well from an ad hoc Zionist National Emergency Committee on Palestine, signed by 51 Senators, 154 Representatives, and 30 Governors, urging President Roosevelt to work to reverse the British policy. Still, the leaders of ZOA had been reluctant to mobilize these self-seeding Christian movements, contenting themselves with some modest financial support for the Conference. This reluctance is explained by the advice that they were receiving from Stephen Wise that Franklin Roosevelt could best use his enormous moral and diplomatic leverage with the British if he did not appear to be acting in response to political agitation from the American Jews.

Early in 1939, Hitler told the Reichstag:

> We will have to solve the Jewish question. There is enough room in the world, but we must free ourselves of the opinion that God chose the Jewish people and therefore they have the right to be parasites nourished by the bodies of other productive nations ... If international Jewish money, whether inside or outside Europe, succeeds in drawing the nations into another world war, then the result will not be world Bolshevization – and with it victory for the Jews – but the extermination of the Jewish race of Europe.

Shortly thereafter, the British Government's White Paper of 1939 was issued and the details were now public: within ten years, an independent State of Palestine would come into existence, and, to guarantee that it would have an Arab majority, total Jewish immigration in the interim would not exceed 75,000. In Cabinet, on 12 February 1940, the Secretary of State for Colonies and author of the White Paper, Malcolm MacDonald, summed up the political equation:

> It would be an error of judgement to exaggerate the influence of the Jewish element in the United States. We had been told at the time of the White Paper that the Jewish element would sway public opinion in that country against us, but this has not, in fact, proved to be the case.[11]

All this time, Stephen Wise fell deeper and deeper under the spell of Roosevelt's promises of action. Witness this public tribute to Roosevelt's labours on behalf of world Jewry, jointly signed by Stephen Wise and Solomon Goldman (then President of the ZOA) to FDR, 17 May 1939, following the London Conference, where the Zionists had failed to dissuade the Chamberlain Government from issuing its fateful White Paper on Palestine:

> In this hour of sorrow over the betrayal of Jewish faith and hope by the Chamberlain government, we feel impelled to say to you that we are mindful of all that you have sought to do on behalf of our cause in recent years.

On several occasions it was your understanding and your intervention in London that averted disaster. Today, alas, your earnest and devoted effort has not availed; and the British government has, at one and the same time, the melancholy satisfaction of violating its pledged word by Balfour, and of refusing to see justice done to our people.

World Jewry and particularly the Jews of Palestine will not, dear Mr President, forget all that you have done or sought to do on our behalf. We shall remember and be grateful always.[12]

12

American Zionist Emergency Council and the Christian Zionists

Not before the Jew is crushed can the forces of darkness attain the other citadels of humanity – humanism, democracy, and Christianity, the three daughters of Judaism ... If the Christian church would yet, at this late hour, understand the signs of the times and realize that the attacks on the Jews, as they multiply in our day, are but a prelude to an assault on Christianity's own foundations ... if the realization would penetrate and deepen in Christian circles that the salvation of the Jewish people through the re-building of the Holy Land is a phase of the struggle for the establishment of the Kingdom of God on earth, I believe, there is still hope. And not only hope of saving the Jewish people from frightful disaster, but hope of saving society! ... Such a Church of Christ, having regained its independence and its courage, would dare to speak to England in Nathan's words: 'Thou art the Man!'

Pierre Van Paassen, 1939[1]

THE EDUCATION OF EMANUEL NEUMANN

On 22 August 1939, the day that the Hitler–Stalin Pact was announced, the twenty-first Zionist Congress was meeting in Geneva. Business was quickly wrapped up, and the delegates fled to their homes. As in the summer of 1914, it was feared that the world leadership would be scattered – or worse; and so, on the precedent of August 1914, an Emergency Committee for Zionist Affairs (ECZA) (later renamed American Zionist Emergency Council – AZEC) was established in the United States. Emanuel Neumann, a member of the World Zionist Executive, was brought back into the centre of Zionist activity in the United States by the leaders of the newly formed ECZA, where he was given charge of its Department of Public Relations and Political Action.

Neumann's first priority was to rally the Christian conscience on behalf of the Jewish Homeland. Himself an observant man, and therefore something of a rarity in official Zionist circles, Neumann had been taught by

Stephen Wise and Louis Brandeis that there was such a thing as a Christian conscience, and that its deepest source in America was the biblical Christianity of the Puritans, on which the Blackstone Memorial drew.

We have already noted that Emanuel Neumann has left out of his autobiography any trace of his own responsibility for the neglect of APC and PPF at the time. Indeed, he does not even mention PPF. Yet he was a teachable man; and apparently he came by 1939 to believe that the neglect of these efforts had been a calamitous mistake. This failure, in turn, followed, he now saw, from a fundamental political error – namely, the decision to close ranks around President Roosevelt and the Democratic Party. Those now close to Franklin Roosevelt reported that though he was a single-minded friend of Zion, he did have certain minor frailties – among them, that he did not like to be put in the position of seeming to make decisions in response to publicly visible organized pressure groups; and another, related to the first, that he did not remain friendly to individuals or groups who were simultaneously working the other side of the partisan-political street. In this light, official Zionists had turned cool on the idea of recruiting the Christian conscience publicly, on the outside of Government.

These calculations were rarely discussed out loud in the 1930s, but in the mid-1940s they came back with a vengeance, as it became impossible to avoid the truth that Franklin Roosevelt had failed the Zionists and the Jews of Europe and Palestine. A terrible price was being paid daily for the retreat from the wise policy that had been behind the initiation of PPF and APC. What resulted was a classic example of the seduction of the innocent by the allurements of 'access' – or, in the language of the Psalmist, of putting one's trust in princes.

In recent years, Emanuel Neumann had become one of the most vocal of those American Zionists denouncing the leadership and policy of Chaim Weizmann – above all, Weizmann's faith in quiet diplomacy with the elected Governments of the United States and Great Britain. Earlier in this story, Neumann's anti-Weizmann policy had put Neumann in the same camp with Stephen Wise, but now Wise was effectively allied with Weizmann as a champion of the policy of working with the statesmen. Wise, the friend of Franklin Roosevelt, was now the anchor on the American end of that policy.

Rabbi Abba Hillel Silver of Cincinnati, a friend and an ally of Neumann since the days when they had attended the same Zionist youth club in New York City. was now a powerful rival of Stephen Wise within ZOA. Together, Neumann and Silver argued for a return to the politics that went with the policies that had been in place before 1933 – that is, before FDR. There must be pro-Zionist channels of opinion in all the arenas of public influence. There must be pro-Zionist Republicans as well as pro-Zionist Democrats, and they must live in fear of each other.

Put crudely, the difference between the policy of Wise and Weizmann, on the one hand, and Neumann and Silver, on the other, turned on whether there was more Christian conscience to be tapped on the inside or the outside of the White House. If the Christian conscience of the White House was of the octane described by Stephen Wise and David K. Niles, Ben Cohen, Samuel Rosenman, and other prominent Jews who got close enough to it to test it, it would be a great disservice to Zion to put it in political jeopardy by noisy politicking on the outside. If, however, Christian conscience within the population at large was of the octane that Neumann believed it to be, it should not be turned off, but should be harnessed and used for all it was worth, everywhere you could find it – in political circles, in the market-place of ideas, in the churches.

This same fundamental line of division has always run through Zionist counsels, and does so today.

APC *REDIVIVUS* (1941)

Neumann's philosophy was spelled out in a document circulated a few weeks after his appointment:

> There is an impatience, understandable but nonetheless deplorable, with any discussion of postwar arrangements at a time when the conflict is in acute stage and the issue undecided. Moreover, we Jews, in common with others whose mental temper is liberal and optimistic, have a way of taking for granted that 'this time' things will turn out differently and well. The progressivist frame of mind is incurable ... [Thus, most Zionists] would have Zionist policy proceed on the assumption that the restoration of Palestine as a Jewish commonwealth will drop on the council table of the nations like manna from heaven.
>
> It will do no such thing. The forces arrayed against us are many and powerful and after the struggle of war will come the struggle of peace ... [We face] the task of spreading an understanding of Zionism among our Christian friends, of mobilizing their support.

Some months later, at the Biltmore Conference in May 1942, where the American Jewish community committed itself to demanding unlimited Jewish immigration to Palestine and the early creation of the Jewish Commonwealth there, Neumann spelled out the vital part to be played by public relations:

> [W]e have to convince all those who are in public life of their own united desire and determination to see the Zionist program through and ensure their support ... [We must impress] church unions, organizations of clergy and laity, great publicists, teachers and preachers who speak for the Conscience of America. We have to present this to them as a great moral problem, involving great moral issues ... We must reach thoughtful America.

Neumann's first major project in his new portfolio was the reconstituting of the American Palestine Committee – something that took some *chutzpah*, given the way in which the official Zionists had walked away from their responsibilities to the organization that originally bore this name, nearly a decade earlier. The very large number of holdover members from the first organization who agreed to join the second APC is testimony to the genuineness of their commitment.

As with the original APC, a major role in recruitment was played quietly by Justice Louis Brandeis (who died, 5 October 1941). Again as with the original APC, the new APC was publicly inaugurated at a dinner meeting – this time at the Shoreham Hotel in Washington, 30 April 1941. By this time, two-thirds of the members of the United States Senate had been enrolled.

Senator Robert F. Wagner of New York, a stalwart friend of Zionism for many years, agreed to become Chairman. Carl Hermann Voss, who worked closely with the Senator over many years in the work of rallying Christian support for the Jewish homeland, attributed Wagner's zeal in this cause to his admiration of Jews and Judaism: he was, that is to say, an example of the classic Christian philo-Semite, who was particularly distressed by the disgrace which Hitlerism had brought to his parents' native Germany.[2]

In one of the earliest press releases, Senator Wagner described both the purpose and the strategy of the APC:

> What is to be the program of our Committee? What can it do to advance the cause it has exposed? Our Committee is wholly non-official; it has neither executive nor administrative, nor legislative powers, but it has access to a power which is enthroned above all these, the sovereign power of public opinion. It is our intention to speak to the conscience of America and of all Christendom.

Others in the executive included Dr Daniel L. Marsh, Chairman, President of Boston University, Prof. William F. Albright, Johns Hopkins University, Dr Henry Atkinson, Prof. Carl J. Friedrich, Harvard University, William Green, President of the AFL, Eric A. Johnston, President of the US Chamber of Commerce, John W. McCormack, Majority Leader of the House of Representatives, Philip Murray, President of the CIO, Senators Claude Pepper and Arthur Vandenburg, Daniel Poling, Editor of *Christian Herald*. and Msgr. John A. Ryan of the National Catholic Welfare Council.

Immediately on its organization, the American Palestine Committee published its Statement of Aims and Principles, describing itself as 'the vehicle for the expression of the sympathy and goodwill of Christian America for the movement to re-establish the Jewish National Home in Palestine'. The link to the Blackstone Memorial is clear:

> The fulfilment of the millennial hope for the reunion of the Jewish people
> with the land of its ancient inheritance, a hope that accords with the spirit
> of Biblical prophecy, has always commanded the sympathy of the liberal
> Christian world.

This Statement was followed by a steady stream of press releases and
published statements, letters to the editors, and full-page newspaper ads.
These, we know, were noted in the White House, where it was appreciated
that the Senatorial membership in the APC added up to the number
required by the Constitution for ratification of treaties. The AZEC, in
striking contrast to the Zionist leaders back in the early thirties, gave literally
the top priority to this work, and funding was generous. The AZEC assigned
fieldworkers to seek out friendly clergymen in every sizable community in
the land, and used the contacts of these clergymen to build eventually more
than seventy-five local ACP chapters. These chapters were exhorted to
provide their Christian Zionist neighbours with funds, clerical services, and
moral support. All this work was underwritten generously by the AZEC:
more than $72,000 per year in the first years, raised to $150,000 annually
by 1947–48. To his troops, Neumann conveyed this motto: 'Sympathy is
like any other force: it is effective only when properly channeled.'

The Second Annual Dinner of the American Palestine Committee, held
at the Mayflower Hotel in Washington on 25 May 1942, and broadcast coast-
to-coast on NBC Radio, observed the twentieth anniversary of the adoption
by the Senate and House of Representatives of their Joint Resolution
favoring the Establishment in Palestine of a National Home for the Jewish
People. It was announced that membership 'now numbers 725 men and
women prominent in every sphere, including 67 members of the United
States Senate, 143 members of the House of Representatives, 22 Governors
of States, jurists, educators, clergymen, publishers, editors, writers and
civic leaders'. A message of commendation from President Roosevelt was
read, and there were many addresses. Best remembered by those who
attended was one delivered by radio from Britain, from Lord Josiah
Wedgwood, a prominent English Christian Zionist.

> I have tried to save for my own countrymen the glory of rebuilding Jerusalem
> – of doing justice and creating freedom. It's no use. They won't do it! I can't
> help ... [T]he responsibilities of the world have lain on our shoulders long
> enough. It's your turn now. The mantle of Elijah has fallen upon Elisha, not
> only in Palestine. It is your rendezvous with destiny.[3]

In response, Chaim Weizmann said:

> [I]f we close our eyes for a minute, we might think these are truly Messianic
> times. For the first time in our history, ladies and gentlemen, the Jews have
> allies. We have paid a heavy price, but for the first time we really do not stand

alone ... The struggle today is a struggle between *Mein Kampf* and the Sermon on the Mount.

Six or seven years ago this struggle, which was obvious to us, was considered by others as only an internal affair of Germany. The nations of the world did not realize that this challenge to the Jews was a challenge to the Christian civilization in which we live and for which we struggle now. It is never too late to make amends, and the atmosphere which prevails here tonight justifies the hope that when the struggle is over we shall not be forgotten. Should you try to forget, we shall be there to remind you.

On 2 November 1942, to mark the 25th Anniversary of the Balfour Declaration, the APC issued its declaration, 'The Common Purpose of Civilized Mankind', re-affirming the 'traditional American policy' in favor of a Jewish homeland, bearing the signatures of 68 Senators and 194 Congressmen. It was submitted to FDR, and afterwards distributed in tens of thousands of copies.[4]

In March 1944 (to get somewhat ahead of the time-frame of this present chapter), the APC sponsored a National Conference on Palestine, at which the demand was made for maximum Jewish immigration to Palestine and the establishment of a Jewish Commonwealth there – all this bringing the APC fully in line with the Biltmore platform. A few months later, lobbying by leaders of the APC in both houses of Congress contributed to the passage of a Resolution favoring these principles.

By 1946, there were 15,000 members of the American Palestine Committee, organized in more than 75 chapters.

THE CHALLENGE OF RECRUITING LIBERAL OPINION

It is significant that Emanuel Neumann undertook to bring the politicians into line first (through the formation of APC) before going to the intellectuals and the churchmen. This strategy reflected the Zionists' knowledge, borne out again and again in the weight of letters to Congressmen and letters to editors, of overwhelming popular support for restoration of the Jewish to a Jewish state. Step two in Neumann's game plan was to reach the opinion-making elites.

The problem, Neumann discovered, was that

[T]he American press ... had paid virtually no attention to the Jewish problem. Articles appeared dealing with various postwar issues, but I found no word about the future position of the Jews and their problem – as if there was a conspiracy of silence despite Hitler and the Nazi terror. It was incomprehensible![5]

Inexcusable it may have been; incomprehensible it certainly was not. The liberal journals, which had routinely castigated British imperialism during the 1920s and 1930s, had changed their tune by the end of 1941. Henceforth, it was an unwritten rule of liberal editorializing that Britain was not to be undermined in her present war effort by criticism from America which bore upon her conduct in those parts of the world (steadily being reduced during 1941) where she could actually work her will. What made Palestine problematical for the friends of Great Britain, was the fact that here, in Palestine, Britain was fully in control and was already carrying out her postwar policy – the policy abundantly spelled out in the White Paper of 1939. Most liberals had used up whatever outrage they felt about Britain's Palestine policy during the first year following the publication of the White Paper of 1939. After Pearl Harbor, few were keen to resuscitate that debate.

Ironically, Jewish intellectuals especially felt the need for restraint. The *New York Times*, owned and substantially manned by Jews, was frankly hostile to Zionism. In light of all this, Neumann, recalled, 'I went to see Freda Kirchwey, editor of *The Nation*, drew her attention to this situation and expressed my surprise that even *The Nation*, so liberal in its policy and so largely supported by Jews, should be remiss in this respect. She readily pleaded guilty.' Together they agreed that the most effective spokesman for the cause of the Zionists would be Reinhold Niebuhr.

REINHOLD NIEBUHR (1893–1971)

Reinhold Niebuhr was born the year before Emanuel Neumann, in 1892, in a small Missouri town. His father had emigrated from Germany and had become a pastor of the Evangelical Reformed Church, a doctrinally conservative Protestant denomination, serving almost exclusively German-Americans. He pastored a number of churches in small-town Missouri and Illinois.

Reinhold had himself become a pastor, after attending the denomination's theological school and receiving his MA at Yale Divinity School. In 1915, he undertook his first and only full-time pastorate, at Bethel Evangelical church in Detroit, serving there until 1928. Ambitious for a larger audience, he turned out many articles for church papers, then found admission to the liberal journals of opinion. He quickly established a reputation for reflective commentary on contemporary religion and on political matters, domestic and international, and turned out, on average, an article a week to be published in journals that ranged from his denomination's house organ, through *Christian Century* (the principal journal of opinion of the Protestant mainstream of the time), *The Nation*, the *New Republic*, several of the University quarterlies, theological journals, as well as a quarterly edited in part by himself (*Radical Religion*, later renamed *Christianity and Society*), and, beginning in February, 1941, a biweekly, entirely edited by himself with the title, *Christianity and Crisis*.

On the basis of his brilliant writing and his powerful preaching before student Christian audiences around the country, Niebuhr was appointed Professor of Christian Ethics at Union Theological Seminary in New York in 1932. Liberal theologians of the older type disdained Niebuhr for his 'Neo-Orthodoxy', while secular liberals, though they usually welcomed his incisive commentaries on current political affairs, mocked him for his residual supernaturalism. But a steadily growing audience of admirers proclaimed his 'Christian realism'.

By the eve of the Second World War, he was one of very few American intellectuals whose work seemed to interest Europeans. In the spring of 1939, as war clouds gathered over Europe, Niebuhr was in Edinburgh, Scotland, giving the first part of a two-part series of lectures for the prestigious Gifford Lectureship; and in the fall, after Great Britain had gone to war, and as America's long agony of watchfulness began, he returned to deliver the second part, with the sound of falling bombs literally accompanying his words. These lectures were then reworked to become his major work, *The Nature and Destiny of Man: A Christian Interpretation*.

Like most of his generation who had been Wilsonian idealists – Stephen Wise, for instance – Niebuhr had shifted to socialism and pacifism in the 1920s. He had voted for the Socialist Party candidates down through 1936, but in 1938 he clashed publicly with the leader of the Party, Norman Thomas, over Thomas's determination to keep the Party neutral with regard to the conflicts unleashed by the Nazis and Fascists. Concerned equally about lingering Stalinism in leftist circles and about the growth of conservative forces within the Democratic Party, Niebuhr led in the founding of the Union for Democratic Action, in April, 1941. In the first year of its existence UDA came to the forefront of supporters of 'all aid short of war' to Great Britain. Throughout the war, it bombarded the public, through advertisements and public meetings, with denunciations of those actions of the Government of the United States which were not in line with its own characterization of the war as one for the liquidation of totalitarianism and the establishment of the Four Freedoms. The President of the United States was certainly aware of the political weight of the UDA, and several members of his official family paid it the respect of signing its petitions about various matters and appearing at its programs – as did Mrs Roosevelt.[6] Of particular interest here is UDA's persistent clamour for removal of all paper obstacles to the rescue of the victims of the Nazi régime in Europe.

In sum, Niebuhr had played a large role in directing the independent left of American politics into a role of greater political effectiveness, able to bring pressure upon the Roosevelt Administration to remain faithful to its New Deal agenda and to be realistic and humane in its foreign policy.

REINHOLD NIEBUHR AND THE JEWISH QUESTION

It has been said of Reinhold Niebuhr that 'he wrote more articles and editorials on the subject of the Nazi assault on the Jews than any other American Christian'.[7] Before audiences of American Jews he spoke of what he called 'my sense of shame that an allegedly Christian civilization can sink to such depths of cruelty'.[8] Niebuhr knew Germany well and had, through his friends in German Church circles and German political circles, abundant sources of knowledge about its real daily life. He played a major role in the work of rescue of German, and after 1938, Austrian, and after June, 1940, French academics and intellectuals, principally through the Friends of German Freedom, the American Friends of the Captive Nations, and an unpublicized network of contacts within the Nazi empire. He helped create the Christian Committee to Boycott Nazi Germany, which sought to persuade Americans not to travel on German ships or buy German products, or 'to set foot on the territory of the Third Reich'. At the same time, he was active in a constellation of organizations at home dedicated to achieving social justice for the disadvantaged, including the Fellowship of Socialist Christians.

As early as February 1941, long before most Jews were ready to face this truth, he was prepared to say in print: 'Nazi tyranny intends to annihilate the Jewish race.'[9] Most Protestant denominations, through their official agencies and through the Federal Council of Churches (the principal institutional expression of mainstream Protestantism), the *Christian Century*, the Student Christian Association – all the accredited voices of the Protestant establishment, had discredited themselves as prophets by persisting as late as the day of Pearl Harbor in advocacy of pacifism and American neutrality. To meet the need for expression of 'Christian realism' in this period of comfortable prophecy, Niebuhr had founded a journal under his editorship, *Christianity and Crisis*, which first appeared in February 1941. The very first of Niebuhr's signed articles in *Christianity and Crisis* declared his thesis:

> That there are historic situations in which refusal to defend the inheritance of civilization, however imperfect, against tyranny and aggression may result in consequences even worse than war ... Nazi tyranny intends to annihilate the Jewish race, to subject the nations of Europe to dominion of a 'master' race, to extirpate the Christian religion, to annul the liberties and legal standards that are the priceless heritage of Christian and humanistic culture, to make truth the prostitute of political power, to seek world dominion through its satraps and allies, and generally to destroy the very fabric of our civilization.

'JEWS AFTER THE WAR'

Reinhold Niebuhr's pro-Zionism had been nurtured for some years by his friends Rabbis Philip Bernstein and Milton Steinberg, both now active on AZEC's Committee on Christian Clergy. Among his other good friends were Stephen Wise and Felix Frankfurter. Neumann found no difficulty at all in persuading Niebuhr to undertake the article, given that he was able to provide both Felix Frankfurter and Isaiah Berlin to provide research material and other guidance.

The article, entitled 'Jews after the War', appeared in two parts in the *Nation*[10] – 'the first articles on this subject', Neumann later claimed, 'to appear during the war years in any American periodical outside the Jewish press'. The piece drew very great attention at the time, and over the next few years large numbers of reprints were distributed by AZEC, CCP/ACPC, and other organizations friendly to Zionism.

Here we will note only a few passages from Niebuhr's two-part article, to remind us of the historical setting:

> The problem of what is to become of the Jews in the postwar world ought to engage all of us, not only because a suffering people has a claim upon our compassion but because the very quality of our civilization is involved in the solution ... The Nazis intend to decimate the Poles and to reduce other peoples to the status of helots; but they are bent upon the extermination of the Jews ... The Jews require a homeland, if for no other reason, because even the most generous immigration laws of Western democracies will not permit all the dispossessed Jews of Europe to find a haven in which they may look forward to a tolerable future ... Whether the Jews will be allowed to develop a genuine homeland under their own sovereignty within the framework of the British Empire depends solely upon the amount of support that they secure in the two great democracies, for those democracies will have it in their power if Hitler is defeated to make the necessary political arrangements ... The Anglo-Saxon hegemony that is bound to exist in the event of an Axis defeat will be in a position to see to it that Palestine is set aside for the Jews, that the present restrictions on immigration are abrogated, and that the Arabs are otherwise compensated.

The AZEC was justifiably confident that it had found in Reinhold Niebuhr the best possible instrument for its purpose, that is, to bring into the arena of discussion their concerns about the future of the Jews. Yet we should note that, while the AZEC promoted the *Nation* articles then and for many years thereafter, there are at least two places in the articles where Niebuhr deviated conspicuously from the official Zionist viewpoint.

First, Niebuhr noted bluntly that

> The Zionist leaders are unrealistic in insisting that their demands entail no 'injustice' to the Arab population since Jewish immigration has brought new

economic strength to Palestine. It is absurd to expect any people to regard
the restriction of their sovereignty over a traditional possession as 'just', no
matter how many other benefits accrue from that abridgement ... The
solution must, and can, be made acceptable to the Arabs if it is incorporated
into a total settlement of the issues of the Mediterranean and Near Eastern
world; and it need not be unjust to the Arabs in the long run if the same
'imperial' policy that established the Jewish homeland also consolidates and
unifies the Arab world.

There was in official Zionist ranks at that time little patience for the view
that the Arabs, when all was said and done, had suffered from the presence of
the Jews in Palestine. This argument was likewise pursued by most Christian
friends of Zionism at that time, and for a while at least it seemed to take
hold in the Roosevelt administration. It is typical of Reinhold Niebuhr that
he should argue that a disinterested perspective on these matters was not
possible, that the friends of Zion had swept too quickly to their verdict on
the benign effects of Jewish immigration and investment in Palestine.

If on the issue of the validity of Palestinian Arab complaints dissent was
rare in Zionist ranks, on a second matter, raised by Niebuhr in the last
paragraph of his second article, dissent had not been heard for years, even
decades. This was the sacrosanct matter of the location of the Jewish State.

> It must be noted in conclusion that there are both Jews and Gentiles who do
> not believe that Palestine is a desirable locus for a Jewish homeland, though
> they do believe that a homeland must be created. They contend that there is
> as yet no evidence of Palestine's ability to maintain an independent economic
> existence without subsidies; that the co-operative agricultural ventures of
> the Jews, impressive in quality but not in size, offer no hope of a solid
> agricultural basis for the national economy; that the enmity of the Arab world
> would require the constant interposition of imperial arms; that the resources
> of Palestine could not support the millions whom the Zionists hope to settle
> there; and that the tendency to use Arab agricultural labor may once again
> create a Jewish urban caste. It is difficult to know to what extent such
> criticisms are justified ... However, even if fully borne out, it would not affect
> the thesis that the Jews require a homeland. It would simply raise the question
> whether a different or an additional region should be chosen. It is barely
> possible that a location ought to be found in Europe.

THE NATURE OF REINHOLD NIEBUHR'S PRO-ZIONISM

That Reinhold Niebuhr could entertain, even for a moment, the notion of
another 'locus' for the Jewish homeland gives away the fact that his pro-
Zionism was not grounded in Christian Restorationism. The source of his
pro-Zionism was, rather, a sturdy philo-Judaism, which in turn derived
from personal experience and religious philosophy.

In autobiographical passages, Niebuhr speaks of having learned in his Midwestern boyhood 'the power of stereotypes' of the Jews. His later adult dealings with Jews provided him with certain generalized truths of a different character. In later years, he spoke of his discovery of the life of the Jews of Detroit:

> If one claims that the Jewish capacity for civic virtue frequently excels that of Christians, the claim rests upon the Jewish capacity for critical devotion to the community which frequently excels the more traditional loyalties of the Gentile community and the typically benevolent goodness of the Christian business man. My judgements may be colored by years of political activity left of center. Whether the problem was one of challenging a nationalistic isolationism or of amending the traditional libertarian attitudes of the business community, Jewish men of wealth were more emancipated from the prejudice of their class than Christian business men. They were discriminate in their judgements of social policy. They were usually more generous in the support of communal projects which transcended the loyalties of a particular group.[11]

Whether or not they recognize it, Christians of serious religious stripe are often drawn to Jews and to Judaism by the hope of finding expression there of the promises and expectations which they have been taught to find in the Church, or in Christian character, or in the life of prayer, or of Christian social action – and which they have failed to find, or, rather, have found so entangled in the dross of unredeemed character as to seem hardly worth having. There is, in other words, a romantic dimension to this story. The soul-less Christian individualist whom Niebuhr portrays standing across the great gulf from the socially sensitive Jew is an unworthy caricature – a stereotype. Many areas of Christian faith and practice embarrassed Reinhold Niebuhr, the Professor of Christian Ethics of New York's Union Theological Seminary. Though reared in a conservative theological tradition and churchly milieu, he had become downright contemptuous of Evangelical Christianity. There was, first of all, the shallowness of its scholarship; then there was the whole embarrassing business about personal witnessing; and above all there was what he came to consider the scandal of revivalism. In later years, the very mention of the name, Billy Graham, would throw him into a rage.

Given Niebuhr's credentials as a theologian, it is at first sight odd that there is so little reference to the religious dimension of Zionism. This reflects his pride in his 'realism' and his loathing of 'idealism'. Reinhold Niebuhr entered the ranks of the Christian champions of the Jewish claim to Palestine in the late 1930s, when the pending holocaust of the Jews made it necessary for liberals of goodwill to deal with the question of the future of the Jews as an urgent and an exceptional issue. Biblical literalists, by contrast, have always understood the past, present and the future of the Jews to be a subject in every sense exceptional. To biblical literalists, arguments about the 'relative justice' of the case for the Arabs in 1938, and agonizings about the legitimate concerns of the British Empire in the Near East, were no more (but also no less) timely than arguments about justice for the Canaanites or agonizings about the future of relations between the XIIIth Dynasty of Egypt and the Hittites. To Reinhold Niebuhr, it seemed that liberals like himself had an advantage (to put it mildly) over the biblical literalists in that their case for Zionism was made in the language of justice, and that the world would find it more or less credible in so far as it addressed the realities of the great power struggles of the day. Thus, the friendly case presented by Reinhold Niebuhr, the Protestant theologian, could be couched in the same vocabulary as the case made by the friendly secularists.

Drawn to the issue of the future of the Jews by the exceptional world-historical circumstances of the moment; perfectly aware of the requirements of the moment in the light of the Christian morality, but scared to death by the language of traditional 'Restorationism' – Reinhold Niebuhr felt much less free than Chaim Weizmann to use the language of biblical prophecy. Nowhere in his commentary, either pre- or post-1948, is there any talk of God's purposes with regard to the Restoration of the Jews. His credibility as an academic theologian depended on his having no allies to the theological right. He was willing to stir the vocabulary of Christian moral philosophy into his astute and well-informed commentaries on contemporary politics, but the least gesture of sympathy for biblical literalism, he believed, would immediately wipe out anything of value that he might bring to the defense of Zionism. In any case, he was not in the least disposed to flirt with Christian Restorationism, which was just one face of all those many forces of popular Christianity which had become so uncongenial, so embarrassing to him since he had left the pulpit for the academy.

AFTERWARD

In a telephone conversation in 1990, I asked Carl H. Voss about this matter: did Reinhold Niebuhr ever comment, in your presence, on the fact that the Restoration of the Jews had always been steadfastly predicted by biblical literalists? Did he concede that they had been vindicated by 1948 and by 1967? Voss recalled Niebuhr saying with some annoyance, but also with reluctant wonder: 'To think that THEY predicted this!' However, it was, apparently, the sort of wonder that a scientist reserves for the *idiot savant* – the technical 'moron', who sits down at the piano and plays Chopin without instruction, or who knows all the years in history when March the third fell on a Thursday, even though he cannot add up double-digit numbers!

In his article 'The Relations of Christians and Jews in Western Civilization' (1958) Niebuhr writes:

> Many Christians are pro-Zionist in the sense that they believe that a homeless people require a homeland; but we feel as embarrassed as anti-Zionist religious Jews when messianic claims are used to substantiate the right of the Jews to the particular homeland in Palestine ... History is full of strange configurations. Among them is the thrilling emergence of the State of Israel.[12]

Niebuhr's published references to Israel after 1948 are few and far between, clustering almost entirely around the two moments of crisis which he lived to see: 1956 (Suez) and 1967 (The Six Day War). The case for America's interest in Israel was now subordinated, in his commentary, to the general world-view called forth by the Cold War. After 1948, Reinhold Niebuhr never reminded his readers that there was anything exceptional about the historical processes that had put Israel on the map and among the United Nations. He was alarmed to note the continuing political signi-ficance of orthodox Judaism in Israel, interpreting these matters in the light of general observations about European and American experience with the bane of 'fundamentalism'.

Still, all things considered. Reinhold Niebuhr remained distinctly friendly to Zionism and to Israel. In this, he was increasingly at odds with most Protestant liberals. In his last years he became very distressed by the uncritically pro-'Palestinian' – that is, pro-Arab – position taken by official voices of mainstream Protestantism, and he was especially distressed by the line taken by the journal he had founded, *Christianity and Crisis*. Paradoxically, this meant that, on this issue, Niebuhr was lined up on the same side with the despised 'Fundamentalists', facing nearly the whole phalanx of liberal-Protestant churchmen and theologians! That intolerable circumstance meant that he had actually to escalate the rhetoric of contempt for 'Messianism', for 'chiliasm', 'millenarianism'. If these embarrassing people insisted on announcing the 'Hand of God' in, for example, the reclaiming in 1967 of Judaea and Samaria, or in the gathering of the exiled Jews of Morocco, Iraq and Yemen – then Niebuhr would persist in seeing only history's 'strange configurations'.

THE CHRISTIAN COUNCIL ON PALESTINE AND THE AMERICAN CHRISTIAN PALESTINE COMMITTEE

Neumann's dealings with Reinhold Niebuhr in the matter of the *Nation* articles set him to thinking more actively about rallying well-disposed Christian leaders. The first fruit of this labour was the Christian Council on Palestine.

Sometime during 1938–39, an organization of Christian friends of Zionism had sprung up, apparently spontaneously, to protest the White Paper, and had then apparently evolved into a lobbying group with an incredibly cumbersome name: the Committee of Christian Leaders, Clergymen and Laymen, on Behalf of Jewish Immigration into Palestine. Many of the names we find here we have met already in the Pro-Palestine Federation. The Committee's statement of policy declared 'that the destiny of the Jews is a matter of immediate concern to the Christian conscience, the amelioration of their lot a duty that rests upon all that profess Christian principles'. Rabbi Philip Bernstein was assigned by Emanuel Neumann to work with this group on behalf of AZEC.

In December 1942, about forty members of the 'Emergency Committee', including Methodist Bishop Francis McConnell, Henry A. Atkinson, W. Russell Bowie, Reinhold Niebuhr, and Carl Voss, met at the Pennsylvania Hotel in New York where, responding to recommendations of Rabbi Philip Bernstein and Emanuel Neumann, they decided to form 'The Christian Council on Palestine'. According to his own memorandum on the meeting, Neumann found that the hardest part of his job was explaining how CCP would differ from APC – to which many of those present already belonged. APC, said Neumann, is 'primarily interested in keeping before the public the question of Zionism, particularly the political phases of the question', while the proposed CCP would concentrate on winning clergymen and leaders of Christian opinion. A policy statement declared the CCP to be 'committed to the establishment of a Jewish commonwealth in Palestine in relation to the overall settlement in the postwar era', while 'urg[ing] as immediate policy the admission now of Jewish exiles into other countries, including the United States, as well as Palestine'. The Executive Committee included Carl Voss, Reinhold Niebuhr, James Luther Adams (a Unitarian clergyman and scholar), Daniel Poling,[13] Paul Tillich, William F. Albright, Pierre Van Paassen (one of the most influential of the serious journalists of the day), Carl Friedrich (a distinguished professor of philosophy), John Haynes Holmes, Eduard Lindemann and Walter Clay Lowdermilk.[14] Carl Voss later recalled Chairman Henry Atkinson saying: 'As soon as the British see that list of men on our stationery – Niebuhr, Tillich, McConnell, Albright, Sockman, and Poling – they'll open the gates of Palestine and let those Jewish refugees come pouring in. Then we'll disband the committee. It's as simple as that.'[15]

The names on CCP's masthead represent a substantial range of denominational affiliations and of theological loyalties – but not extending to the Evangelical/Fundamentalist end. Poling was perhaps the most 'conservative', while Niebuhr and Tillich were in those days described as 'Neo-Orthodox'. Holmes was a non-denominational liberal, a noted champion of the 'Modernist' side in the conflicts with the biblical literalists in the 1920s. Carl Voss, the Executive Secretary, was a Unitarian. Lindemann is described by Voss as 'a humanist/naturalist/non-theist' but nonetheless 'as deeply religious as they' (whatever that may mean!). It is clear that CCP, steered by Voss and Niebuhr, deliberately avoided approach to the Fundamentalist-to-Evangelical side of church world.

In the months that followed, many pamphlets and books appeared under CCP auspices, many public meetings were held, Letters to the Editor were written, and full-page advertisements appeared in the *New York Times*. By 1946, some 3,000 prominent clergymen and lay Christian leaders belonged to CCP. As was the case with ACP, all but a token portion of the funding came from official Zionist and other Jewish sources. Later, these two original organizations (APC and CCP) were incorporated as sub-divisions of the American Christian Palestine Committee (ACPC), having their own letterheads and their own officers.

THE WORLD COMMITTEE FOR PALESTINE

In the fall of 1945, an effort was begun, principally under American Zionist auspices, to establish a network of 'Pro-Palestine Committees' throughout the world. The process began at an 'International Conference for Palestine', wherein twenty-five nations were said to be represented, and which met in Washington, 1–2 November 1945. While no hint of this appears in the publications of the World Committee, the documents make clear that the lion's share of time and money and energy went into the work of penetrating Latin America, where (as is noted in the minutes of the Executive Committee) 'there are twenty nations with twenty votes in the United Nations Organization, regardless of size of country or size of population', and where there is also 'a woeful lack of information on the Jewish problem'. All in all, there were to be World Committee Information Bureaus in Washington, London, Toronto, Mexico City, Paris and Montevideo, all supplied and supported from the World Zionist information bodies in Jerusalem, London and Washington.

All of this would cost money. To the founding Committee,

> Dr Le Sourd explained briefly, and in confidence, the financial set-up of the World Conference for Palestine, which, because of its world coverage, was subsidized by the Jewish Agency. He explained that the American Christian Palestine Committee, is subsidized by the American Zionist Emergency Council, a combination of Zionist organizations in the United States. The Jewish Agency is at work around the world organizing Zionist groups in various countries. Ultimately, it is expected that these local Zionist groups will be able to finance the activities of the pro-Palestine Committees in their

respective countries, and to pay the expenses of the delegates from these countries to the international meetings … Dr Le Sourd [further] explained that it is well established that membership in the ACPC involves no financial obligations, voluntary contributions come in daily and are encouraged wherever possible … It was generally conceded that it is uncomfortable for the non-Jews to come to the Jews and ask them to finance their work. It was felt that the Jewish Agency should instruct local Zionists to offer such co-operation to the non-Jewish supporters of the cause of the Jewish people.

At a Joint Meeting of the World Committee for Palestine and the Jewish Agency, 8 November 1945, 'The Plan of Co-operation of World Pro-Palestine Committees' was adopted, and an executive chosen. These included Mrs Orde Wingate (Great Britain), Senator Gabriel Gonzales Videla (Chile), and several distinguished Christian politicians and men of letters from Europe and Latin America. Virtually the entire senior leadership of the Jewish Agency attended: Louis Lipsky, Dr Nahum Goldman, Meyer W. Weisgal, Eliahu Epstein, Reuven Zaslani, Arthur Lourie, and, of course, Emanuel Neumann. Nahum Goldmann undertook, on behalf of the Jewish Agency, to guarantee full funding of the work of the various Committees. In May 1946, Senator Sir Ellsworth Flavelle of Canada was elected Chairman, and among its Vice Chairmen was Senator Robert Wagner. The World Committee for Palestine undertook:

> 1. To coordinate the activities of the various Pro-Palestine committees, supporting the Jewish National Homeland and Commonwealth in Palestine.
> 2. To plan for a more effective expression of the aroused conscience of Christendom to its responsibility for the establishment of Jewish security.
> 3. To further the awakening of men's minds to the true tragic plight of the destitute and still persecuted Jews of Europe.
> 4. To promote an intelligent, articulate concern among the nations of the world that Palestine become legally and in fact the Jewish National Homeland.
> 5. To support the Zionist objectives to make Palestine a democratic Jewish Commonwealth as an indispensable factor in the solution of the world Jewish problem, the extension of democracy, and the establishment of permanent peace.
> 6. To foster an interchange of ideas, literature, speakers and programs among the Pro-Palestine Committees for the attainment of greater unity and more effective procedures of education.

The profile of ACPC/WCP was raised considerably by the success of the AZEC's leadership in recruiting the former Undersecretary of State, Sumner Welles, as Chairman of its Maryland Chapter. He had been won to the Zionist cause in reaction to what seemed to him the shameless policy of the British which Welles had been observing from the inside of the

Roosevelt Administration for many years. He contributed a lively book to the debate about Palestine (*We Need Not Fail*, 1948), and he made many public statements as well as appearances at ACPC- or WPC-sponsored functions. Perhaps most important, he was put to good use by the Jewish Agency as an interlocutor with crucial persons in the State Department and in the UN delegation of the United States.[16]

PART FOUR

'I AM CYRUS'

13

The Issue of Palestine in the Wartime Years

FDR AND THE ZIONISTS (1942–45)

We have described many imaginative and energetic efforts by the American Zionist leadership, working largely through the AZEC, to rally the Christian conscience on behalf of the Zionist cause. They had every reason to be proud of these efforts and to be confident that they would bear the anticipated fruit.

The European and the Palestinian Zionists, however, had much less confidence than did the Americans in the value of these efforts. Reporting to the Jewish Agency on his visit to the United States in 1942, Moshe Shertok complained of administrative confusion, divided leadership, and lack of zeal in the ranks of the ZOA: as a result 'I grieve to inform you that the Zionist movement has few supporters among American Jewry. To our sorrow the 5,000,000 American Jews place too much faith in what the neighbours think, and feel that open admission of their race and open support of the Zionist movement will render them victims of anti-Semitic action.'[1] Chaim Weizmann, too, gave low grades to the American leaders, but was inclined to believe that what really mattered in the end was not the quality of the leaders of AZEC nor their efforts at rallying of public opinion but, rather, successful wooing of the American administration from the inside. His report to the Zionist executive meeting, London, 5 July 1943, was therefore more positive:

> There were, of course, many excellent people – for instance there were some 6,000 Jews in the administration, from Morgenthau down to typists, and among them there were some brilliant young men. Mr Sieff had grouped around himself a number of people in Washington ... who were ready and willing to do whatever was possible ... There was a good deal of vague sympathy in Washington. They could always get a row of names for a Jewish cause which would astonish people outside America, but it really meant little ... The whole thing turned on the President and on the immediate entourage of the White House.[2]

Chaim Weizmann's trust in FDR seemed at this stage of things to match that of Stephen Wise. Weizmann was first brought to meet FDR in February of 1940, when he had an opportunity to put the Zionist case, and, in particular, to answer the President's well-informed queries about the 'absorption' possibilities of Palestine. It was all quite 'theoretical', Weizmann later recalled. Weizmann was called to a second interview in July 1942, primarily so that he could explain the military applications of his scientific work. On that occasion, Weizmann followed the advice of Mr Winant (the US Ambassador in London) that he could 'serve the Zionist cause more effectively' on that occasion by not digressing from 'the rubber problem'. A third meeting took place in June 1943. On that occasion, FDR agreed with Weizmann that there must soon be a conference on the future of Palestine, at which FDR, Churchill, and Jewish and Arab leaders would all be present, and where they would hammer out a plan for Palestine's future. FDR told Weizmann that (in the latter's paraphrase) 'he believed that the Arabs are purchasable'. But simultaneously, we now know, Roosevelt's State Department was working with the British Foreign Office on a joint Anglo-American statement of their intention to postpone any declaration of their commitments regarding Palestine until after the successful conclusion of the war. From these encounters Weizmann went away confident that 'our difficulties were not connected with the first-rank statesmen', and that therefore 'the obstinate, devious and secretive opposition' that he knew existed in the State Department would be overcome in the end by the President's authority.[3]

It certainly was not true, as Weizmann implies in his memoirs and categorically states in his memos at the time, that the American Zionists did not understand the value of contacts on the inside. AZEC officials, and notably Neumann, worked assiduously to keep the very men mentioned by Weizmann well disposed, but they had learned the hard way that no amount of goodwill on the inside would win the day unless the insiders could be shown that the American public wanted what the Zionists wanted. Thus, while the 'Sieff group' met to co-ordinate their efforts on the inside on behalf of the Jewish people and the Jewish Homeland, and while Stephen Wise and Chaim Weizmann (during his several extended visits to the United States between 1939 and the establishment of the State in 1948) cultivated the goodwill of the Secretary of State and the President, the AZEC leadership wisely put their best efforts into keeping public opinion supportive. These efforts were often frustrated by the commitment that Weizmann and Stephen Wise had made to the notion that 'the first-rank statesmen' could work best on behalf of the Zionist cause if not distracted by agitation of the Zionist agenda in the public arena.

The great turning point in this story of the evolution of Zionist political strategy was the extraordinary Zionist conference held at the Biltmore Hotel in New York in May 1942. During these proceedings the day was won by Ben-Gurion and Abba Hillel Silver, advocates of a maximum effort to rally opinion outside the seats of power in support of the immediate establishment of the Jewish Commonwealth.

There was much that was, to say the least, paradoxical in the new alignment of powers within American Zionism. Abba Hillel Silver, Rabbi of the very prosperous and very liberal Temple of Cleveland from 1917 until his death in 1963, was not enthusiastic for the New Deal, while most American Jews certainly were. Yet neither was Silver a committed Republican; in fact, in Presidential elections since 1920 he had voted for Norman Thomas, Robert La Follette, Alfred E. Smith, and for FDR in both 1936 and 1940. Currently, however, his most active political contacts were all with Republicans – notably Senator Robert Taft (one of the most constant political friends of the Zionists) and Thomas Dewey, Governor of New York – the two most likely candidates of the party for the Presidency in 1944. Following Silver's strategy, the official Zionists worked both sides of the political street in the mid-term elections of 1942 and during the Presidential elections of 1944. From here on in, Silver proclaimed, 'quiet diplomacy' was out, 'loud diplomacy' was in.[4] In still cruder terms: 'It is too late for court Jews.'[5]

Both Franklin Roosevelt and Harry Truman after him took a deep dislike to Abba Hillel Silver. It was true that he was a graceless individual, in his official capacity as the voice of the suffering Jewish people, but it was also true that both Roosevelt and Truman could get along with graceless individuals when they had to. The deeper cause was the resentment both Democratic presidents felt at Silver's incitement to Jewish voters to work the other side of the street.

'We'll force the President to swallow our demands', Silver declared. Chaim Weizmann took the strongest exception to this new policy and to its champion, whom he called 'The Mufti from Cleveland'. Stephen Wise and Chaim Weizmann, bitter rivals in the organizational infighting of the World Zionist movement in the early thirties, now agreed in most of their judgements of persons, issues, and opportunities. Not coincidentally, Weizmann was losing his grasp on the Jewish Agency just as Wise was losing his grip on the AZEC. After a moment of disarray when Wise and Silver had denounced each other in the fiercest language and resigned, the AZEC had worked out a fragile power-sharing agreement between Silver and Wise that was in effect, on and off, through the whole of this period down to 1946.

This was not American Zionism's shining hour. Wise was driven by the need to vindicate his political life by proving to the World Zionist Organization and to Jews in general that he personally had the keys that gave access to the White House, but Zionists who had previously been his closest friends were now bluntly affirming that having that access had done the cause no good – that Wise, in effect, had let himself be used by the government of Franklin Roosevelt. In illustration of Franklin Roosevelt's procedures, we might take the case of his meeting with the official Zionist delegation, consisting of Rabbis Silver and Wise on 9 March 1944 – following which a statement was issued by Silver and Wise:

> The President has authorized us to say that the American government has never given its approval to the White Paper of 1939. The President is happy that the doors of Palestine are today open to Jewish refugees [*sic!*], and that when future decisions are reached, full justice will be done to those who seek a Jewish National Home, for which our government and the American people have always had the deepest sympathy and today more than ever, in view of the tragic plight of hundreds of thousands of homeless Jewish refugees.[6]

Following a Cabinet meeting the next day, Vice-President Wallace recorded a discussion on the Jewish and Palestine questions:

> The President held forth at some length about how ... Stephen Wise and Rabbi Silver were in to see him, and how he had started out by attacking them vigorously by saying, 'Do you want to be responsible for the loss of hundreds of thousands of lives? Do you want to start a Holy Gehad [*sic*]?' The President continued along this line, quoting his conversation with regard to the dangers of attacks from the enraged Arabs. It is exactly the same line he had pulled on Monday when I raised the question. And yet I knew because Silver had talked to me at length the night before that the bulk of the President's conversation had undoubtedly been to cause Wise and Silver to believe that he was in complete accord with them and the only question was the timing ... The President certainly is a waterman. He looks one direction and rows the other with utmost skill.[7]

Long years of dealing with the Administration and the person of Franklin Roosevelt had done much damage to the moral integrity of the American Zionists.

A truly agonizing question mark hung over the policies and the activities of President Roosevelt in his last year of office and of life. In the summer of 1944, both parties' convention platforms had in effect endorsed the position of the Wagner–Taft Resolution, by declaring in favor of the Jewish State in Palestine. In the course of his campaign, FDR, to the consternation of his State Department, explicitly endorsed the Palestine plank, but then, after the election, the Administration reverted to its previous line, that, while the President whole-heartedly supported the idea of working towards the Jewish state, this matter should await a general review of the postwar possibilities, which would follow upon the Allied victory, expected soon. In effect, Roosevelt was saying to the Zionists: Trust my judgement. Do not require me to carry to the Great Power Conference (which turned out to be Yalta) a Congressional Resolution which compels me to tell Winston Churchill that he must declare Palestine immediately open to unlimited immigration of the Jews. First let me hear out Churchill's vision for Palestine, and together we will work out a solution along Zionist lines, which we will then announce to the whole world as an unbridgeable commitment of the Great Powers.

With the official Zionist leadership quietly acquiescing, the Wagner–Taft Resolution was tabled by the Senate Foreign Relations Committee on 11 December 1944 – something they all regretted later.

THE JEWISH QUESTION IN THE LAST MONTHS OF
THE PRESIDENCY OF FRANKLIN ROOSEVELT

American Zionism was at a fateful crossroads. On 1 March 1945, when FDR presented his report to Congress on the Yalta Conference, Wise and the Zionists learned, along with the rest of the world of the President's secret meeting with Ibn Saud on the Great Bitter Lake – something not projected in any of FDR's previous meetings with them. Panic struck in all their hearts at once, when they heard him say before the whole world, 'I learned more about that whole problem, the Moslem problem, the Jewish problem, by talking with Ibn Saud for five minutes than I could have learned in the exchange of two or three dozen letters' – as though he was, in that moment, publicly sweeping the slate clean of all the years of their painful efforts to educate him. Now that the Jews of Europe were nearly all gone, Franklin Roosevelt had told the world (or so it had sounded) that he had to think it all through again, having sat for a few hours at the feet of one the Arab world's tyrants. Afterwards, characteristically, FDR had quickly reached out to reassure the Zionists, calling Stephen Wise to the White House (16 March 1945.) Wise gained the President's permission to make a statement to the Press. As reported in the *New York Times*:

> 16 March. President Roosevelt re-affirmed today his support of a free and democratic Palestine, after a conference with Dr Stephen S. Wise, chairman of the Zionist Emergency Council.
> Dr Wise talked with the President for three-quarters of an hour, and an official statement issued later quoted the President as saying:
> I made my position on Zionism clear in October. That position I have not changed and shall continue to seek to bring about its earliest realization ... Dr Wise is understood to be preparing a report of his conference with the President which will be submitted to the executive committee of the American Zionist Emergency Council.[8]

But with Wise scarcely out the door, FDR had fired off cablegrams to all the Arab capitals, reassuring them, in turn, of his commitment not to proceed any further without fully involving them. One of these, addressed to the President of Syria, 12 April 1945, is the last item in the volume of the *Foreign Relations of the United States* devoted to the Middle Eastern policy of the Roosevelt Administration.[9]

Had Roosevelt lived, that would doubtless have been the pattern for the indefinite future: reassurance fired off in one direction, then the other, until everybody's patience broke down, with the United States losing credibility, and therefore leverage, in the end. Following FDR's address to Congress on the Yalta and the Great Bitter Lake meetings, the official American Zionists – those who had had access to FDR until now – had immediately broken into two camps. The first believed, against all evidence, that the effort to convince FDR should be resumed along the old lines; the other, growing in strength every day, cursed the waste of effort and of trust of a decade of dealings with the Democratic administration, and called for a bolder strategy, one of demanding justice for the Jews in the larger political arena. One of the leaders of this second camp was Emanuel Neumann, whose ultimate verdict is harsh:

> Whatever his attitude toward the Jews and the apparent absence of anti-Semitism in his makeup, there is no doubt that Roosevelt did nothing effective to stay the hands of the Nazis in their extermination of European Jewry, and little or nothing to help Hitler's victims find a refuge in the United States or to induce England to admit Jewish refugees to Palestine ... [Within the Zionist movement] he was regarded as a devoted friend of the Jewish people, an implacable foe of Hitler and a loyal ally of Great Britain in her struggle against Nazi Germany. He came to be looked upon by American Jews not only as their champion, but as the personification of all that was noble in the American character. As this feeling grew he came to be revered and adored by the Jewish masses; to criticize him was blasphemy ... I came to realize that Roosevelt's favorable attitude to our cause was not much more than 'platonic love' or, as Abba Hillel Silver came to describe it in his own inimitable way, a case of 'uninvolved benignancy'. I gradually came to doubt even the 'benignancy' and considered it a misfortune that at such a critical time the government of the United States should be headed by a President who was clothed with great power and imperturbable charm, but who seemed determined to do nothing of substance for our people and its cause.

Paradoxically, what these two camps had in common was their all-absorbing pre-occupation with Franklin Roosevelt. And then suddenly, FDR was gone.

14

Harry Truman and the Zionists

HARRY TRUMAN AND THE JEWISH QUESTION

In most of the general accounts of his Presidency, Harry Truman is
described as disoriented and confused by the welter of Zionist and anti-
Zionist arguments with which he was abruptly confronted in the first weeks
of his presidency; but in fact Truman was well schooled in the polemics
about Zion, much more so than Franklin Roosevelt, and his loyalty to the
Zionist program, much more authentic than Roosevelt's at any time, had
been effectively secured before 1941.

There is good evidence that Truman received his basic pro-Zionist
instruction from the best possible authority, from Justice Louis Brandeis.
In the days when Senators Truman and Burton K. Wheeler were carrying
out their investigations regarding railroad financing (which culminated in
the Wheeler–Truman Transportation Act of 1940), Truman became
acquainted with Max Lowenthal, counsel to Wheeler's subcommittee, who
in turn introduced him to Justice Louis Brandeis, who retained his lively
interest in public questions, especially those having to do with financial
practices and with the Government's role in direction of the economy, and
who wanted to learn from Truman about the pending legislation. Evidently,
Brandeis and Truman got along well, and Truman became a regular visitor
at the Brandeis weekly teas – an honor much coveted among legislators, as
it amounted to certification of one's right to be considered in the progressive/
liberal/Wilsonian succession, without which, Harry Truman could never
have become Vice-President. After his first appearance at the Brandeis
home, Harry Truman wrote home to Bess: 'Both he and Mrs Brandeis are
as nice as they can be. It was a rather exclusive and brainy party. I didn't
exactly belong but they made me think I did.'[1] Although Truman does not
record anywhere that Zionism featured in the discussions he had in the
Brandeis home, it makes sense that it did – as Brandeis, we know, never
missed an opportunity to indoctrinate any promising contact on this, the
cause closest to his heart.

Truman was a member of the American Palestine Committee – as, indeed were two-thirds of United States senators at the time – and thus formally and publicly committed to the principle that Britain should abandon limitations on Jewish immigration to Palestine. Harry Truman seems to have taken his membership more seriously than most, and made speeches to several Zionist groups. Truman's exceptional effort to be helpful to Jewish constituents in matters of appeals regarding refugees had won high praise from Jewish groups. In May 1939, he denounced the White Paper: 'The British government has used its diplomatic umbrella again, this time on Palestine. It has made a scrap of paper out of Lord Balfour's promise to the Jews. It has just added another to the long list of surrenders to Axis powers.' On 14 April 1943, he had addressed the Chicago United Rally to Demand Rescue of Doomed Jews.[2]

He did not, however, follow the APC leadership in the matter of the Wagner–Taft Resolution, introduced early in 1944, calling for immediate declaration by the Government of the United States in favour of creation of a Jewish Commonwealth. Rather, he followed the instructions of the President, who wanted the issue of the Jewish Homeland set aside for discussion in the context of the Great Power meetings which must come towards the end of the War. The embarrassment Truman felt as he sought to rationalize his position shines through the fabric of tangled metaphors in this letter to a Zionist constituent, Phineas Smaller:

> I do not think it is the business of senators who are not on the Foreign Relations Committee to dabble in matters that affect our relations with our Allies at this time. With the difficulty looming up between Russia and Poland, and the Balkan States and Russia, and with Great Britain and Russia absolutely necessary to us in financing the war I don't want to throw bricks to upset the apple cart, although when the right time comes I am willing to help make the fight for Jewish homeland in Palestine.[3]

For this retreat from the position of the Biltmore Platform, he received complaints from articulate Zionist constituents.

The truth was, of course, that Truman could not have been chosen Vice-Presidential candidate in 1944 had he not been regular on the foreign policy matters that most concerned President Roosevelt. Aware that the Palestine issue was potentially the greatest of the obstacles to continuing good relations with Britain, Franklin Roosevelt would not permit his allies in Congress to support the Wagner–Taft Resolution in the spring of 1944, notwithstanding the fact that Wagner–Taft was nothing but a more explicit reading of the pledges which Roosevelt had made to the Jewish leadership many times in the past. Truman's dilemma was temporarily resolved later in the year, when, during the 1944 Presidential election campaign, the President publicly endorsed the Democratic Party's platform. But then, no sooner was the election over than the Administration reverted to its previous line, that while the President whole-heartedly supported the idea of working towards the Jewish state, this matter should await a general review of the postwar possibilities, which would follow the Allied victory, expected soon.

SUCCESSION: THE ZIONISTS WEIGH THEIR PROSPECTS WITH THE NEW PRESIDENT

During the entire three months of his Vice-Presidency, Harry Truman saw President Roosevelt only twice, both times briefly – except at Cabinet meetings, and, as Truman himself has noted, 'Roosevelt never discussed anything important at his Cabinet meetings'.[4] About 'important things' he knew only what he read in the newspapers. The Jewish Agency, however, was not unprepared. On 13 April 1945, Truman's first day in the Oval Office, it was able to circulate in the ranks of its 'Political Department' a memo entitled, 'Note on the New President of the United States'.[5] This reviewed Truman's record on the interlocked questions of the plight of the Jews of Europe and the future of Palestine – which we have just briefly reviewed.

The story of President Truman's deliberations on the Zionist question begins with a visit on 20 April 1945, from Stephen Wise, the chairman of the American Zionist Emergency Council, and it continues through a long chain of visits from leaders of all the various Jewish organizations, including several who brought him anti-Zionist messages. By the middle of 1946 – a mid-term election year – he was heartily fed up. The lowest point in this story came on 2 July 1946, when Rabbi Abba Hillel Silver, now the titular leader of the American Zionist movement, literally pounded on the President's desk – as if to awaken him from imagined indifference.[6] Thereafter, the word was out: no Zionist spokesman, nor anyone presenting himself to speak on the question of Palestine and its future was to get past the office of the President's Secretary. No exceptions. People who think in clichés at once spread the judgement that the new President, in shocking contrast to his liberal-minded and gentlemanly predecessor, was ... one of *them*!

Internal Zionist correspondence from these days yields much evidence of low esteem for President Roosevelt's successor. For example, Gershon Agronsky, of the Jewish Agency has left a record of a conversation between Felix Frankfurter and Henry Morgenthau, Jr., 19 July 1945, in which Frankfurter speaks of the despair that they all feel dealing with a new 'number one' so unlike FDR, who 'had a mind and sources of his own'. Morgenthau and Frankfurter agree 'to ask Stephen S. Wise to send No. 1 a note on the immigration phase of the question ... [expressed in] terms which a man from Missouri like No. 1, would understand, that the *Bnai Brith* were behind this, etc.'[7]

Yet the fact was that Truman's attitudes both towards Jews and towards Zionism had been fixed positively long ago, and it was for this very reason that he resented being led by the hand by people who for so long still thought of him as needing instruction. When these same people dealt with President Roosevelt, they had never let it show that they believed that he needed instruction – only gentle reminding or refreshing of his memory.

THE SOURCES OF TRUMAN'S PRO-ZIONISM

In his *Memoirs*, Truman recalls himself, at the meeting of 20 April 1945, drawing Rabbi Wise's attention to a memo from Under-Secretary Stettinius, urging that he take no actions until the State Department has had an opportunity to explain it all to him; and, both to Wise and the reader of his *Memoirs*, he expresses his resentment and astonishment at the implication that he has somehow been living all these years in ignorance of this important issue.

> Since I was in agreement with the expressed policy of the Roosevelt administration on Palestine, I told Rabbi Wise that I would do everything possible to carry out that policy. I had carefully read the Balfour Declaration, in which Great Britain was committed to a homeland in Palestine for the Jews. I had familiarized myself with the history of the question of a Jewish homeland and the position of the British and the Arabs. I was skeptical, as I read over the whole record up to date, about some of the views and attitudes assumed by the 'striped-pants boys' in the State Department. It seemed to me that they didn't care enough about what happened to the thousands of displaced persons who were involved. It was my feeling that it would be possible for us to watch out for the long-range interests of our country while at the same time helping these unfortunate victims of persecution to find a home. And before Rabbi Wise left, I believe I made this clear to him.[8]

The meeting in question was very brief; it was one item in 'what I was told was the longest list of scheduled callers in the memory of any member of the executive office staff'. It is difficult to credit that Truman accomplished in what was supposed to be merely a courtesy meeting all that he describes in the *Memoirs*. By the time that he sat down with Merle Miller, a decade and a half later, however, the story of the interview[9] had improved considerably:

> I had a long list of appointments that day, and one of them ... was with Rabbi Wise. I saw him late that morning, and I was looking forward to it because I knew he wanted to talk about Palestine, and that is one part of the world that has always interested me, partly because of its Biblical background, of course.

This note prompts an excursion into the theme of the Bible, and its influence on his life:

I told you, I've always done considerable reading of the Bible. I'd read it at least twice before I went to school[!] ... [ellipsis in original] I liked the stories in it. I never cared much for fairy stories or Mother Goose, not that I'm sure we had any Mother Goose at our house, but I just didn't care for that *kind* of thing.

The stories in the Bible, though, were to me stories about real people, and I felt I knew some of them better than *actual* people I knew.

This leads to a digression within the digression, wherein he complains about 'those damn new translations [of the Bible] that they've got out lately':

The King James version of the Bible is the best there is or ever has been or will be, and you get a bunch of college professors spending *years* working on it, and all they do is take the poetry out of it ...

But as I started to say ... [ellipsis in original] it wasn't just the Biblical part about Palestine that interested me. The whole history of that area of the world is just about the most complicated and most interesting of any area anywhere, and I have always made a careful study of it. There has always been trouble there, always been wars from the time of Darius the Great and Rameses on ...

But getting back to what you were asking about, that morning I saw Rabbi Wise. It was late in the morning, and I remember he said, 'Mr President, I'm not sure if you're aware of the reasons underlying the wish of the Jewish people for a homeland'.

He was just as polite as he possibly could be, but I've told you in those days nobody seemed to think I was *aware* of anything. I said I knew all about the history of the Jews, and I told the rabbi I'd read all of Roosevelt's statements on Palestine, and I'd read the Balfour declaration, and of course, I knew the Arab point of view ... But I said as far as I was concerned, the United States would do all that it could to help the Jews set up a homeland. I *didn't* tell him [This contradicts the version in the Memoirs] that I'd already had a communication from some of the 'striped pants' boys warning ... [ellipsis in original] in effect telling me to watch my step, that I didn't really understand what was going on over there and that I ought to leave it to the experts ... And I said that some of the *experts*, the career fellas in the State Department, thought that they ought to make policy but that as long as I was President, I'd see to it that *I* made policy. Their job was to carry it out, and if there were some who didn't like it, they could resign anytime they felt like it.

Did Truman, in this interview with Rabbi Wise, truly link his intentions for Israel in this way with an explicit declaration of his allegiance to the Bible (even assuming that the digressions about the authors of the Gospels, the problems of textual authority in the Gospels, the merits of the various translations, and the other matters that Truman went into with Merle Miller did not get aired before Rabbi Wise that day?) There is no hint of any of this in the account in the *Memoirs*, nor in Stephen Wise's account of the meeting; but in a real way, this latter-day testimony, though doubtless less accurate as a résumé of what was said that day, is more valuable for our purposes, in that it expresses strikingly how Truman liked to remember that meeting which began his association as President of the United States with the Zionists – how he sought to assure them, how he described himself to them, the arguments and the thinking that now, long years after, made sense of his dealings with the Zionists and of his devotion to their cause.

HARRY TRUMAN WAS A BAPTIST

Clark Clifford, who worked closely with President Truman in the months leading to the decision for recognition of the State of Israel on 14 May 1948, later recalled: 'From his reading of the Old Testament he felt the Jews derived a legitimate historical right to Palestine, and he sometimes cited such Biblical lines as Deuteronomy 1:8: "Behold, I have given up the land before you; go in and take possession of the land which the Lord hath sworn unto your fathers, to Abraham, to Isaac and to Jacob".'[10]

In one of the autobiographical fragments preserved in his personal papers and many years after his death published, along with other fragments, by Robert Ferrell as *The Autobiography of Harry S. Truman*, Truman wrote: 'I'm a Baptist because I think that sect gives the common man the shortest and most direct approach to God.'[11] At the time of Harry's birth, his parents were active in the Baptist Church at Grandview, Missouri. Later, while they lived in Independence, Harry was enrolled in the Sunday School at the First Presbyterian church at Lexington and Pleasant, which, he says, the family attended 'every Sunday regularly or as long as we lived in Independence' – which would have been until 1903, the year the family moved to Kansas City. There, when he was eighteen, he joined the Baptist Church by baptism, later transferring his membership to the Grandview Baptist church in 1906 when he went back to work on the family farm, and maintaining it there for the rest of his life.

Many years after his retirement from the presidency, Harry Truman spoke to the National Baptist Convention, the principal body of Black Baptists, which held its convention in his home town of Independence, Missouri (8 September 1959). 'I am', he declared,

> a Baptist by education and by belief that John the Baptist recognized and baptised the Savior of the World, Jesus, and, my friends, he did not sprinkle him with Jordan water; he reverently lowered him bodily below the surface of the sacred Jordan and raised him as a symbol that sin could be washed away.
> [At the time that Jesus came to be baptised by John,] the Jews had long

been awaiting a prophet who would give them a revival of the teachings of Moses, Samuel, Amos and Isaiah, and when he came, they failed to recognize him. He came to rescue the poor and the indigent from the special privilege classes. He was born in a manger. He grew up as the son of a carpenter and was one himself, but remember, he carried his mission to the people who needed the mercy of God.

He constantly called attention to the Law and the prophets. He told the people, who believed that they were better than the poor, where they stood … He reminded them of the Good Samaritan who had helped his neighbour – and Samaritans were, in that day in Jerusalem, regarded as people of your color have been in some parts of the United States …

Jesus Christ preached the Law and the prophets – the XXth Chapter of Exodus, the Vth Chapter of Deuteronomy, the preachings of Amos, Mikah, Isaiah and Jeremiah.

Study the Sermon on the Mount, the 5th, 6th and 7th Chapters of the Gospel according to St Matthew, the 10th Chapter of St Luke, and then turn back to Matthew 22–15 [*sic*] and find obedience to the law of the land.

The Old Testament and the New will give you a way of life that will cause you to live happily.[12]

It would be difficult to think of another president of our time (excepting only Jimmy Carter) and very few public figures of any rank, prepared, in the broad light of day, to make a declaration of such a straightforward Christian creedal character. Yet, from other sources, we know that, as a young man, Harry Truman permitted himself some unorthodox reading. He liked to recommend Thomas Jefferson's *The Life and Morals of Jesus Christ of Nazareth, Extracted textually from the Gospels of Matthew, Mark, Luke, and John* – popularly known as 'The Jefferson Bible' – an entirely unorthodox work. What Truman seems to have taken away from the 'Jefferson Bible' is Thomas Jefferson's proud posture of defiance against priests and superstition. In truth, 'Truman had little interest in theological issues, although he had an almost fundamentalist reverence for the Bible'[13] – something that no one would say of Thomas Jefferson.

As we saw in his address to the National Baptists, Truman was much pre-occupied by the question of the link between religious faith and public morality. Once, at a press conference, he was asked (out of nowhere):

On several occasions recently, sir, you have said that your own political philosophy and that of the administration is based on the Sermon on the Mount.

THE PRESIDENT. That's right.

Q. Would you care to expand, sir, on that theme and point out in what way?

THE PRESIDENT. My best advice to you is to turn to the fifth, sixth, and seventh chapters of the Gospel according to St Matthew in the King

James translation, and read it very carefully, and you will find out without any comment from me. [Laughter]

Q. Mr President, some of us are not so familiar with the Bible. Is that the fifth, sixth, and seventh?

THE PRESIDENT. Fifth, sixth, and seventh chapters of the Gospel according to St Matthew, the King James version. Read those three chapters – won't take you but 20 minutes.

Q. Mr President, we can't hear.

THE PRESIDENT. The Sermon on the Mount – talking about the Sermon on the Mount and my political philosophy. I advised him to read the Sermon on the Mount.

Q. Do you agree with the Sermon on the Mount?

THE PRESIDENT. I do. I am in complete agreement with it.[14]

When he was 66 years old, Truman noted in his diary that it was when he was eighteen years old (that would have been in the year of his baptism, if his recollection of both these matters is exact) that he had written down a prayer, which he then carried with him in his wallet, and read once every day:

> Oh! Almighty and Everlasting God, Creator of Heaven, Earth, and the Universe:
>
> Help me to be, think, to act what is right, because it is right; make me truthful, honest and honorable in all things; make me intellectually honest for the sake of right and honor and without thought of reward to me. Give me the ability to be charitable, forgiving and patient with my fellowmen – help me to understand their motives and their shortcomings – even as Thou understandest mine!
>
> Amen, Amen, Amen.
>
> The prayer on the other side of this page has been said by me – by Harry S. Truman – from high school days: as window washer, bottle washer, floor scrubber in an Independence, Mo, drug store, as a time-keeper on a railroad contract gang, as an employee of an untruthful and character-assassinating newspaper, as a bank clerk, as a farmer riding a gang plow behind four horses and mules, as a fraternity official learning to say nothing at all if good could not be said of a man, as a public official judging the weaknesses and shortcomings of constituents, and as President of the USA.[15]

(It is, incidentally, refreshing to note that the rule, 'to say nothing at all if good could not be said of a man', still left one free to note the facts about 'an untruthful and character assassinating newspaper'.)

With precisely the same degree of confidence in the same special providence of God, he said of his nation:

> Divine Providence has played a great part in our history. I have the feeling that God has created us and brought us to our present position of power and strength for some great purpose.
>
> It is not given to us to know fully what that purpose is, but I think we may

be sure of one thing, and that is that our country is intended to do all it can, in cooperating with other nations to help create peace and preserve peace in the world. It is given to defend the spiritual values – the moral code – against the vast forces of evil that seek to destroy them.

This is a hard task. It is not one that we have asked for. At times we would like to lay it down, and, as we go on with it, we see it is full of uncertainties and sacrifices, but we need not be afraid, if we have faith.[16]

Liberal theologians long ago became embarrassed by that kind of talk. The *Christian Century* more than once scolded Truman for his simplistic religious talk, notably, for his references, from time to time, to the 'Christian' heritage of the nation, and even to its 'Christian mission' in world affairs.[17]

TRUMAN'S PHILOSOPHY OF HISTORY

It would be a mistake, however, to think that the beginning and end of the truth about Harry Truman was that he was a Baptist. Truman was very proud of having worked out his own philosophy of life, something which marked him out from persons of less active intellect – including the rank and file of Baptists, and in this philosophy of life, the foundation was his theory of history.

All the witnesses to the early life of Harry Truman agree with his own recollection that he was a passionate and indefatigable reader. (It does seem to be stretching things a bit, however, to claim, as he repeatedly did, to have read all the books, including the encyclopedias, in the Independence, Missouri, library before he finished high school – by Truman's reckoning, three thousand books – 'and some of them twice'.)[18] Apart from the resources of the public library, there was a good library at home. His favorites included the complete Dickens collection, Gibbon, Greene, Plutarch, and above all a four-volume set of biographies, *Great Men and Famous Women*, edited by Charles Francis Horne.

Truman presented himself as a man of vast historical learning; and he could prove it on the spot by giving you a list as long as your arm of the proper names of the men whose lives and accomplishments (if you would take the trouble to look them up) would prove the point at issue. He seems to have been constantly rehearsing these lists – out loud, if there was an ear to be bent, and in his mind, if there was none – as though he were practicing scales. In his diary, 1–2 January 1952, for example, entirely without an audience, he moves from reference to Bess's problem with a sore throat and the problems that family members have been telling him about in letters, to the gloomy prospects for peace in the world; and these cause him to reflect that,

We face the greatest age in history. I wish I was seventeen instead of sixty-seven, with the same urge I had at seventeen to learn and to know world history. I spent a lot of time reading about the World's Great. Moses, Joshua, David, Solomon, Darius I and Cyrus the Great his uncle, Alexander, Hannibal, Caesar, Antoninus Pius, Hadrian, Titus, Marcus Aurelius Antoninus, Rameses III, Cleopatra, Mark Antony, Augustus Caesar, Thothmes III, Plato, Socrates, Pericles, Demosthenes, Cicero, the Catos, both of them, and then Charlemagne, his father Charles Martel, Roland, John Hunyadi at Belgrade, Saladin, Suleiman the Magnificent, Jenghis Khan, Kubla Khan, Tamerlane, John Sobieski, Richelieu, Gustavus Adolphus of Sweden and Charles XII of Sweden, Alfred the Great, William of Normandy, the greatest of the French Kings, Henry IV of France and King of Navarre, Francis I of France, and Charles V of Spain, Elizabeth of England and Mary of Scotland, Sir Francis Drake and Captain Kidd, Martin Luther, Frederick the Great and Maria Theresa of Austria, Wellington and Lord Russell, Disraeli, Gladstone, Washington, Jefferson, Jackson, Lincoln, Grover Cleveland, Wilson, Franklin Roosevelt and the end![19]

When responding to inquiries about his views on history or public life, he could drop as many stanzas from the list as seemed to be needed:

MEMORANDUM:
July 8. 1953.
    When you contemplate a career think only of the service you can render to your fellowmen.
    Study the lives of great men – the truly great men, men who have made sacrifices for the betterment of the world and their individual countries and communities.
    There are all sorts of men and women who have made history – Abraham, Isaac, Jacob, Joseph, Moses, Joshua, the Great Prophets of Israel, Hammurabi the great Sumerian law-giver, Solon, Lycurgus, Aristides, Cyrus the Great, Darius the Great, Alexander, Hannibal, Caesar, Jenghis Khan, Tamerlane, the Great Mogul, Saladin, Suleiman the Magnificent, Charles Martel, Charlemagne, Napoleon to name a few.
    Then there were Buddha, Jesus, Cincinnatus, George Washington, Abraham Lincoln, Woodrow Wilson.
    Some men of great name were destroyers of mankind, some were law-givers, some were just plain patriots, some were philosophers, some left the world worse off than they found it, some left it better off.
    The moralists and philosophers left the world a much greater heritage than did most of the rulers and conquerors.[20]

If these lists and these maxims were the only evidence of what Harry Truman learned from history, one might be tempted to dismiss him as a mentally arrested schoolboy show-off, but the fact is that no other American President since Theodore Roosevelt, and not excluding Woodrow Wilson, spent more time reading history and brooding upon it. Truman read a wide range of newly published books from academic historians, mainly biographies and narrative histories, mostly on American political and military history. He had little patience for theoretical approaches, and was convinced that most academic historians had betrayed the real purpose in telling history.

This reading and this brooding shaped his self-understanding; and it should be given pride of place in our efforts to understand his motivation at those moments when his actions were at odds with the advice he was receiving from advisors and friends and pundits. In this category we must include such items as the decision to seek the Presidency in 1948, the decision to sack General MacArthur, the decision to denounce the steel strikers in 1946, – and, most spectacular of all, the decision to recognize the State of Israel on 14 May 1948.

It was not a sophisticated theory of history. It is a kind of poor man's Carlyle: '[R]eal history', he said, 'consists of the life and actions of great men who occupied the stage at the time.' Yet it was honestly won, through the exercise of much reading of scholarly and popular history. In any case, the scholarly validity of his theorizing about history is not the matter at issue here. What is at issue is his conception of himself, and what that owed to his theorizing about history.

Two principles stand out. One is that there is such a thing as 'historical greatness', and that this is rooted in character:

> In reading the lives of great men, I found that the first victory they won was over themselves and their carnal urges. Self-discipline with all of them came first. I found that most of the really great ones never thought they were great; some of them did. I admired Cincinnatus, Hannibal, Cyrus the Great, Gustavus Adolphus of Sweden, Washington and Lee, Stonewall Jackson and J.E.B. Stuart … I was not very fond of Alexander, Attila, Ghengis Khan, nor Napoleon, because while they were great leaders of men they fought for conquest and personal glory. The others fought for what they thought was right and for their countries. They were patriots and unselfish.[21]

The second principle is that this sifting out of the great characters of history is under the Providence of God. Despite the professed discipleship to Thomas Jefferson, and despite the Tom Sawyer persona that he liked to assume from time to time, Truman was thoroughly convinced of the Divine directing of his life and everybody else's. For instance, in a diary item of 27 May 1945 (at the end of his sixth week in the presidency) the account of last night's poker game leads to this:

> For some reason I was lucky enough not to lose any money. Luck always seems to be with me in games of chance and in politics. No one was ever luckier than I've been since becoming the Chief Executive and Commander in Chief. Things have gone so well that I can't understand it – except to attribute it to God. He guides me, I think.[22]

Harry Truman, unlike Franklin Roosevelt, was a rigorous thinker, if not a profound one. His major decisions proceeded from hard-earned convictions about the process and direction of the history unfolding before his eyes. This vision of history had two sources – one theological, the other philosophical. The theological source nurtured an unsophisticated, virtually 'fundamentalist' faith, and what the theologians call a 'high view' of the authority of Scripture, as well as deep conviction of Divine guidance of his personal life. From the philosophical source he derived what might be called a fundamentalist-Carlylean 'great man' theory of history. Every day of his presidential life, Truman pondered resolutely on the extraordinary circumstances that brought him where he was. He studied soberly his own strengths and weaknesses – fully at peace about the fact of his humble origins. And he came to the perfectly calm conclusion that he *was* *Cyrus*.

It was not a manner of speaking, but the largest possible truth, that someone, someday, would be called upon to play the role of *Cyrus redivivus*. This was what his teachers taught him in his Sunday School; it was what McDonald and Blackstone had preached; it was what the signers of the Blackstone Memorial had endorsed; it was what moved Woodrow Wilson to endorse the Balfour Declaration.

THE INHERITANCE: AMERICAN POLICY TOWARD PALESTINE, IN APRIL 1945

From the beginning of his presidency, Harry Truman was committed to the pursuit of the best interests of the Jews of the world, and never doubted that in serving these he would encounter no conflict with the best interest of the United States or, for that matter, of the United Nations. Like most Americans of that time, he was not yet irresistibly convinced that the immediate creation of a sovereign Jewish commonwealth was the best way to serve these interlinked interests – those of the global community, those of the United States, those of the Jews; but he did come to that conclusion eventually, more or less in tandem with most American Jews. Like most American Jews, he was willing to hear the case for continuation of the British Mandate in some form or other down to mid-1946, by which time it was all too clear that Britain's government intended to stay in the Middle East on terms that permitted – perhaps, in her view, even required – the abandonment of the Jews of Palestine to an ancient and unappeasable enemy.

In his *Memoirs*, Truman recalled:

> I was always aware of the fact that not all my advisers looked at the Palestine problem in the same manner I did. This was nothing unusual, of course. It is the job of the military planners to consider all matters first and always in

the light of military considerations. The diplomat's approach is – or in any case should be – determined by considerations of our relations to other states ... The Department of State's specialists on the Near East were, almost without exception, unfriendly to the idea of a Jewish state.[23]

In the very last days of FDR's life, the State Department's senior permanent staff were beginning to believe that they had regained the advantage in their contest with the Zionists for the heart and mind of the president. A memorandum, dated 6 April 1945 (a week before Roosevelt's death), from Deputy Director of the Office of Near Eastern and African Affairs, Paul H. Alling, to Assistant Secretary of State, James C. Dunn outlines the Department's policy:

> [To] counteract ... the unfavorable impression caused in the Near East by his [FDR's] continuing to give encouragement to the Zionists ... [T]he recurring indications of support of Zionist aspirations in certain influential government quarters are affecting most gravely our standing in the entire area ... Of course, if we were actually to implement the policy which the Zionists desire, the results would be disastrous ... [We must persuade the President to] make public on some suitable occasion the assurances we have given the Arab governments that no solution of the Palestine problem will be reached without consultation with both Arabs and Jews.[24]

In pursuit of this policy, a statement was drawn up for the President's signature, to be read by FDR on the occasion of a visit of the Regent of Iraq. Dated 12 April, it was never read by Franklin Roosevelt, who died that very day.[25]

The first item of record for students of the near eastern policy of the new president is a memorandum from Secretary of State Stettinius to President Truman, Wednesday, 18 April 1945 (Harry Truman's sixth day in the new job):

> It is very likely that efforts will be made by some of the Zionist leaders to obtain from you at an early date some commitments in favor of the Zionist program which is pressing for unlimited Jewish immigration into Palestine and the establishment of a Jewish state.
>
> As you are aware, the government and people of the United States have every sympathy for the persecuted Jews of Europe and are doing all in their power to relieve their suffering. The question of Palestine is, however, a highly complex one and involves questions which go far beyond the plight of the Jews in Europe. If this question shall come up, therefore, before you in the form of a request to make a public statement on the matter, I believe you would probably want to call for full and detailed information on the subject before taking any particular position in the premises. I should be very glad, therefore, to hold myself in readiness to furnish you with background information on the subject at any time you may desire.[26]

Of this memo, Peter Grose writes:

> It made an impact of enduring and far-reaching consequence – and not at
> all along the line the diplomats intended ... Perhaps the layers of experts
> accustomed to drafting messages for presidential attention honestly thought
> they were being helpful and responsive to the needs of the moment, but they
> did not yet know Harry Truman. In their patronizing tone, appropriate from
> a board of senior prefects to a new boy in the lower form, the Palestine experts
> committed in the first week a miscalculation from which their relations with
> the President would never recover.[27]

FORGING AN AMERICAN POLICY IN THE LIGHT OF
POST-WAR PROSPECTS

As Harry Truman was preparing to pick up at Potsdam where Roosevelt
had left off at Yalta, he received a telegram from the National Conference
of the American Palestine Committee meeting at Princeton (2–8 July 1945),
urging him to get the Palestine issue addressed by the Big Three at the
forthcoming meeting. Some weeks later, at a three-day conference held in
mid-October, some two thousand 'Christian educators' heard distinguished
speakers, including Reinhold Niebuhr, Carl Friedrich, Walter Lowdermilk,
and Senator Owen Brewster defend the Zionist solution to the Jewish
problem. Representative Helen Gahagan Douglas said that America should
demand that Britain fulfill the Balfour pledge, and she denounced Britain
for her inhuman handling of the refugee situation. 'The Jews in Palestine
today', she said, 'are making the Bible's prophecies come true; they are
consciously attempting to build a society worthy of their ethical heritage
... What Jewish Palestine has already done by force of example gives us
assurance as Americans that it is the key to the democratization of the Arab
lands and that its development is, therefore, to America's own interest.'[28]

Yet on this matter, Truman fared no better at Potsdam than Roosevelt
did at Yalta. At this early stage of things, the government of the United
Kingdom was not expecting formidable resistance to its hegemony on the
Palestinian scene. The British were, of course, aware that the new president,
like the former one, would be subject to Zionist pressures. Lord Halifax,
British Ambassador to the US, reporting to Foreign Secretary Anthony
Eden, 1 July 1945, weighed up the political prospects:

> It should in the first place be borne in mind that there are five million United
> States citizens who are Jews (forming about half the remaining Jews in
> the world). Many of them occupy prominent positions around the White
> House, in the Administration, and in the press. In the key electoral state of
> New York, the Jewish vote may be sufficient to turn the scale in election
> years. The Jews are able therefore to exert considerable pressure on the

Administration, in Congress and on public opinion, but they are not by themselves as powerful as they are vocal. Their influence will always mainly depend on whether or not on any given issue they are able to carry non-Jewish opinion with them, and in particular win the support of leading non -Jews in the Administration and in Congress.

Apart from groups and individuals here and there, non-Jewish opinion is not on the whole greatly interested in the merits or demerits of particular solutions of the Palestine problem except as these affect the issue of immigration ... The average citizen does not want them in the United States, and salves his conscience by advocating their admission to Palestine. On this issue the Jews can therefore carry with them both liberal humanitarians and many anti-Jews ...

The State Department itself is more favorable to the Arab than to the Jewish cause ... The United States of America is concerning itself with the Middle East: first, because of American oil interests, in Saudi Arabia and in Persia; second, because of the opportunities for civil aviation and commercial expansion; and third, because in her present mood America is feeling that she can no longer remain aloof from any area of the world in which a threat to the peace of the world may arise ... Soviet Russia is simultaneously beginning to interest herself in the whole Middle Eastern theatre, with as yet unpredictable consequences for the territorial integrity and social structures of countries situated there ...

Mr Byrnes, the Secretary of State, should be influenced by the views of intimate friends of his such as Mr Benjamin Cohen and Mr Justice Frankfurter. President Truman himself has one or two unimportant but intimate Jewish friends.[29]

On this issue, Truman's first substantial action after Potsdam was his appointment of a commission to study the situation of displaced persons in Europe, to be headed by Earl G. Harrison, formerly Commissioner of Immigration and Naturalization, and in 1945 Dean of the University of Pennsylvania Law School. Harrison's Report, made in August 1945, dispelled from all but the most cynical minds any doubt about the desperate need of the European Jews. Harrison reported: 'As matters now stand, we appear to be treating the Jews as the Nazis treated them except that we do not exterminate them ... With respect to possible places of resettlement Palestine is definitely and pre-eminently the first choice.'[30]

About this time Truman wrote to Senator George: 'My only interest is to find some proper way to take care of these displaced persons, not only because they should be taken care of and are in a pitiful plight, but because it is in our own financial interest to have them taken care of because we are feeding most of them.'[31] Truman knew that American public opinion was overwhelmingly hostile to the first option (liberalizing the immigration laws, so as to make possible massive immigration to the United States). To accomplish the other option, Truman would have to persuade the British to throw away the White Paper policy, to open the doors of Palestine, and to face down the Arab's opposition to implementing the Balfour pledge.

Inspired by Harrison's Report, and giving the back of his hand to his State and War Departments, Truman kept up publicly and privately the pressure upon the British to admit at least 100,000 Jews immediately. Truman was now under tremendous domestic political pressure from Jewish and also from non-Jewish citizens at a time when minds were turning to the mid-term elections due in November 1946. The British Embassy in Washington reported on the situation to the Foreign Office in February 1946:

> Zionist hopes have turned to disillusion ... Six months ago American Zionists were hoping for the moon. They know now that they are not going to get it ... The belief that the fundamental cause of the Jewish tragedy is Jewish homelessness gains widening currency, overrides common sense and logic and banishes historical perspective.[32]

Confident that American opinion would not remain engaged on the issue over the long haul, the British kept insisting that the whole matter needed more study – causing everyone's thoughts to go back to the sorry history of that string of Royal Commissions of the 1920s and 1930s, and the steady chipping away at the Balfour commitment. Truman outfoxed the British by agreeing to their proposal for a Joint Anglo-American Committee of Inquiry, but attaching the condition that the two issues of the future of the Jews in Europe and the future of Palestine be explicitly linked in the terms of reference.

Pro-Zionist advisors in Truman's inner circle, managed to secure the appointment of several good friends of Zionism among the American appointees. One was James G. McDonald, formerly the League of Nations High Commissioner for Refugees and later the first American Ambassador to the State of Israel); another was Bartley C. Crum, a lawyer, active in civil liberties matters, a liberal Republican, close to Wendell Willkie in 1940, Chairman in 1944 of Republicans for Roosevelt – and a good friend of ACPC.

ACPC presented its brief to the Joint Committee early in its proceedings. The argument includes elements both of the old 'Blackstonian' message and the liberal-secular language of Roosevelt's 'Four Freedoms' speech of 1940:

> It is the belief of Christian churches, based on the Bible, that God called the Jews to nationhood for conspicuous service to mankind.
>
> Christians believe, as do the Jews, that Palestine was divinely selected as the site of the Jewish nation and that the continuance on that site of Jewish culture, philosophy, and idealism under the protection of national status would meet with divine blessing and approval.[33]

Reinhold Niebuhr appeared before the Committee on behalf of CCP, 10 January 1946. His was a more realistic, less idealistic, less theological, message than ACPC's institutional statement.

> There is in fact no solution to any political problem. The fact, however, that the Arabs have a vast hinterland in the Middle East, and the fact that the Jews have nowhere to go establishes the relative justice of their claims and of their cause ...
> Christians are committed to democracy as the only safeguard of the sacredness of human personality ... The opposition to a Jewish Palestine is partly based on the opposition of Arabs to democracy, western culture, education and economic freedom. To support Arab opposition is but supporting feudalism and Fascism in the world at the expense of democratic rights and justice.[34]

In its Report, 20 April 1946, the Committee of Inquiry did not call for immediate implementation of the Balfour pledge – to the distress of the Zionists; but it did call unanimously for the immediate issuance of 100,000 certificates for immigration to Palestine, and this had the effect of forcing the British into an impossible public relations crisis. If it granted the certificates, it would lose the Arabs. If it did not, it was declaring to the world that it would never let the problem of the Jews of Europe be solved in the only way that an impartial and officially appointed body of notable citizens of both countries could find to solve it.

At that point, Truman began to demand that Britain permit massive Jewish immigration to Palestine. From this day forward, it would become more and more obvious that President Truman was not in step with his official family of advisors. As just one instance of many that could be cited: Loy Henderson, Chief of the Near Eastern Division of the State Department, in his zeal to see the Zionists thwarted and the British upheld, did not hesitate to betray President Truman – as we see from a cable forwarded by the British Ambassador to his Foreign Office, 7 May 1946:

> *This telegram is of particular secrecy and should be retained by the authorized recipient and not passed on.*
>
> CABINET DISTRIBUTION: FROM WASHINGTON TO FOREIGN OFFICE: IMPORTANT SECRET.
> ... Henderson has told members of my staff that State Department, including himself, made every effort to head off the unilateral statement by the President on Palestine. Both he and Acheson had telegraphed Byrnes in Paris on the matter ... but forces had been at work in the White House, which the State Department had been quite unable to control. Henderson deeply regretted the occurrence, as he knew it had added to the difficulties of the Palestine question.[35]

British–US official relations hit a new low when the British Foreign Secretary, Ernest Bevin, told the annual meeting of the British Labour Party at Bournemouth: 'I hope it will not be misunderstood in America if I say, with the purest of motives, that it was because they did not want too many of them in New York.'

It was certainly true that President Truman was coming more and more under pro-Zionist influence; and also true that domestic political considerations played a substantial part. Among those most active in getting Truman aligned on the Zionist side of the Palestine issue was Bartley Crum. Just a few months after his service on the Inquiry, he had published a book (*Behind the Silken Curtain: A Personal Account of Anglo-American Diplomacy in Palestine and the Middle East*, 1946), which was in fact largely the work of a small group of ghost-writers appointed by AZEC, and headed by Gerold Frank. The book was on the best-seller lists for many months in 1946–47 – 'the first Zionist best-seller in the country', bragged an AZEC executive in an internal memo. At the same time, Bartley Crum was appearing before ACPC audiences, lending the weight of his new literary fame to the company of Christian pro-Zionists.[36]

Having come to this, the British decided in fury that the only way out was to hand over the problem to the United Nations. On 25 February 1947, they announced their intention to do so before the end of May, 1948. Thereafter, the main thrust of British policy in this matter was to do everything possible to improve the military position of the Arab nations and their diplomatic position at the United Nations, looking to the inevitable failure of the effort of the Jews to create a viable state. In the months that followed, the governments of Harry Truman and Clement Attlee failed to find a basis for agreement on any aspect of the multi-faceted dilemma of Palestine. Diplomatic exchanges on this theme in this period are unusually terse, sometimes verging on rude.

At the same time, Truman became increasingly impatient with efforts of those around him to base the American Government's decisions squarely on the agenda of the Zionist leaders. To James McDonald, sent to him in July 1946, by the Zionist leadership to secure his public support for immediate partition, Truman responded testily: 'Hell, you can't satisfy those people.' Foolishly, McDonald responded by saying: 'Roosevelt understood some of these imponderables. He understood what the people felt.' Truman's furious reply to that was: 'I am not Roosevelt. I am not from New York. I am from the Middle West.' Not intimidated, McDonald responded: 'I know, but you can win the support of the Jewish people, if you will only stick to this ...' Truman, however, was not worn down: 'You can't satisfy these people', he repeated. 'They are not interested in the United States.

They are interested in Palestine and the Jews.' And again: 'I am not from New York. I am from the Middle West. I must do what I think is right.'[37]

In the spring of 1947, the UN established its Special Committee on Palestine (UNSCOP), which in September reported in favor of a partition of the territory held under the mandate into two States: one Arab, one Jewish, with Jerusalem set aside under the jurisdiction of the United Nations. The Jewish Agency accepted the report; the Arabs rejected it.

During all this time, Zionists and their friends lobbied ceaselessly. Truman's annoyance at the heavy-handed techniques employed by the Zionists and their friends bursts out again and again in correspondence to friends and advisers. In contradiction of the legend of Truman's bloody-minded pursuit of the Jewish vote, we find much evidence in these months of the President's studied non-cooperation with the political advisers who sought to get him out front on the issue. A meeting with Emanuel Cellar and other New York Congressmen in July of 1946 did not go well. Something of the content of the meeting was evidently leaked to the *New York Times* – in itself, a deed that cost the Zionists heavily in Presidential goodwill – whose story on the meeting prompted the British Ambassador (now Lord Inverchapel) to write gleefully to his Foreign Office:

> Mr Truman's reception of his visitors appears to have betrayed testiness at the continuous Zionist badgering to which he is almost uninterruptedly subjected. He said that he knew all about Palestine and had no time to listen, he was working on broader problems of displaced persons generally, and that while he did not blame Congressmen for coming, as they were up for election in the autumn, it was time someone came to see him about a United States problem for a change ... All this bears out Acheson's remark to me that the President is unhappy about the whole business. It also seems to indicate that he is wearying of Zionist pressure.[38]

To the Chairman of the Democratic Party's State Committee for New York, Truman wrote testily: 'The Jews are doing everything they possibly can to upset the applecart, as they did before when we had the thing almost settled. I would suggest that you advise them to keep still.'[39]

On 4 October 1946, in time for the mid-term elections, Truman did issue a forceful statement (remembered as 'the Yom Kippur statement') expressing his disappointment in the policies of the British government on the Palestine issue. 'Substantial immigration into Palestine cannot await a solution to the Palestine problem', he insisted, 'It should begin at once ... The immigration laws of other countries, including the United States, should be liberalized', and, finally, he spoke of looking to 'a solution along the lines of' that proposed by the Jewish Agency – thus just stopping short of endorsing Partition. When by mid-1947 it had become clear that only formal partition would serve to save the *Yishuv* and the homeless Jews of

Europe, Truman formally embraced that solution, and imposed it as American policy upon a recalcitrant, and indeed frequently disloyal, State Department.[40]

CHAIM WEIZMANN AND HARRY TRUMAN

Of the champions of Zionism whom Harry Truman met in the first weeks of his presidency, not one struck him as a reliable and stable character, and certainly none appealed to his notions of what great historical actors looked and sounded like. At the same time, in the course of his discussions with policy advisers inherited from the FDR presidency, Harry Truman had taken note of the fact that everyone who had had occasion to mention Chaim Weizmann's name to him spoke of him as of a breed apart.

Though there had been considerable periods of time since the accomplishment of the Balfour Declaration when Weizmann had been at odds with the rest of the Zionist leadership, in Europe, in Palestine, and in America, it was generally conceded that none of his rivals was ever, in truth, more than the leader of a faction within Zionism. Norman Rose writes: 'Weizmann stands out as a leader in the history of Zionism in that he led no party or faction; he led the movement or he did not lead at all.'[41]

Like Harry Truman, Weizmann 'thought of himself as "a deeply religious man, although not a strict observer of the religious ritual"'.[42] He attended synagogue on High Holidays, and normally observed the festivals in his home.

Again like Harry Truman, Chaim Weizmann was 'possessed by a sense of destiny' that had one root in his religious self-awareness and another in a privately acquired theory of history. In the aftermath of the hard work of lobbying for the Mandate in 1922, he rejoiced in his achievement:

> [W]hen I look at the Jewish community ... in all the Western countries, when I remember the destruction in the East, my heart freezes, and I come to the conclusion that only the Chosen Ones who have acquired all their moral strength from the only true Jewish source – only they are prepared and fit to assume the burden of work for the sake of others, and they will succeed in reviving the dry bones. [See Ezekiel 37.] So let us not complain of our destiny; it may be difficult, but it is beautiful.[43]

Elsewhere in his diaries we read: 'They [his rivals in the Zionist movement] will perish without me, as soon as I turn my back ... everything will fall apart ... I know that no other man in the world would have been able to accomplish anything like this – I know it, even though I do not suffer from megalomania.'[44]

The trouble was that by the end of the year 1946, Chaim Weizmann had been stripped of his formal leadership of the Zionist movement, and it was beginning to appear that his own egotistical assessment of the situation of World Zionism might be true: everything *had* fallen apart by February 1948. At the Biltmore Conference of May, 1942, Weizmann and the generation which had clung to the hope of a negotiated solution to the Jewish question was repudiated. The Jewish community was now demanding that the Jewish Agency be given control of immigration to Palestine, and 'that Palestine [must] be established as a Jewish Commonwealth integrated in the structure of the new democratic world'. Weizmann and Wise, though bound to uphold this unanimously adopted program, were known to be assuring the 'princes' (Churchill and Roosevelt, and later Attlee and Bevin and Byrnes), that the Jewish people could be satisfied for now with generous attention to the problem of refugee relief.

The twenty-second World Zionist Congress, held at Basle, in December 1946, adopted the Biltmore program. In an emotional speech Weizmann restated his confidence in the path of negotiation. Unfairly, he spoke as though all those who were expressing any degree of doubt about the primacy of the path of negotiation were aiding and abetting terrorism. '*Lo zu haderech*', he said: 'This is not the road.' At one point, someone shouted out: 'This is demagoguery.' Weizmann caught the remark at once:

> Would that my tongue were tipped with flame, and my soul touched with the strength of our great prophets, when they warned against the paths of Babylon and Egypt which always led Jewry to failure ... Go and read Isaiah, Jeremiah, Ezekiel, and test that which we do in the light of the teachings of our great prophets and wise men ... *Zion will be redeemed through righteousness* – and not by any other means.[45]

The Zionist Congress voted 171–154 against attending the conference which the British were proposing to hold in London. No president was nominated to replace Weizmann, nor was he elected to the Jewish Agency executive.

Thus, suddenly at the outset of the year 1947, Chaim Weizmann was no longer a leader of the World Zionist movement. The new American leaders, Silver and Neumann, believed that time had passed Weizmann by – that he did not understand how politics really worked. Yet their behaviour had utterly alienated the President of the United States. Since the desk-pounding incident of August 1945, Harry Truman would not meet with the elected leadership.

Weizmann had shared the hope of the American Zionists that Franklin Roosevelt would prove a constant champion, but he had formed an early appreciation of Roosevelt's inconstancy. Now Weizmann shared the other Zionists' disappointment in Truman. After hearing Truman's report on the Potsdam meeting during his Press Conference of 16 August 1945,

Weizmann said: 'Truman's statement is phoney. He takes away with one hand what he gives with the other, and here again I see nothing but disappointment ahead of us. He will never jeopardize his oil concessions for the sake of the Jews, although he may need them when the time of elections arrives. He wants immigration and also Arab consent!'[46]

Yet Weizmann's judgement of the character of Harry Truman was changed abruptly by his first face-to-face meeting with Truman after the latter became President. Given the brevity of that meeting (7 December 1945), it would be safe to say that intuition played a large part in Weizmann's assessment of Truman's character. Before the meeting, Weizmann had been coached by David Niles who told him that Truman was still under the influence of recent interviews with anti-Zionist Jews. Weizmann took it upon himself, then, to describe to Truman the Zionists' vision of the Jewish state – how it would realize the ancient hope by being a place where the Jewish faith could be realized in practice, while still being 'a secular state, based on sound democratic foundations with political machinery and institutions on the pattern of those of the United States'. Truman was quite impressed.[47]

This initial meeting took place while Weizmann still held formal office as president of the WZO, although well after his influence over the other leaders had suffered the steep decline that followed the Biltmore conference. When the Zionist leaders turned to him in desperation again, in October 1947, he was without formal office in the WZO, but it still remained the case that President Truman would not talk to any of Zionism's elected officers. This time, the immediate crisis was caused by a softening of the position being taken by the US delegation at the UN regarding the borders of the Jewish State that would emerge from the Partition to be proposed in November. As the President would speak to no-one but Weizmann, the leadership swallowed their pride, and despatched him to explain the case for including the Negev in the state. The Jewish Agency's principal representative at the UN, Abba Eban, accompanied Weizmann to the meeting of 19 November 1947, and he has left a colorful account of Weizmann's deft appeal to Truman's fascination with history and geography. Truman phoned directly from the interview to a meeting of State Department officials and Jewish Agency officials taking place at UN headquarters, issuing his instructions to reverse the US position: the borders must include the Negev.[48]

Afterward, Weizmann wrote to him: 'It is the first time in my life that I have met a President who can read and understand maps.'[49] Weizmann's genius as a diplomat – as we have seen already – was not in using flattery, but in knowing the object well enough to know exactly where it must be applied.

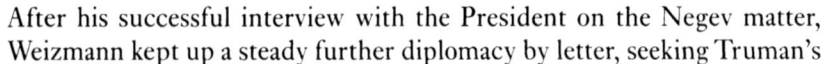 After his successful interview with the President on the Negev matter, Weizmann kept up a steady further diplomacy by letter, seeking Truman's

help on the main issue of the Partition vote to come in November. When the time came for him to address the United Nations General Assembly directly, Weizmann made a point of appealing, frontally and vigorously, to what, after a long lifetime of dealing with Christian statesman, he knew to be the powerful residual appeal of biblical language. He chose as his text, Isaiah 11:11–2:

> The LORD shall set His hand again the second time to recover the remnants of His people. And He shall set up an ensign for the nations, and shall assemble the outcasts of Israel and gather together the dispersed of Judah from the four corners of the earth.[50]

Many of those closest to the scene were persuaded that this appeal made the decisive difference.

A vote of two-thirds of the members was required. On 29 November 1947, the United Nations General Assembly voted for Partition by a vote of 33–13. All 11 of the Moslem states were among those voting against. Britain abstained.

OFF COURSE: AFTERMATH OF THE PARTITION DECISION

Since November 1947, when the American delegation at the UN had played its part in winning the General Assembly's support for Partition, things had gone badly for the Jews. The American public had not been properly prepared for what would follow. Most people who were paying any attention to the issue seemed to be assuming that the Arabs would grind their teeth, and then get in line with world opinion – that the heroic part of the story was over. Few understood that the Arab States were eternally opposed to letting the Jewish State come into existence when the British mandate ended in May 1948. Few were therefore prepared for the violence of the Arab effort to prevent the Jewish leadership from functioning, or for the violence of Jewish response. Few had understood, in November 1947, that Britain intended to refuse co-operation with the leaders of the state-to-be, and to ingratiate herself with the leaders of the present Arab states and the Arab population of Palestine – sure to be victorious in the unequal contest ahead.

In the light of all this, the majority in the State and War Departments, opposed to American support for the Jewish State – and this company included both the Secretary of State (Marshall) and the Secretary of Defense (Forrestal), as well as the Under Secretary of State (Robert Lovett), the Assistant Secretary for the United Nations (Dean Rusk), the Director of the Near Eastern desk at the State Department (Loy Henderson) and most of those assigned to the UN – now resumed their campaign to prevent the Jewish State actually coming into existence. They managed to persuade the President to allow the US Ambassador to the UN, Warren Austin, to hold in readiness a statement, to be presented 'if and when necessary', to the effect that the US now supported creation of a United Nations Trustee-ship for the whole of Palestine, to be in effect for ten years. The rationale to be offered ('if and when necessary') would be that the unanticipated magnitude of opposition of the Arabs had demonstrated the need for more time to work out the problems, and thus for a postponement of the Partition, due to take place in May 1948, so that a more equitable solution with better prospects of long-term success could be negotiated.

To the Zionists it was obvious that no room existed for negotiations with the Arabs, and that this is what the UN would find all over again during any period of Trusteeship; it would all go back to the UN Assembly ultimately, with an outcome different from the previous one – no Jewish State.

Motives of the architects of this proposal varied. Secretary Marshall seems to have been genuinely persuaded that to allow the Jews to proceed was to encourage them to their collective death. Others believed that, whether or not the Jews would die collectively, the Arab states would never forgive the Americans and the Europeans for permitting the Jewish state to come into existence: they would withhold their oil, and would realign themselves politically and diplomatically with the Soviet Union. It is safe to say that none of the proponents of the Trusteeship Plan seriously expected that a sovereign Jewish State would be on the map after the period of Trusteeship should pass.

Inspired stories appeared in the newspapers in March and April of 1948, to the effect that American policymakers were turning towards a 'trusteeship solution'. There is good reason to believe that, at the beginning of March 1948, Truman was, at least subliminally, contemplating a retreat from Partition – that there was at least a part of him that wanted to be persuaded by the Trusteeship idea. The Zionists' friends in the Administration – notably, David K. Niles, and Clark Clifford, both responsible for keeping Truman electable through 1948 – alerted the Zionist officials.

What was the point of alerting these officials however, when none of them could get into the White House?

Truman was by now completely estranged from the Zionist leadership because of an extremely brazen campaign that brought tons of letters and telegrams into the White House. Very early in the process someone had actually put up Truman's mother to write to him about the Palestine issue – and it became necessary for him to write to her with unwonted harshness: 'Don't let anyone talk to you about foreign affairs!'[51] The self-destructive possibilities in this effort could be seen by anyone who had taken a realistic measure of the character of Harry Truman. Yet the sad truth is that some of the Zionist leaders seemed to be taking satisfaction from Truman's rejection of them. 'It shows we're getting under their skin!' said Rabbi Silver, who hoped, and like everybody else, expected, that Truman would be defeated in November, and whose political friends were Republicans: 'What Truman says or does does not mean a damn thing.'[52] The perverse aspect of this is, of course, that long before the Republican Administration might come to office, the Jewish State might come into this world and then right out of it again – if the current Truman Administration acted wrongly.

The pattern was abundantly clear. On every previous occasion when the Zionists had needed action from the President to overcome the anti-Zionist energies of the State Department, it was an intervention by Chaim Weizmann that had turned the trick. Now, after the euphoria of November 1947, there came another such moment of crisis. The Jewish Agency in New York sent an urgent call to Chaim Weizmann in England to come to the United States and play the role that only he could play at such a critical time. It was a painful confession that their 'mass politics' had failed. 'We have just left New York', Weizmann told his wife, 'and now the idiots want us to go back.'[53] He did come, of course, but then he immediately came down with a fever – which cost several more precious days. Then, on 10 February, Weizmann sent a message to the President, pleading for 'a few moments of your precious time' in order to prevent 'a catastrophe not only for my people but for Palestine and for the United Nations'.[54] To everybody's horror it now developed that Truman was sticking by his promise to himself. This time, Chaim Weizmann was included in the general ban. It was not that Truman had changed his view of Chaim Weizmann – but merely that, as he put it, 'he had heard it all before' – no more Zionist propaganda, from anyone.

At this point it apparently occurred to several people at once that the only force that might conceivably open the door of the White House to their message again might be the combined weight of Chaim Weizmann plus Eddie Jacobson.

15

A Significant Friendship

President Truman himself has one or two unimportant but intimate Jewish friends.

Lord Halifax, British Ambassador to the US, 1 July 1945

Surely, there has never been a more significant friendship between a Christian and a Jew.

Editor, American Jewish Archives, April 1968

EDDIE JACOBSON (1891–1955)

Edward Jacobson, born in 1891 in Leavenworth, Kansas, was one of the six children of David and Sarah Jacobson, described by their son as 'victims of Russian oppression' who fled to the United States, where David became 'a poor shoemaker'.[1] Around 1906, the family moved to Kansas City, Missouri. At the age of 15, Eddie quit school, apparently by his own wish, and began work as a stockboy for a haberdasher. At that time he was casually acquainted with Harry Truman, then 21 years old and working at the Union National Bank.

Their lives were linked in 1917, when Eddie enlisted, becoming eventually supply sergeant in the 129th Field Artillery, later attached to the 35th Division, serving under junior First Lieutenant, later Captain, Harry Truman. They became partners in managing their battery's co-operative canteen. It was an astonishing success. On the strength of their obvious personal compatibility and their complementary gifts, they decided to go into business together after the Armistice. Most biographers feel certain that Truman did not for a moment intend to end his days as a haberdasher, and had not given up on larger ambitions in law or politics or both. However, the business failed, after only a little over two years – a victim of the recession of 1921–22. Significantly, the shared experience of this failure seems to have strengthened the bond of trust between the two partners, who remained close and caring friends thereafter. Truman refused to take protection under bankruptcy laws from his share of the debt, and eventually paid back all the creditors. Jacobson spent most of the next twenty-odd years on the road as a travelling salesman, before he recovered enough credit to return to the haberdashery business.

Harry Truman thought he had the makings of a good businessman. In fact, he once bragged in writing to his fiancée, Bess, of 'my Jewish ability'. While at training camp in 1917, he wrote: 'I have a Jew in charge of the canteen by the name of Jacobson and he is a crackerjack. Also the barbershop is run by a Jew, Morris Stearns by name.' Later, en route to the front, he wrote home about a disappointing day spent in the much overrated New York City: 'If only I could have stayed in Kansas City instead of this Kike town.'[2]

The biographers have found many such racial-stereotypical observations in Truman's personal correspondence. Perhaps the worst is this, from a letter to Bess, 22 June 1911:

> Uncle Will says that the Lord made a white man from the dust, a nigger from the mud, then threw up what was left, and it came down a Chinaman. He does hate Chinese and Japs. So do I. It is race prejudice, I guess, but I am strongly of the opinion that negroes ought to be in Africa, yellow men in Asia, and white men in Europe and America.[3]

The best that can be made of this embarrassing material is perhaps to say that these are the attitudes of a teenager and a young man, expressed in the most private of contexts.

In August 1940, he wrote to Bess of a troublesome political acquaintance: ... 'I am really disgusted with that damned Jew ... [A]s soon as I can cut the smart Hebrew loose, I shall do it', but on the next page, on a different matter, he speaks of two constituents: 'Nice Jewish boys. I am going to get them jobs.'[4]

Michael Cohen, who offers a generally cynical analysis of Harry Truman's dealings with Jews, with Zionists, and with Israel, guesses that 'Eddie could hardly have imagined, and would have no doubt been shocked to read some of the comments his business partner and friend was writing in private about the Jewish race'.[5] We should doubt this. Harry Truman was not a refined man. Neither was Eddie Jacobson. The only known witness (other than Truman's secretary and lifelong friend, Matt Donnelly) to any part of the many off-the-record meetings between President Truman and Harry Jacobson was Abraham J. Granoff, a Kansas City lawyer. He recalled years later something of the shock and embarrassment that he felt at the way they behaved.

Eddie never, either with me or alone, ever asked for an appointment. We came to Washington, first making sure that the President was in Washington, and called the White House ... And we would get an appointment within a few hours. No limitation as to time ... ushered in through the back door, so to speak ... no reporters ... all off-the-record, with one or two exceptions ... [Truman would say:] 'Sit down, you bastards, sit down'. That's the way we talked.[6]

The substance of their discussions and the general tone was like that of two old regimental buddies (which they were): inquiries after each other's families, recollections of pranks they had played together at company reunions, and so on. Eddie Jacobson surely never doubted that Truman, in other company than his own, dipped into his own deep Missouri cracker-barrel from time to time and came up with jokes and one-liners about the Jews.

But what did Harry Truman know about Jews? Probably, quite a good deal. His first Jewish contacts were his near-neighbours, the Viner family, for whom he served as *shabbos goy*.[7] Besides Eddie, there were several other Jews in Truman's circle of friends in Kansas City. Apart from their working days together, Harry Truman visited the Jacobson home regularly in his Kansas City days, usually for card games.

During Truman's days in Independence and Kansas City, Harry Jacobson did not make a big deal of his Jewish belonging. Raised by extremely Orthodox parents, he slipped out of the practice of his faith until the later 1920s, when he began attending the Reform Temple to which his wife belonged. Thereafter, he became active in Temple activities and Jewish men's groups: first *B'nai Jehudah*, then, after the Second World War, *B'nai B'rith*. He never joined any Zionist organizations. The members of his own Temple inclined to the anti-Zionist side, and his rabbi was vehemently opposed. What impressed him most about Zionism, apparently, was its ability to tear congregations apart – especially in his part of the country. Stubbornly, he insisted through all the many months of his activity at the behest of the Zionist leaders, and indeed until his death, that he was not a Zionist, but that in his support of the case for the Jewish state after the War he was entirely motivated by his deep concern to find refuge for the Jews of Europe. After the creation of the State, it becomes hard for us to follow this rationale, especially when we learn that he acted, on the request both of President Truman and President Weizmann, as, in effect, the first unofficial agent of the State during the first weeks of its existence, running messages between the two Presidents.

THE PRESIDENT'S FRIEND

As Rabbi Frank Adler puts it: 'Truman's unexpected elevation to the Presidency lifted Eddie Jacobson from obscurity to public notice with equal suddenness.'[8] Just a few days earlier, he had realized the dream of the previous twenty-odd years, by opening the Westport Men's Shop at Thirty-Ninth and Main Streets, in Kansas City. His trade thereafter may have owed something to the belief of many that Eddie Jacobson would serve as a conduit for their requests for the President's attention. If so, they were mistaken. Harry Truman is adamant about this: 'In all my years in Washington he had never asked me for anything for himself.'[9] Quite a different matter was the need of the Jewish people at the moment. Eddie quickly made clear to Harry Truman that he believed he had the right, out of old friendship, to speak bluntly and from his heart about this matter – which sometimes caused Harry to set his jaw a little when it happened, but did not diminish his willingness to have Eddie show up in Washington virtually at any time and ask for an unscheduled and unminuted meeting.

It can be shown, however, that Eddie Jacobson played some part in demonstrating to Harry Truman the domestic political value of a correct position on the Palestine issue – a factor of increasing importance through the period from late fall 1947 to Election Day 1948. In December 1947, Jacobson and Granoff co-authored an editorial which appeared in the *B'nai B'rith National Jewish Monthly*, in which they stated: '[I]t was our own American President who, more than any other individual, was responsible for the two-thirds UN vote ... President Truman took a personal hand in the matter. He directly saw to it that the American delegation at Flushing Meadow used its influence to obtain the two-thirds vote' – something which Truman, in his *Memoirs*, directly denies doing. 'Under these circumstances, President Truman emerges as one of the greatest champions of justice. He takes his place with other noble Christians who, in our time, led the good fight that has now been won – with Lord Balfour, Lloyd George, Woodrow Wilson, Franklin D. Roosevelt, James G. McDonald, Bartley Crum, and other heroes and statesmen whom we honor.'[10] We know that Truman was pleased by the article. The thought occurs that something he said in his unminuted interview with Jacobson and Granoff on 9 December 1947, might have nudged them in this direction. In any case, the article was an early item in the very active propaganda effort of the friends of the Administration to secure the Jewish vote in 1948.

Eddie Jacobson's indubitable moment as a maker of history, however, did not come until March 1948. In a moment of time, he entered into a most improbable partnership with the most commanding figure in World Zionism – Chaim Weizmann – and in effect demanded the attention of President Truman, winning from him the decision that saved the Zionist dream.

CHAIM WEIZMANN RECRUITS THE PRESIDENT'S FRIEND

Zionist leaders had not missed the Jacobson connection in their research on the past of Harry Truman. Jacobson's Zionist friends in his Temple in Kansas City and in *Ben Jehudah* had been working on him in friendly ways for years – without success. Max Bretton, owner of a restaurant and the leader of the Kansas City Jewish Community Centre, brought Dr Israel Goldstein, President of the ZOA and a Conservative rabbi, to meet Jacobson in May 1945 in the hope of making a Zionist at last of the latter. Bretton used the most powerful argument he could think of, quoting Esther 4:14: 'Who knows whether you have not come to high estate for such a time as this?'[11] Yet it was to no avail. Eddie, the President's friend, would not declare for Zionism. The Zionist leaders were aware of these approaches by rank-and-file Zionists to Eddie Jacobson, but made no use of them. The reason for this is simply that they completely misjudged their own resources. Stephen Wise, Abba Hillel Silver, Emanuel Neumann and the others, were all men with large egos, and it took them many months before they would admit to themselves, let alone to others, that there was no hope of their getting back into the White House. After it was all over the Zionist chieftains all sought to minimize the role of Eddie Jacobson. The name of Eddie Jacobson does not even appear in the memoirs of Chaim Weizmann! Abraham Granoff's son Loeb astutely summed it up many years later: 'Never would the Zionists have stooped to the use of the likes of Eddie Jacobson if they had not been totally desperate.'[12]

We know that by early 1948 David Niles was impressing upon the Zionist officials the significance of Eddie Jacobson's privileged access to his friend the President. Finally, after the checkmate of their efforts to get Weizmann back into the President's office in February 1948, Frank Goldman and Maurice Bisgyer, the president and the secretary respectively of *B'nai B'rith*, called Eddie Jacobson sometime after midnight on 21 February urging him to speak to the President about meeting Chaim Weizmann. Immediately Jacobson sent a telegram to the President's secretary:

> Would appreciate it much if you will place the following message on the President's desk so that he will get to it at once. Mr President I know that you have very excellent reasons for not wanting to see Dr Chaim Weizmann. No one realizes more than I the amount of pressure that is being thrown on you during these critical days, but as you once told me this gentleman is the greatest statesman and finest leader that my people have. He is very old and heartbroken that he could not get to see you. Mr President I have asked you for very little in the way of favors during all our years of friendship, but I am begging of you to see Dr Weizmann as soon as possible. I can assure you I would not plead to you for any other of our leaders. If you wish me present I will fly to Washington at once as I would deem it an honor to be with you gentlemen. I am praying that you will be able to see us. Please wire.[13]

The President, however, on vacation in Key West, Florida, put him off:

> My schedule was just so crowded that I couldn't get him [Weizmann] in.
> There wasn't anything he could say to me that I didn't already know ... The
> Zionists, of course, have expected a big stick approach on our part, and
> naturally have been disappointed when we can't do that. I have about come
> to the conclusion that the situation is not solvable as presently set up.

In an uncharacteristically stubborn gesture, Jacobson now phoned the
White House as soon as the President had returned, and asked for an
appointment. Then, on 13 March, there took place what has come to be
remembered as the Andy Jackson interview:

> For a few minutes we discussed our families, my business, in which he has
> always shown a brother's interest, and other personal things.
>   I then brought up the Palestine subject. He immediately became tense and
> grim, abrupt in speech and very bitter in the words he was throwing my way.
> In all the years of our friendship he never talked to me in this manner.
>   He made it almost impossible for me to continue when he said sharply
> that he didn't want to discuss Palestine or the Jews or the Arabs or the British;
> that he was satisfied to let these subjects take their own course through the
> United Nations.
>   I then actually argued with him and I am now surprised at myself that I
> had the nerve to do it. I reminded him of his feelings for Dr Weizmann,
> which he had often expressed, that the doctor was an old and sick man and
> had made his long journey to the United States especially to see him, but
> the President remained immovable.
>   I could not think of any more arguments to give him to soften his anger
> ... His turndown of my request left me crushed and then, believe it or not,
> I happened to rest my eyes on a beautiful model of a statue of Andrew Jackson
> mounted on a horse which I had noted passingly the many previous times I
> had been to the White House. I then found myself saying this to the President,
> almost word for word:
>   'Harry, all your life you have had a hero. You are probably the best read
> man in America on the life of Andrew Jackson. I remember when we had our
> store together and you were always reading books and papers and pamphlets
> on this great American. When you built the new Jackson County courthouse
> in Kansas City you put this very statue, lifesize, on the lawn right in front
> of it where it still stands. Well, Harry, I too have a hero, a man who is, I think,
> the greatest Jew who ever lived. I too have studied his past and I agree with
> you, as you have often told me, that this is a gentleman and a great statesman
> as well. I am talking about Chaim Weizmann, who is a very sick man, almost
> broken in health, but who traveled thousands of miles just to see you to plead
> with you the cause of my people.
>   'I wouldn't be here if I didn't know that if you will see him you will be
> properly and accurately informed on the situation as it exists in Palestine,
> and yet you refuse to see him.'
>   Just as I finished I noticed that the President began drumming on the desk

with his fingers and as I stopped talking, he abruptly turned around while still sitting in his swivel chair and started looking out the window into what in the summer is a beautiful rose garden, gazing just over the pictures of his mother, wife, and daughter. I knew the sign. I knew that he was changing his mind. I don't know how many seconds passed in silence but it seemed like centuries. All of a sudden he swiveled around again, faced his desk, and looked me straight in the eye and said the most endearing words I ever heard: 'You win, you baldheaded son-of-a bitch I will see him.'[14]

Jacobson was then taken directly to New York (14 March) to meet Chaim Weizmann and to stay nearby until confirmation came that the President truly did intend to meet him. Weizmann said to those around: 'Our people are waiting and dying. I am waiting for weeks to see President Truman. If he does not see me, my entire trip to the States and my mission will have been in vain. I have always placed my trust in him. The world has forsaken us. He must not forsake us.'[15] On 15 March the President's secretary phoned with the news that an off-the-record meeting would take place, 18 March. To avoid alerting reporters Dr Weizmann must come without Eddie Jacobson and must come through the East Gate.

Chaim Weizmann and Harry Truman met secretly, 18 March 1948. No minutes exist for this off-the-record meeting. We have only Truman's vague summary in his *Memoirs*, three equally vague lines in Weizmann's memoirs, and Weizmann's subsequent letter of thanks to the President, but its substance and its significance are summed up by Peter Grose: 'Once again, the extraordinary current of mutual respect and sympathy which had animated their first meeting dominated their conversation ... Truman changed his mind and returned to his original convictions.'[16]

THE AUSTIN STATEMENT

Since November, as we have seen, the Zionists had been receiving signals suggesting the Administration's intention to retreat from the commitment to Partition. Despite their well-placed contacts, the Zionists probably did not know how bad the situation actually was. Both the Policy Planning Staff and the CIA were advising the President that a Jewish State could not survive, and that Partition must be prevented – to save the Jews.

On 19 March 1948 – the very day after Harry Truman had privately assured Chaim Weizmann that his commitment to Partition was now firm – Ambassador Warren Austin seized headlines across the world by announcing at the United Nations that the United States now believed that Partition could not succeed 'as long as existing Arab resistance persists', and therefore proposed the setting up of a temporary trusteeship.

The Zionists of course were shocked. David Ben-Gurion denounced this as 'a surrender'. Truman was very angry. In his diary he wrote:

> This morning I find that the State Department has reversed my Palestine policy. The first I know about it is what I see in the papers! Isn't that hell? I'm now in the position of a liar and a double-crosser. I've never felt so low in my life.
>
> There are people on the 3rd and 4th levels of the State Dept. who have always wanted to cut my throat. They've succeeded in doing it.[17]

The matter of the degree of Truman's own responsibility for this debacle has been thoroughly worked over by all the scholars, and the student can chose from a range of verdicts. All agree that at some point Truman had given permission for a line of action in contradiction to his Administration's stated policy; then there is a moment of public consternation when two policies seem to be being pursued; then it becomes obvious that someone must climb down to allow it to appear that the President had been perfectly clear about the matter from the beginning. It is clear that on 18 March Austin had been given State Department approval to proceed under what all understood was standing authorization to issue some such statement as he made. Immediately after the Austin speech, Secretary Marshall called a news conference, describing this as 'the wisest course', and confirming that he had recommended it to the President and that the President had approved; but it is also on record that Truman had insisted at the beginning that he see the final draft of the Trusteeship speech before its actual delivery. There is room for believing that the Department's overlooking of this commitment at the last minute may have been willful.

FINDING A WAY BACK TO PARTITION

There is much that is painful and embarrassing in the story that follows, between 19 March and 14 May. For the short term, it seemed obvious that there was much more to lose than to gain if Truman were to repudiate the Austin statement. All his usefulness would be lost if he were seen to be admitting in the broad light of day that he was not in charge of the nation's foreign policy. It seemed necessary, therefore, to try to make American foreign policymaking seem more sophisticated and mysterious than it was by letting people guess how the new proposal could be squared with the old proposal in favor of Partition. Thus, at his Press Conference of 25 March, Truman calmly read out that the position of the United States 'has been accurately presented by Ambassador Austin in his speech before the Security Council'.[18] In the meantime, Truman assigned Samuel Rosenman to 'Go find Chaim Weizmann wherever he is. Tell him I meant every word of what I said. I promised we would stick to our guns on Partition and I meant it.' The errand was repeated a few days later. Weizmann, to his credit, stood by his side of the friendship by refusing to react publicly to the Austin statement, while privately circulating words of confidence to the Zionist insiders. Among these were his words by telephone to Eddie Jacobson (22 March): 'Don't be disappointed and do not feel badly. I do not believe that President Truman knew what was going to happen in the United Nations on Friday when he talked to me the day before ... You have a job to do; so keep the door of the White House open.'[19]

On 9 April, Weizmann wrote to strengthen the President's resolve: 'The choice for our people, Mr President, is between statehood and extermination. History and providence have placed this issue in your hands, and I am confident that you will yet decide it in the spirit of the moral law.'[20] A few days earlier he had written from New York to Oscar Wolfsberg in Jerusalem: 'The present enemies of today, in spite of their number, in spite of their arrogance, in spite of the support which they might get from various quarters, in spite of the fact that they find us standing alone and almost friendless, will fail because God will protect His people.'[21]

Thus, the Administration had to let the Austin statement stand. Lord Inverchapel, British Ambassador to US, to the Foreign Office, 20 March 1948, was one who took it at face value, as a definitive reversal of policy, fully sanctioned by the President and revealing a new realism – that is, a last-hour conversion to Britain's understanding of the Middle Eastern scene:

> There can be do doubt that, in the situation, the President and Secretary of State have felt constrained to give greater weight to the views of the Secretary of Defense and the Chiefs of Staff ... [I]n the light of the fact that even loyal Democrats now despair of his re-election, the President himself may well have lost patience with all domestic pressures and arguments which have hitherto militated against the assessment of the Palestine problem on its own merits ... In all the circumstances, I think it is proper to suggest that the Administration is now deriving a new found independence of judgement on this particular issue.[22]

Britain, in the meantime, had declared her intention to end her responsibilities in the former Mandate at midnight, 14 May 1948 (6 p.m., 14 May, in Washington). Two days before that deadline, President Truman held an exceptional meeting, ostensibly to review the options of the United States government in the prospect of a declaration of a Jewish State. Present were Secretary of State Marshall, Under Secretary of State Lovett, Clark Clifford and David Niles. In effect, the President was sounding his official family to see what support he could expect for the decision that he was in honour committed to.

Marshall made the case for continuing with support at the UN for the Trusteeship proposal, while urging the Jewish Agency to back down from its intention to declare the State on 14 May. President Truman then turned to Clark Clifford, to whom he had a few days earlier assigned the task of presenting the brief for the other side, but before Clifford could get properly launched, General Marshall exploded: 'I thought this meeting was called to consider an important and complicated problem in foreign policy. I don't even know why Clifford is here. He is a domestic adviser and this is a foreign policy matter.'

Truman responded firmly: 'Well, General, he's here because I asked him to be here.' But to every one's astonishment, this did not stop the General: 'These considerations have nothing to do with the issue. I fear that the only reason Clifford is here is that he is pressing a political consideration with regard to this issue. I don't think politics should play any part in this.'

Lovett joined in: 'It is obviously designed to win the Jewish vote.'

This was not the low point, however. That came a little later, when Marshall interjected: 'If you follow Clifford's advice, and if I were to vote in the Election, I would vote against you.'

Afterwards, Truman praised Clifford privately for his presentation, but, ominously, he also said, 'I can't afford to lose General Marshall.'[23]

Already on 8 May, Marshall had spoken bluntly to Moshe Sharrett of the Jewish Agency about 'the difficulties they had experienced with American Zionists'. The time might come (he seemed to threaten) when they might all speak out about 'all the political pressure, the blustering, the misleading assurances, etc., etc., that was going on'. He warned them, on the basis of his unparalleled experience with military realities: 'Believe me, I am talking about things that I know ... How can you hope to hold out?' Then he brusquely dispatched Sharrett to advise the Jewish Agency not to declare the State on 14 May. Chaim Weizmann got to Sharrett as he was departing to convey the gist of a second message from Rosenman that Truman would support Partition when it was announced. 'Don't let them weaken', Weizmann urged him to say to Ben-Gurion and the others: 'Don't let them spoil the victory. Proclaim the Jewish State, now or never.'[24]

TRUMAN RECOGNIZES THE STATE OF ISRAEL, 14 MAY 1948

On 12 May it had seemed obvious that Truman would have to choose between honoring his pledge to the Jews (given through Chaim Weizmann) or losing his Secretary of State, with all the awful consequences that would follow; but in the last few hours before the Recognition decision had to be made and announced, Marshall conveyed to the President his assurance that he would not make public his opposition to the decision, that he would carry out the policy, and see to it that it was carried out down through the ranks. We know, however, that he honestly believed that when the decision for Recognition was announced, there might be a mass resignation in the State Department, and that he, the loyal captain, would have no crew. Clifford, once told by the President that Marshall's loyalty had been secured, called in Eliahu Elath, of the Jewish Agency, to say : 'You'd better write a letter asking us for recognition'.[25]

Thus at eleven minutes after 11 a.m., Washington time, 14 May, a message went to the press from the White House:

> This government has been informed that a Jewish State has been proclaimed in Palestine, and recognition has been requested by the provisional government thereof.
> The United States recognizes the provisional government as the *de facto* authority of the new State of Israel.

Truman's announcement of recognition was not conveyed in advance to the delegation at the United Nations. When Dean Rusk broke to the Ambassador the news of the announcement from the White House, Warren Austin, 'incredulous and terribly angry', simply put on his hat and went home.[26]

AFTER: 'I AM CYRUS'

In the years of his retirement Truman frequently insisted that the most infuriating moments of his Presidency were those when he had to fight off the persistence of the Zionists. These people, he said, were the only people who ever stood in his presence and spoke to him as though their cause was the only cause in the world, as though their people were the only people who suffered, and as though that suffering gave them the right to speak to him as though the office of President of the United States meant nothing to them. No other visitors ever pounded on his desk!

Nevertheless, in retirement Truman looked back upon his role in bringing about the establishment of the state of Israel as among his proudest achievements. He would reckon among his fastest friends the individuals who had persuaded him to make the cause of Zion the cause of the government of the United States. Among his proudest memories would be those moments when he acceded to the request of the Zionist chieftains – for support of Partition, for inclusion of the Negev, for recognition of the state of Israel – throwing his State and War Departments into consternation, and significantly, he invariably hit upon these moments to illustrate the point that the President must do what is right, even if all the expert advice is running the other way – the point of the famous motto on the desk: 'The Buck stops here.'

When the former president took visitors on tour of the Truman Library, he liked to show them the Torah scroll and its Ark, presented to him by the President of Israel. Then there was Truman Village, which he could not show off literally, but to which he could direct his friends when they visited Israel. This truly extraordinary gift was presented to President Truman at a dinner in Washington in May 1952, with these words from the Israeli Ambassador, Abba Eben:

> We do not have orders or decorations. Our material strength is small and greatly strained. We have no tradition of formality or chivalry. One thing, however, is within the power of Israel to confer. It is the gift of immortality. Those whose names are bound up with Israel's history never become forgotten. We are, therefore, now writing the name of President Truman upon the map of our country. In a village of farmers near the airport of Lydda at the gateway to Israel, we establish a monument, not of dead stone but of living hope. Thus when the eyes of men alight on Truman Village in Israel they will pause in their successive generations to recall the strong chain which, at the middle of the 20th century, drew the strongest and the smallest democracy together with imperishable lines.

Eban recalls that, 'As I left the rostrum I saw the tough-minded President burying his face in a handkerchief without any effort to restrain his emotion. The next day he sent me a letter asking me for a text of my address: "You spoke so flatteringly about me that for a moment I had the impression that I was dead".'[27]

Moshe Davis has left us record of a visit which Harry Truman made a few months after the end of his Presidency to the Jewish Theological Seminary, together with Truman's friend, Eddie Jacobson. Jacobson introduced Harry Truman to the professors: 'This is the man who helped create the State of Israel', but Truman corrected him: 'What do you mean "helped to create"? I am Cyrus. I am Cyrus.'[28]

It seems that the analogy to Cyrus had already been suggested to President Truman by the Chief Rabbi of Israel, Isaac Halevi Herzog, on the occasion of a visit to him in the White House early in 1949. The rabbi went on to assert: 'God put you in your mother's womb so you would be the instrument to bring about Israel's rebirth after two thousand years.' We are told by a witness that, 'On hearing these words, Truman rose from his chair and, with great emotion, tears glistening in his eyes, he turned to the Chief Rabbi and asked him if his actions for the sake of the Jewish people were indeed to be interpreted thus and the hand of the Almighty was in the matter'.[29]

These words of Truman's – 'I am Cyrus' – were uttered neither casually nor ironically. We must take them with the fullest seriousness, and when we do, we will have the key to understanding Truman's constant pro-Zionism.

Harry Truman frequently turned over the name of 'Cyrus the Great' as he rehearsed the names of the 'Great Men of History' – a mental exercise which he performed regularly, as a concert pianist performs scales. The American democratic process, he knew, had put him in the place where *Cyrus redivivus* was expected. His awareness of all this is what explains the consistency of his refusal to allow himself to be worn down by the emotional and sometimes brutal arguments of the Zionists, fully as much as it explains his serenity in the face of the arguments from anti-Zionist Jews, the pro-Arab blandishments coming from the State Department, the 'realistic' military judgements coming from George Marshall and George Kennan, and the economic-geopolitical arguments of James Forrestal.

To doubt his personal fitness for this great role would have been the same as to doubt the fitness of the American political system which had put him in place. To set his own name at the end of that long catalogue of the Great Men (in which Cyrus always figured) was not, he believed, an act of vanity, but a requirement of fidelity to received religion and to his own self-confidence as a student of history.

In the light of all this, he could not have acted differently.

Notes

1: THEODOR HERZL AND WILLIAM HECHLER

1. A small but important collection of materials by and about William Hechler is in CZA/Box K11/9/Files ## 1 and 2 (where Hechler's pamphlet is to be found) and CZA/Box A145/file # 21. (For assistance in translating some German-language items in this file I am indebted to Helga Jaakkimainen, Ottawa, Canada.) In this chapter, all direct quotations of the words of Theodor Herzl are from *CDTH*, unless otherwise indicated.
2. Amos Elon, *Herzl* (New York: Rinehart & Winston, 1975), p. 16.
3. Ernst Pawel, *The Labyrinth of Exile: A Life of Theodor Herzl* (New York: Farrar, Straus & Giroux, 1989), pp. 69–70.
4. Ibid., p. 44.
5. William Hechler, 'The First Disciple: The British Chaplain Who Aided Herzl in His Activities', in Meyer W. Weisgal (ed.), *Theodor Herzl: A Memorial*, published by *New Palestine* (official magazine of ZOA) (New York, 1929), pp. 254–6.
6. 'Herzl, Hechler, the Grand Duke of Baden and the German Emperor: Documents found by Hermann and Bessai Ellern, trans. Harry Zohn', in Raphael Patai (ed.), *Herzl Year Book*, vol. IV (New York: Herzl Press, 1962), p. 208.

2: WILLIAM HECHLER'S VISION

1. CZA/Box K11/file # 9. (Two autobiographical fragments written by Dietrich Hechler.)
2. R. W. Greaves, 'The Jerusalem Bishopric 1841', *English Historical Review*, 64 (1939), p. 334.
3. Barbara Tuchman, *The Bible and the Sword: England and Palestine from the Bronze Age to Balfour* (New York: Ballantine, 1956), pp. 177–8.
4. Ibid., p. 179.
5. Geoffrey B. A. M. Finlayson, *The Seventh Earl of Shaftesbury, 1801–1885* (London: Methuen, 1981), p. 157.
6. Edwin Hodder, *The Life and Work of the Seventh Earl of Shaftesbury, K.G.* (London: Cassell, 1887), vol. I, p. 378.
7. Finlayson, *The Seventh Earl*, p. 160; Tuchman, *The Bible and the Sword*, p. 207.
8. Claude Duvernoy, *Le prince et le prophète* (Jerusalem: Département des publications de l'Agence Juive, 1966), trans. P. C. Merkley, pp. 83–4.

9. William II, former Emperor of Germany, *My Early Life*, trans. from German (1926; New York: AMS Press, 1971), pp. 100–1.
10. Ibid., pp. 34, 66–7, 89–93; William II, *The Kaiser's Memoirs*, trans. from German (New York: Harper, 1922), pp. 208–22.
11. William II, *My Early Life*, p. 93.
12. Robert K. Massie, *Dreadnought: Britain, Germany, and the Coming of the Great War* (New York: Random House, 1991), p. 297.
13. Ibid., p. 298.
14. 'Herzl, Hechler, the Grand Duke of Baden and the German Emperor: Documents found by Hermann and Bessai Ellern, trans. by Harry Zohn', in Raphael Patai (ed.), *Herzl Year Book*, vol. IV (New York: Herzl Press, 1962), pp. 210–13.
15. Ibid., pp. 213–14.
16. Howard M. Sachar, *A History of Israel: From the Rise of Zionism to Our Time* (New York: Knopf, 1979), p. 63.
17. Norman H. Finkelstein, *Theodor Herzl* (New York: Impact, 1987), p. 114.
18. Henriette Hannah Bodenheimer, 'A Memory of the Early Zionists', in *Christian Zionism and its Biblical Basis*, pamphlet (Jerusalem: International Christian Embassy, 1988), p. 11.

3: HECHLER, HERZL AND THE KAISER

1 'Herzl, Hechler, the Grand Duke of Baden and the German Emperor: Documents Found by Hermann and Bessai Ellern, trans. Harry Zohn', in Raphael Patai (ed.), *Herzl Year Book*, vol. IV (New York: Herzl Press, 1962), pp. 210–13.
2. Ibid., pp. 222–3.
3. Ibid., pp. 223–4.
4. Ernst Pawel, *The Labyrinth of Exile: A Life of Theodor Herzl* (New York: Farrar, Strauss & Giroux, 1989), p. 342.
5. Claude Duvernoy, *Le prince et le prophète* (Jerusalem: Département des publications de l'Agence Juive, 1966), p. 80.
6. Ibid., p. 70.
7. Ibid., pp. 77–8.
8. Ibid., p. 79.
9. Martin Gilbert, *Jerusalem: The Rebirth of a City* (New York: Viking, 1985), pp. 224–5.
10. Pawel, *The Labyrinth of Exile*, p. 391.
11. William Hechler, 'The First Disciple: The British Chaplain Who Aided Herzl in His Activities', in Meyer W. Weisgal (ed.), *Theodor Herzl: A Memorial*, published by *New Palestine* magazine (New York, 1929), p. 51.
12. Duvernoy, *Le prince et le prophète*, p. 130.
13. David Pileggi, 'Vicarious Zionist', *Jerusalem Post* (8 November 1988), p. 5.

4: THE RESTORATIONIST TRADITION IN BRITAIN

1. Franz Kobler, *The Vision Was There: A History of the British Movement for the Restoration of the Jews to Palestine* (published for the World Jewish Congress, British Section; London: Lincolns-Praeger, 1956), p. iii.
2. David S. Katz, *Philo-Semitism and the Readmission of the Jews to England, 1603–1655* (Oxford: Clarendon Press, 1982), p. 190.

3. Cited in Alan Edelstein, *An Unacknowledged Harmony: Philosemitism and the Survival of European Jewry* (Westport, CT: Greenwood, 1981), p. 143.
4. Kobler, *The Vision Was There*, p. 38.
5. Ibid., pp. 38–9.
6. Barbara Tuchman, *The Bible and the Sword: England and Palestine from the Bronze Age to Balfour* (New York: Ballantine, 1956), p. 163.
7. Kobler, *The Vision Was There*, p. 50.
8. Israel Finestein, 'Early and Middle 19th Century British Opinion on the Restoration of the Jews: Contrasts with America', in Moshe Davis (ed.), *With Eyes Toward Zion. Vol. II: Themes and Sources in the Archives of the United States, Great Britain, Turkey and Israel*, Second International Scholars Colloquium on America–Holy Land Studies (New York: Praeger, 1986), p. 72.
9. Tuchman, *The Bible and the Sword*, p. 175.
10. Ibid., pp. 190–1.

5: GERMANY DECLINES THE MANTLE OF CYRUS, AND BRITAIN TAKES IT UP

1. *LPChW*, vol. I, # 1.
2. Chaim Weizmann, *Trial and Error: The Autobiography of Chaim Weizmann* (London: East and West Library, 1950), p. 46.
3. Norman Rose, *Chaim Weizmann* (New York: Viking, 1986), p. 35.
4. Weizmann, *Trial and Error*, p. 61.
5. Leonard Stein, *The Balfour Declaration* (1961; 2nd edn, Jerusalem/London: Magnes Press, Hebrew University, 1983), p. 18; Rose, *Chaim Weizmann*, p. 131.
6. Weizmann, *Trial and Error*, p. 137.
7. Ibid., pp. 142–4; cf. Blanche Dugdale, *Arthur James Balfour*, 2 vols. (New York: Putnam's, 1937), vol. I, pp. 324–6.
8. Weizmann, *Trial and Error*, p. 210.
9. Ibid., pp. 194–5; Stein, *Balfour Declaration*, pp. 139–46.
10. Weizmann, *Trial and Error*, p. 195; cf. Stein, *Balfour Declaration*, pp. 147–65.
11. Weizmann, *Trial and Error*, p. 200.
12. Stephen S. Wise, *Challenging Years: The Autobiography of Stephen Wise* (New York: Putnam's, 1949), pp. 190–1.
13. Weizmann, *Trial and Error*, pp. 224–6 and 200.

6: THE RESTORATIONIST TRADITION IN THE UNITED STATES

1. Joseph Gaer and Ben Siegel, *The Puritan Heritage: America's Roots in the Bible* (New York: Mentor, 1964), pp. 20, 26.
2. John McDonald, *Isaiah's Message to the American Nation* (Albany, 1814). Reprinted as one of three items in *Call to America to Build Zion* (New York: Arno Press, 1977).
3. Alice Felt Tyler, *The Foreign Policy of James G. Blaine* (Minneapolis: University of Minnesota Press, 1927), pp. 270–9; *FRUS*, vols. for 1891 and 1892; Frank E. Manuel, *The Realities of American–Palestine Relations* (Washington, DC: Public Affairs Press, 1949), pp. 57ff.

7: WILLIAM BLACKSTONE AND THE BLACKSTONE MEMORIAL

1. *ECZA Bulletin/1941* at ZAL. See also A. M. Margolith to Emanuel Neumann, 31 January 1932, CZA/Box A123/file # 423.

2. Yona Malachy, *American Fundamentalism and Israel* (Jerusalem: Hebrew University, 1978), pp. 141–2.

3. Cited in *One Hundred Years of Blessing: The Centennial History of the American Messianic Fellowship (1887–1987), Including a Biographical Introduction to its Founder, William E. Blackstone* (Lansing, IL: American Messianic Fellowship, 1987), p. 48.

4. CZA/Box A404 (Papers of Jacob de Haas)/file # 45.

5. Beth M. Lindberg, *A God-Filled Life: The Story of William E. Blackstone* (Chicago: American Messianic Fellowship, 1985), n.p.

6. See the articles 'Scofield, Cyrus Ingersol', and 'Scofield Reference Bible', in *DCA*.

7. William E. Blackstone, *Jesus is Coming* (1st edn, 1878; 3rd edn, Chicago: Fleming H. Revell, 1908), pp. 161, 167, 169, 176.

8. Ibid., pp. 234–5.

9. Ibid., p. 236.

10. Ibid., pp. 238–9, and 241.

11. Ya'akov Ariel, *On Behalf of Israel: American Fundamentalist Attitudes toward Jews, Judaism, and Zionism* (Brooklyn, NY: Carlson, 1991), pp. 65–6.

12. Timothy P. Weber, *Living in the Shadow of the Second Coming: American Premillennialism, 1875–1982*, enlarged edn (Grand Rapids: Zondervan/Academie, 1983), p. 137, citing Gabelein, *Has God Cast Away His People?* (1905).

13. Ariel, *On Behalf of Israel*, pp. 63–4.

14. Ibid., p. 70.

15. Frank E. Manuel, *The Realities of American–Palestine Relations* (Washington, DC: Public Affairs Press, 1949), p. 71; Ariel, *On Behalf of Israel*, pp. 78–9.

16. LDB to Nathan Strauss, 26 April 1916; LDB to Richard Crane, Secretary to Robert Lansing, Secretary of State, 26 April 1916; Robert Crane to LDB, 23 May 1916, University of Louisville. *Correspondence from the Collection of the Late Justice Brandeis Relating to Zionism and Palestine, 1913–1939* (microfilm, CZA, reel # 9).

17. These appear in the handwritten notes in *Correspondence from the collection … Justice Brandeis* (microfilm, CZA, reel # 9.) Other responses can be found in Ariel, *On Behalf of Israel*, p. 75.

18. William E. Blackstone, *Palestine For the Jews: A Copy of a Memorial Presented to President Harrison*, 5 March 1891 (Oak Park, IL, 1891). Reprinted in *Christian Protagonists For Jewish Restoration* (New York: Arno Press, 1977), p. 16.

19. Blackstone, *Jesus Is Coming*, p. 235.

20. Lindberg, *A God-filled Life*, n.p.

21. Weber, *Living in the Shadow of the Second Coming*, pp. 105–27.

22. Peter Grose, *Israel in the Mind of America* (New York: Schocken, 1984), pp. 40–1; cf. Manuel, *The Realities of American–Palestine Relations*, p. 70.

8: LOUIS BRANDEIS AND WOODROW WILSON

1. Correspondence from the *Collection of the Late Justice Brandeis relating to Zionism and Palestine, 1913–1939* (microfilm, CZA, reel # 9).

2. 'Are the Jews to Recover Palestine?', *Literary Digest*, 11 (13 July 1895), cited in Isidore S. Meyer (ed.), *Early History of Zionism in America* (1958; reprinted, New York: American Jewish Historical Society, 1977), p. 319.

3. Philippa Strum, *Louis D. Brandeis: Justice for the People* (New York: Schocken, 1984), p. 11.

4. Ibid., pp. 244–5.
5. Ibid., p. 225.
6. Ibid., p. 34.
7. *LLDB*, vol. II, p. 659.
8. Jacob de Haas, *Louis D. Brandeis: A Biographical Sketch* (New York: Bloch, 1929), pp. 51–2; Strum, *Louis D. Brandeis*, p. 231; Alphaeus Thomas Mason, *Brandeis: A Free Man's Life* (New York: Viking, 1946), p. 443.
9. *LLDB*, vol. II, p. 402.
10. *LLDB*, vol. III, pp. 355–6.

9: 'A SON OF THE MANSE'

1. *LLDB*, vol. III, pp. 291–3.
2. Stephen S. Wise, *Challenging Years: The Autobiography of Stephen S. Wise* (New York: Putnam's, 1949), p. 37.
3. The principal source for SSW is the Stephen S. Wise Papers, American Jewish Historical Society Library, Waltham, MA. All references made herein to correspondence to and from SSW are from *SSWP*, unless otherwise indicated. The quotation is from a fragmentary 'Diary' in *SSWP*/Box 172/file # 32; cf. Wise. *Challenging Years*, p. 162; cf. Henry Morgenthau III, *Mostly Morgenthaus: A Family History* (New York: Tichnor & Fields, 1991), pp. 98ff.
4. CZA/box 404/file # 45.
5. Principal source is CZA/Box A404 (Jacob de Haas Papers)/file # 47 (1916 campaign of Woodrow Wilson). Correspondence between SSW and Jacob de Haas is in *SSWP*/box 107/files ## 22–4 and in box 182/file # 3.
6. Cited in *One Hundred Years of Blessing: The Centennial History of the American Messianic Fellowship (1887–1987), Including a Biographical Introduction to its Founder, William E. Blackstone* (Lansing, IL: American Messianic Fellowship, 1987), p. 48.
7. Citations which I offer herein from *Blackstone Papers* are in fact from xeroxed copies generously provided to me by Yaakov Ariel. LDB to WEB, 22 May 1916, *Blackstone Papers*/cf. Ariel, *On Behalf of Zion*, p. 85. This item is not in *LLDB*. In fact, there was much more correspondence between WEB and LDB than the few items to be found in *LLDB* – this, I believe, through no fault of the distinguished editors of those volumes. Yaakov Ariel notes that most of Brandeis' side of the Blackstone/Brandeis correspondence for the period after the War is missing from the Brandeis papers, and he inclines to the belief that either Brandeis or his literary heirs became embarrassed by it. There is a similar situation with regard to the Blackstone/Wise correspondence. Only a portion of Blackstone's Papers have survived intact, and are presently available at the Billy Graham Centre in Grand Rapids. These latter do include what seems to be the bulk of the Brandeis/Blackstone and the Wise/Blackstone correspondence. (Based on author's conversation with Y. Ariel, Jerusalem, September 1992.)
8. *LLDB*, vol. IV, pp. 288–9.
9. LDB to James de Rothschild, 16 December 1917, Weizmann Archives, reprinted in Howard M. Sachar (general ed.), *The Rise of Israel: A Documentary Record from the Nineteenth Century to 1948. A Facsimile Series Reproducing over 1,900 Documents in 39 Volumes* (New York: Garland, 1987), vol. VII (Part 1).
10. An excerpt from this letter is in *LLDB*, vol. IV, p. 278. Urofsky and Levy cite a

letter, LDB to WEB, 26 March 1917 (vol. IV, p. 278) as proof that Brandeis declined this responsibility. But Ariel has shown that indeed Brandeis did accept, and did put the 'Rapture Will' in his own personal strong box (cf. *One Hundred Years of Blessing*, p. 51). No one seems to know what became of it.
11. Blackstone, *Jesus Is Coming*, p. 240.
12. Peter Grose, *Israel in the Mind of America* (New York: Schocken, 1984), pp. 68–9.

10: WORKING ON PUBLIC OPINION

1. *One Hundred Selected Editorials from the Secular Press of America on the Zionist Movement*, pamphlet, 1918, ZAL.
2. Emanuel Neumann, *In the Arena: An Autobiographical Memoir* (New York: Herzl Press, 1976), pp. 71–2.
3. CZA/boxA123 (Emanuel Neumann Archives)/file # 443.
4. *New York Times*, 31 May 1936; 30 August 1936; 9 September 1936; 12 December 1936; 16 December 1936; Samuel Halperin, *The Political World of American Zionism* (Detroit: Wayne State University Press, 1961), pp. 180 and 373 (footnote # 7); FDR to State Department, attaching 'Resolutions adopted by American Christian Conference on Palestine', *FDRL*/Office File # 700.
5. Hertzel Fishman, *American Protestantism and a Jewish State* (Detroit: Wayne State University Press, 1973), p. 28.
6. Ibid., p. 28.
7. Ibid., pp. 31 and 37–8.

11: FRANKLIN D. ROOSEVELT, THE JEWS AND THE ZIONISTS

1. Rexford Tugwell, *The Democratic Roosevelt* (Garden City, NY: Doubleday, 1957), pp. 32–3.
2. Frances Perkins, *The Roosevelt I Knew* (New York: Viking, 1946), pp. 141–2.
3. Peter Grose, *Israel in the Mind of America* (New York: Schocken, 1984), pp. 114–15.
4. Ibid., p. 116.
5. Leonard Dinnerstein, 'Jews', in Otis L. Graham and Meghan R. Wander, *Franklin D. Roosevelt: His Life and Times: An Encyclopedic View* (Boston: G. K. Hall, 1985), p. 217.
6. Harry Fleischmann, *Norman Thomas: A Biography* (New York: Norton, 1964), p. 122.
7. Melvin I. Urofsky, *A Voice That Spoke for Justice: The Life and Times of Stephen S. Wise* (Albany: State University of New York Press, 1982), p. 265
8. Stephen S. Wise, *Challenging Years: The Autobiography of Stephen S. Wise* (New York: Putnam's, 1949), p. 216.
9. *FDRL*/President's Personal File: # 3292.
10. SSW to FDR, 28 August 1936, *FDRL*/President's Personal File: # 3292.
11. Cabinet Records, London, 3 December 1937, reprinted in Howard M. Sachar (general ed.), *The Rise of Israel: A Documentary Record from the Nineteenth Century to 1948. A Facsimile Series Reproducing over 1,900 Documents in 39 Volume* (New York: Garland, 1987), vol. XXVI.
12. *FDRL*/President's Personal File: # 3292.

12: AMERICAN ZIONIST EMERGENCY COUNCIL AND THE CHRISTIAN ZIONISTS

1. Pierre van Paassen, *Days of Our Years* (New York: Hillman-Curl, 1940), p. 420.
2. Author's conversation with C. H. Voss, 1991.
3. CZA/box A123/file # 359.
4. Samuel Halperin, *The Political World of American Zionism* (Detroit: Wayne State University Press, 1961), p. 183; Walter Laqueur, *A History of Zionism* (New York: Schocken, 1989), pp. 550–1.
5. Emanuel Neumann, I*n the Arena: An Autobiographical Memoir* (New York: Herzl Press, 1976), p. 155.
6. James Loeb, oral history interview, 7 November 1979, Eleanor Roosevelt oral history collection, *FDRL*; Paul Merkley, *Reinhold Niebuhr: A Political Account* (Montreal and London: McGill-Queen's University Press, 1975), Ch. 12.
7. Franklin H. Littell, 'RN and the Jewish People', the RN Lecture at Elmhurst College, 1990, p. 13.
8. 'My Sense of Shame', *Hadassah Newsletter* (December 1938), pp. 59–60.
9. 'The Christian Faith and the World Crisis', *Christianity and Crisis* (10 February 1941), pp. 4–5.
10. 'The Jews After the War', *The Nation*, 154 (21 February and 28 February 1942), pp. 214–16, 253–5. Reprinted in Reinhold Niebuhr, *Love and Justice: Selections from the Shorter Writings of Reinhold Niebuhr*, ed. by D. B. Robertson (Philadelphia, PA: Westminster Press, 1957), pp. 132–42.
11. 'The Relations of Christians and Jews in Western Civilization', reprinted in Reinhold Niebuhr, *Pious and Secular America* (New York: Scribner's, 1958), pp. 86–112.
12. Ibid., p. 109.
13. Poling is the only one of the clergymen belonging to CCP who seems to have had an *entrée* to the White House. He was Editor of the *Christian Herald*, and among the most popular Christian writers of his day. When he lost his son, a chaplain, early in the war, he was brought on by the Administration as a spokesman for the war effort. (A. MacLeish to FDR, 1 April 1942, *FDRL*/Office File: # 76 (Church matters), and *FDRL*/President's Personal File: # 7800 (Poling).)
14. Walter Lowdermilk is the one CCP figure whose arguments on behalf of Zionism penetrated to the highest levels of government. We know that President Roosevelt became truly persuaded about the future of a Jewish state in Palestine only after he became persuaded about the virtually limitless possibilities of renewal of the soil of Palestine, and that what finally won him on this score (against the pessimism of the State and War Departments) were discussions and memoranda based upon reports of the Assistant Chief of the Soil Conservation Service of the US, Department of Agriculture, Walter Clay Lowdermilk (*FDRL*/Office File: # 700, especially the report entitled 'Jewish Colonization', 1939); also SSW to FDR, 29 January 1945 (including copy of Lowdermilk's book and observations on FDR's reaction to discussion of the book) (*FDRL*/Office File: # 700). Lowdermilk eventually settled in Israel, where he became Professor of Soil Conservation at the Haifa Technion CZA/Box A123/file # 130 (Walter Lowdermilk).
15. Author's conversation with Carl Voss (1991).
16. CZA/box A123/file # 271 (Sumner Welles) and file # 351 (Moshe Shertok).

13: THE ISSUE OF PALESTINE IN THE WARTIME YEARS

1. Moshe Shertok's report, 27 April 1943, on his visit to London and the United States. FO 371/35035, reprinted in Howard M. Sachar (general ed.), *The Rise of*

Israel: A Documentary Record from the Nineteenth Century to 1948. A Facsimile Series Reproducing over 1,900 Documents in 39 Volumes (New York: Garland, 1987), vol. XXXI.

2. Weizmann's report on his stay in the United States. CZA/box Z4/file 302/27, reprinted in Sachar, *Rise of Israel*, vol. XXXI.

3. Chaim Weizmann, *Trial and Error: The Autobiography of Chaim Weizmann* (London: East and West Library, 1950), pp. 516–35; Norman Rose, *Chaim Weizmann* (New York: Viking, 1986), pp. 362–72; *FRUS, 1943*, vol. IV, pp. 792ff. and p. 867n.

4. Peter Grose, *Israel in the Mind of America* (New York: Schocken, 1984), p. 172.

5. Doreen Brierbrier, 'The American Zionist Emergency Council: an Analysis of a Pressure Group', senior honors thesis, Brandeis University, 1958, p. 32; AHS to Henry Morgenthau, Jr., 26 October 1944, CZA/boxA123/file # 354.

6. *FRUS, 1944*, vol. V, pp. 588 and 588n.

7. John M. Blum, (ed.), *The Price of Vision: the Diary of Henry A. Wallace, 1942–1946* (Boston, MA: Houghton Mifflin, 1973), pp. 312–13.

8. *New York Times*, 17 March 1945, p. 13:2.

9. *FRUS, 1945*, vol. VIII, pp. 698ff.

14: HARRY TRUMAN AND THE ZIONISTS

1. Dec. 13/37, R. H. Ferrell (ed.), *Dear Bess: The Letters From Harry to Bess Truman, 1910–1959* (New York: W. W. Norton, 1983), p. 409. On Lowenthal's advocacy of Zionism, see HST to Lowenthal, April 23/52, HSTL, Post Presidential Name File. Also, HSTL: Palestine folder 1, box 12 and Max Lowenthal, Oral History.

2. HSTL/Senatorial File /Box 71(Jews) and Box 226 (Zionist Organizations); Congressional Record (76 Cong, 1st sess., 1939, Vol. 84, pt. 13, Appendix, pp. 2231–2; Merle Miller, *Plain Speaking: An Oral Biography of Harry S. Truman* (New York: Berkeley, 1974), pp. 389–91.

3. HSTL/Senatorial file/Box 71.

4. Roy Jenkins, *Truman* (London: Collins, 1986), p. 1.

5. 'Copies of Papers in the Weizmann Archives, Rehovoth, Israel, relating to Relations Between the United States and Palestine and Israel, 1945–52' (HSTL/ Palestine folder 1, box 12).

6. David McCullough, *Truman* (New York: Simon & Schuster, 1992), pp. 598–9; Howard M. Sachar, *A History of the Jews in America* (New York: Knopf, 1992), p. 596.

7. Gershon Agronsky, memo, 19 June 1945, CZA/box 525/file 747, reprinted in Howard M. Sachar (general ed.), *The Rise of Israel: A Documentary Record from the Nineteenth Century to 1948. A Facsimile Series Reproducing over 1,900 Documents in 39 Volumes* (New York: Garland, 1987), vol. XXXI.

8. Harry S. Truman, *Memoirs* (Garden City, NY: Doubleday, 1955–56), vol. I, pp. 67–9.

9. Miller, *Plain Speaking*, pp. 230–4.

10. Clark Clifford, *Counsel to the President* (New York: Random House, 1991), p. 8.

11. Robert H. Ferrell (ed.), *The Autobiography of Harry S. Truman* (Boulder, CO: Colorado Associated University Press, 1980), pp. 33–4.

12. HSTL, 'Post-Presidential/Invitations', General-Baptist Misc. folder # 32.

13. Merlin Gustafson, 'Harry Truman as a Man of Faith', *Christian Century* (17 January 1973), p. 76.

14. *PPPHST: 1949*, # 231.
15. R. H. Ferrell (ed.), *Off the Record: The Private Papers of Harry S. Truman* (New York: Harper & Row, 1980), p. 188 (item dated 15 August 1950).
16. Gustafson, 'Harry Truman as a Man of Faith', p. 77.
17. Ibid., p. 76.
18. *The Truman Tapes*, recorded interviews with HST, during 1963–65, by Ben Gradus (New York: Caedmon Records, n.d.).
19. R. H. Ferrell (ed.), *Off the Record*, pp. 224–5.
20. Ibid., pp. 294–5.
21. Autobiographical manuscript, dating from the time of HST's service as a County Judge (14 May 1934), in Ferrell, *Autobiography of Harry Truman*, pp. 136–7.
22. Ferrell, *Off the Record*, pp. 37–8.
23. Truman, *Memoirs*, vol. II, p. 162.
24. *FRUS, 1945*, vol. VIII, pp. 698–703.
25. *FRUS, 1945*, vol. VIII, pp. 704.
26. *FRUS, 1945*, vol. VIII, pp. 704–5; cf. Acting Secretary of State J. C. Grew to HST, 19 June 1945, ibid., p. 708.
27. Peter Grose, *Israel in the Mind of America* (New York: Schocken, 1984), pp. 190–1.
28. CZA/boxF40/files ## 93–101 (Press Releases and Statements, CCP/ACPC).
29. Lord Halifax to Anthony Eden, 1 July 1945, UK Cabinet Record, reprinted in Howard M. Sachar (general ed.), *The Rise of Israel: A Documentary Record from the Nineteenth Century to 1948. A Facsimile Series Reproducing over 1,900 Documents in 39 Volumes* (New York: Garland, 1987), vol. XXXV.
30. *Department of State Bulletin*, 30 September 1945, p. 456.
31. HSTL/OF/Box 204, misc.
32. Confidential memorandum, A. H. Tandy to E. Bevin, Foreign Secretary, 14 February 1946. FO 371/52568, reprinted in Sachar, *Rise of Israel*, vol. XXXI.
33. CZA/box F40/file # 58 (Anglo-American Committee of Inquiry).
34. RN, 'Statement to Anglo-American Committee of Inquiry', Reinhold Niebuhr Papers, Library of Congress; also, CZA/box F40/file # 59.
35. Lord Halifax to Foreign Office, 7 May 1946. Colonial Office, reprinted in Sachar, *Rise of Israel*, vol. XXXV.
36. CZA/box A123/file # 324; HSTL/Vertical file: 'Bartley Crum'; cf. Emanuel Neumann, *In the Arena: An Autobiographical Memoir* (New York: Herzl Press, 1976), pp. 216–18, and 222–37.
37. James McDonald, Report (to AZEC) on his conversation with the President of 17 July 1946 (marked 'SECRET') (HSTL/Palestine folder 1, box 12).
38. Lord Inverchapel to FO, August 1946, FO371/52528, reprinted in Sachar, *Rise of Israel*, vol. 35.
39. HST to Paul E. Fitzpatrick, 8 October 1947, HSTL/Box 204, misc.
40. A memorandum, 'BACKGROUND TO PRESIDENT'S YOM KIPPUR STATEMENT AND ROLE OF "OUR FRIEND"' [David Niles], from Eliahu Epstein to Nahum Goldman, Jewish Agency for Palestine, London, 9 October 1946 (Weizmann Archives, reprinted in Sachar, *Rise of Israel*, vol. XXXV, vol. XXXI); cf. *PPPHST*, 1946 , vol. II, pp. 442–4, and Truman, *Memoirs*, vol. II, pp. 153–5.
41. Norman Rose, *Chaim Weizmann* (New York: Viking, 1986), p. 268.
42. Ibid., p. 267.
43. *LPChW*, vol. II, ## 169, 199; Rose, *Chaim Weizmann*, pp. 219–20.
44. Rose, *Chaim Weizmann*, p, 227; cf. *LPChW*, vol. XII, ## 61, 63.

45. Rose, *Chaim Weizmann*, pp. 418–21; Weizmann, *Trial and Error*, pp. 543–4.
46. Rose, *Chaim Weizmann*, p. 421.
47. Ibid., pp. 407–8; *LPChW*, vol. XXII, # 97; Weizmann, *Trial and Error*, pp. 458–9; Abba Eban, *An Autobiography* (New York: Random House, 1977), pp. 94–5.
48. McCullough, *Truman*, p. 604; *LPChW*, vol. XXIII, # 40.
49. Rose, *Chaim Weizmann*, pp. 428–9; Weizmann, *Trial and Error*, pp. 561–3.
50. Rose, *Chaim Weizmann*, p. 427; Eban, *An Autobiography*, pp. 92–4.
51. HST to 'Dear Mamma and Mary', 11 September 1945, in Ferrell, *Off the Record*, p. 65.
52. Peter Grose, *Israel in the Mind of America*, p. 271.
53. Rose, *Chaim Weizmann*, p. 439.
54. *LPChW*, vol. XXIII, # 21.

15: A SIGNIFICANT FRIENDSHIP

1. 'Eddie Jacobson – autobiographical sketch, *c.* 1948'. Two pages, typewritten (clumsily, and with many strikeovers, evidently by EJ himself) (HSTL/Vertical file: 'Eddie Jacobson').
2. Harry S. Truman, *Memoirs* (Garden City, NY: Doubleday, 1955–56), vol. I, p. 128; R. H. Ferrell (ed.), *Dear Bess: The Letters From Harry to Bess Truman, 1910–1959* (New York: W. W. Norton, 1983), pp. 233 and 254.
3. Ferrell, *Dear Bess*, p. 40.
4. Ibid., p. 443.
5. Michael J. Cohen, *Truman and Israel* (Berkeley: University of California Press, 1990), pp. 8–9.
6. Abraham Granoff, Oral History, HSTL.
7. Sarah Peltzman (a daughter in this Viner family), HSTL/Miscellaneous Historical Documents file.
8. Frank Adler, *Roots In a Moving Stream: The Centennial History of Congregation B'nai Jehudah of Kansas City: 1870–1970* (Kansas City, MO: published by the congregation, 1972), p. 202.
9. Truman, *Memoirs*, vol. II, p. 160.
10. 'Behind the Scenes of the UN Decision', *Bnai B'rith National Jewish Monthly*, in HSTL/Vertical file: Edward Jacobson; cf. advertisement, *Kansas City Star* (29 October 1948), 'I Want the American People to Know the truth ...', in HSTL/Papers of Edward Jacobson.
11. Adler, *Roots in a Moving Stream*, p. 203.
12. Granoff, Oral History, HSTL.
13. 'Two Presidents and a Haberdasher', American Jewish Archives (April 1968), p. 5. (This item contains the full text of EJ's account of his dealings with HST on the Palestine question, conveyed in a letter to Joseph Cohn, 30 March 1952.) Cf. Maurice Bisgyer, *Challenge and Encounter: Behind the Scenes in the Struggle for Jewish Survival* (New York: Crown, 1967), pp. 188–96; Adler, *Roots in a Moving Stream*, pp. 209–10; Truman, *Memoirs*, vol. II, pp. 160–2.
14. 'Two Presidents and a Haberdasher', pp. 5–7. HST tells a reduced version of this same story, reproducing identically portions of EJ's own recapitulation of the dialogue (with the expletive deleted, of course). This suggests that he used EJ's document for his own account (Truman, *Memoirs*, vol. II, pp. 160–1).
15. Bisgyer, *Challenge and Encounter*, p. 193.

16. Truman, *Memoirs*, vol. II, pp. 161–2; Larry Collins and Dominique La Pierre, *O Jerusalem* (New York: Simon & Schuster/Pocket Books, 1972), p. 228; Peter Grose, *Israel in the Mind of America* (New York: Schocken, 1984), pp. 273–4; Norman Rose, *Chaim Weizmann* (New York: Viking, 1986), p. 437; Chaim Weizmann, *Trial and Error: The Autobiography of Chaim Weizmann* (London: East and West Library, 1950), p. 577; *LPChW*, vol. XXIII, # 137.

17. R. H. Ferrell (ed.), *Off the Record: The Private Papers of Harry S. Truman* (New York: Harper & Row, 1980), pp. 126–7; cf. Truman, *Memoirs*, vol. II, pp. 161–2.

18. *PPPHST, 1948*, pp. 190–5.

19. 'Two Presidents and a Haberdasher', p. 10.

20. *LPChW*, vol. XXIII, # 137.

21. *LPChW*, vol. XXXIII, # 131.

22. Lord Inverchapel to Foreign Office, FO 371/68648, reprinted in Sachar, *Rise of Israel*, vol. XXXVIII.

23. Clark Clifford, *Counsel to the President* (New York: Random House, 1991), pp. 1–96; Peter Grose, *Israel in the Mind of America* (New York: Schocken, 1984), pp. 289–93; David McCullough, *Truman* (New York: Simon & Schuster, 1992), pp. 614–7; *FRUS, 1948*, vol. V, pp. 972–8.

24. CZA/Box Z6/file 59, reprinted in Sachar, *Rise of Israel*, vol. XXXIX; Larry Collins and Dominique La Pierre, *O Jerusalem* (New York: Simon & Schuster/Pocket Books, 1972), pp. 358–61; Grose, *Israel in the Mind of America*, pp. 286–8.

25. Clifford, *Counsel to the President*, pp. 18–22 ; McCullough, *Truman*, p. 618.

26. *PPPHST, 1948*, p. 258; Truman, *Memoirs*, vol. II, pp. 164–5; Clifford, *Counsel to the President*, p. 22.

27. Abba Eban, *An Autobiography* (New York: Random House, 1977), pp. 164–5.

28. Moshe Davis, 'Reflections on Harry S. Truman and the State of Israel', in Allen Weinstein and Moshe Ma'oz (eds), *Truman and the American Commitment to Israel* (Jerusalem: Magnes Press, Hebrew University, 1981), pp. 82–5 (excerpt cited is p. 83.); Eliahu Elath, quoted by Davis, in Weinstein and Ma'oz, *Truman and the American Commitment to Israel*, p. 106.

29. Eliahu Elath, quoted by Davis, ibid., p. 106; Alfred Steinberg, *The Man from Missouri* (New York: G. P. Putnam's, 1962).

Bibliography

ARCHIVES

American Jewish Historical Society Library, Waltham, Massachusetts.
Central Zionist Archives, Jerusalem, Israel.
Franklin Delano Roosevelt Library, Hyde Park, New York.
Harry S. Truman Presidential Library, Independence, Missouri.
Jewish Historical Society, Waltham, Massachusetts.
Library of Congress, Washington, DC.
Zionist Archives and Library, World Zionist Organization–American
Section, 515 Park Avenue, New York City.

PUBLISHED DOCUMENTARY COLLECTIONS

Foreign Relations of the United States. Washington: US Government
Printing Office.
Franklin D. Roosevelt and Foreign Affairs (FDRFA). 14 vols: vols. I–III
(January 1933–January, 1937), ed. Edgar B. Nixon (Cambridge, MA:
Harvard University Press, 1969; vols. IV–XVI, ed. Donald B. Schewe
(New York: Clearwater Press, 1979).
Franklin Delano Roosevelt: His Personal Letters (FDRPL). 4 vols, ed. Elliott
Roosevelt (New York: Duell, Sloan & Pearce 1947–50).
Nathan M. Kaganoff (ed.), *Political Relations and American Zionism* (vol. II
of *Guide to America–Holy Land Studies,* general ed. Moshe Davis). (New
York: Praeger, 1982).
A. S. Klieman and A. L. Klieman (eds), *American Zionism: A Documentary
History,* 15 vols (New York: Garland, 1991).
Arthur S. Link *et al., The Papers of Woodrow Wilson,* 63 vols to date
(Princeton, NJ: Princeton University Press, 1956–90).
Barnet Litvinoff (general ed.), *Letters and Papers of Chaim Weizmann,* 23
vols (London: Oxford University Press/Jerusalem: Israel Universities/
New Brunswick, NJ: Transaction Books, 1968–80).

Raphael Patai (ed.), *The Complete Diaries of Theodor Herzl* (*CDTH*), trans. Harry Zohn, 4 vols (New York: Herzl Press, 1960).

Raphel Patai (ed.), *Encyclopedia of Zionism and Israel* (New York: Herzl Press, 1971).

Public Papers and Addresses of Franklin Delano Roosevelt (*PPAFDR*). 13 vols, ed. Samuel I. Rosenman, 13 vols, 1938–50 (New York: Random House, 1938/New York: Macmillan, 1941/New York: Harper, 1950).

Public Papers of the Presidents: Harry S. Truman (*PPPHST*). 8 vols (Washington: US Government Printing Office; vols for the years 1945–48, published 1961–65).

Howard M. Sachar (general ed.), *The Rise of Israel: A Documentary Record from the Nineteenth Century to 1948. A Facsimile Series Reproducing over 1,900 Documents in 39 Volumes* (New York: Garland, 1987).

State of Israel. Israel State Archives/World Zionist Organization: Central Zionist Archives, *Political and Diplomatic Documents, December 1947– May 1948*; and *Companion Volume* (Jerusalem, 1979).

University of Louisville. *Correspondence from the collection of the late Justice Brandeis Relating to Zionism and Palestine, 1913–1939* (available on microfilm at CZA).

Melvin I. Urofsky and Davis M. Levy (eds), *Letters of Louis D. Brandeis*, 5 vols (New York: State University Press, 1972–78).

BOOKS

Cyrus Adler and Aaron M. Margalith, *With Firmness in the Right: American Diplomatic Action Affecting Jews, 1840–1945* (1946; reprinted, New York: American Jewish Historical Society/Arno Press, 1977).

Frank Adler, *Roots In a Moving Stream: The Centennial History of Congregation B'nai Jehudah of Kansas City: 1870–1970* (Kansas City, MI; published by the congregation, 1972).

Ya'akov Ariel, *On Behalf of Israel: American Fundamentalist Attitudes Toward Jews, Judaism, and Zionism* (Brooklyn, NY: Carlson, 1991).

Kenneth R. Bain, *The March to Zion: United States Policy and the Founding of Israel* (College Station, TX: Texas A&M University Press, 1979).

Leonard Baker, *Brandeis and Frankfurter: A Dual Biography* (New York: New York University Press, 1984).

Michael Balfour, *The Kaiser and His Times* (London: Cresset Press, 1964).

Alex Bein, *Theodor Herzl* (New York: Atheneum, 1970).

G. F. A. Best, *Shaftesbury* (London: Batsford, 1964).

Maurice Bisgyer, *Challenge and Encounter: Behind the Scenes in the Struggle for Jewish Survival* (New York: Crown, 1967).

William E. Blackstone, *Jesus is Coming* (1st edn, 1878; 3rd edn, Chicago: Fleming H. Revell, 1908).

William E. Blackstone, *Palestine For the Jews: A Copy of a Memorial Presented to President Harrison*, 5 March 1891 (Oak Park, IL, 1891). (Reprinted in *Christian Protagonists For Jewish Restoration* (New York: Arno Press, 1977).)

John M. Blum (ed.), *The Price of Vision: The Diary of Henry A. Wallace, 1942–1946* (Boston, MA: Houghton Mifflin, 1973).

Paul Boyer, *When Time Shall Be No More: Prophetic Belief in Modern American Culture* (New York: Harvard University Press, 1992).

J. Wesley Bready, *Lord Shaftesbury and Social-Industrial Progress* (London: George Allen & Unwin, 1926).

Frank W. Brecher, *Reluctant Ally: United States Foreign Policy Towards Israel, From Wilson to Roosevelt* (New York: Greenwood Press, 1991).

Doreen Brierbrier, 'The American Zionist Emergency Council: An Analysis of a Pressure Group', Senior Honors Thesis, Brandeis University, 1958.

Call to America to Build Zion (New York: Arno Press, 1977).

Christian Protagonists for Jewish Restoration (New York: Arno Press, 1977).

Clark Clifford, *Counsel to the President* (New York: Random House, 1991).

Bert Cochran, *Harry Truman and the Crisis Presidency* (New York: Funk & Wagnalls, 1973).

Israel Cohen, *Theodor Herzl: Founder of Political Zionism* (New York: Yoseloff, 1959).

Michael J. Cohen, *Truman and Israel* (Berkeley: University of California Press, 1990).

Saul P. Colbi, *A History of the Christian Presence in the Holy Land* (Lanham, NY: University Press of America, 1988).

Larry Collins and Dominique La Pierre, *O Jerusalem* (New York: Simon & Schuster/Pocket Books, 1972).

Virginia Cowles, *The Kaiser* (New York: Harper, 1963).

Kelvin Crombie, *For the Love of Zion: Christian Witness and the Restoration of Israel* (London: Hodder & Stoughton, 1991).

Jonathan Daniels, *The Man of Independence* (Philadelphia, PA: Lippincott, 1950).

Moshe Davis (ed.), *Israel: Its Role in Civilization* (New York: Harper, 1956).

Moshe Davis (ed.), *With Eyes Toward Zion. Vol. II: Themes and Sources in the Archives of the United States, Great Britain, Turkey and Israel*, Second International Scholars Colloquium on America–Holy Land Studies (New York: Praeger, 1986).

Moshe Davis and Yehoshua Ben-Arieh (eds), *With Eyes Toward Zion*, vol. III: *Western Societies and the Holy Land* (New York: Praeger, 1991).

Nelson L. Dawson (ed.), *Brandeis and America* (Lexington, KY: University Press of Kentucky, 1989).

Robert J. Donovan, *Tumultuous Years: The Presidency of Harry S. Truman* (New York: Norton, 1982).

Blanche Dugdale, *Arthur James Balfour*, 2 vols (New York: Putnam's, 1937).

Claude Duvernoy, *Le prince et le prophète* (Jerusalem: Département des publications de l'Agence Juive, 1966).

Abba Eban, *An Autobiography* (New York: Random House, 1977).

Alan Edelstein, *An Unacknowledged Harmony: Philosemitism and the Survival of European Jewry* (Westport, CT: Greenwood, 1981)

Carle F. Ehle, 'Prolegomena to Christian Zionism in America: The Views of Increase Mather and W. E. Blackstone', PhD thesis, New York University, 1977.

Amos Elon, *Herzl* (New York: Rinehart & Winston, 1975).

Henry L. Feingold, *Zion in America: The Jewish Experience from Colonial Times to the Present* (New York: Hippocrene Books, 1974).

Robert H. Ferrell (ed.), *The Autobiography of Harry S. Truman* (Boulder, CO: Colorado Associated University Press, 1980).

R. H. Ferrell (ed.), *Off the Record: The Private Papers of Harry S. Truman* (New York: Harper & Row, 1980).

R. H. Ferrell (ed.), *Dear Bess: The Letters From Harry to Bess Truman, 1910–1959* (New York: W. W. Norton, 1983).

Reuben Fink, *America and Palestine: The Attitude of Official America and of the American People Toward the Rebuilding of Palestine* (New York: Zionist Emergency Council, 1944).

Norman H. Finkelstein, *Theodor Herzl* (New York: Impact, 1987).

Geoffrey B. A. M. Finlayson, *The Seventh Earl of Shaftesbury, 1801–1885* (London: Methuen, 1981).

Hertzl Fishman, *American Protestantism and a Jewish State* (Detroit: Wayne State University Press, 1973).

Harry Fleischmann, *Norman Thomas: A Biography* (New York: Norton, 1964).

Richard W. Fox, *Reinhold Niebuhr: A Biography* (New York: Harper & Row, 1987).

Osmond K. Fraenkel (ed.), *The Curse of Bigness: Miscellaneous Papers of Louis D. Brandeis* (Port Washington, NY: Kennikat Press, 1965).

David Fromkin, *A Peace to End All Peace: The Fall of the Ottoman Empire and the Creation of the Modern Middle East* (New York: Avon Books, 1989).

Joseph Gaer and Ben Siegel, *The Puritan Heritage: America's Roots in the Bible* (New York: Mentor, 1964).

Zvi Ganim, *Truman, American Jewry, and Israel* (New York: Holmes & Meier, 1979).

Martin Gilbert, *Jerusalem: The Rebirth of a City* (New York: Viking, 1985).

Arthur A. Goren (ed.), *Dissenter in Zion: From the Writings of Judah L. Magnes* (Cambridge, MA: Harvard University Press, 1982).

Joseph L. Grabill, *Protestant Diplomacy and the Near East* (Minneapolis: University of Minnesota Press, 1971).

Otis L. Graham and Meghan R. Wander, *Franklin D. Roosevelt: His Life and Times: An Encyclopedic View* (Boston, MA: G. K. Hall, 1985).

Peter Grose, *Israel in the Mind of America* (New York: Schocken, 1984).

Jacob de Haas, *Louis D. Brandeis: A Biographical Sketch* (New York: Bloch, 1929).

Ben Halpern, *A Clash of Heroes: Brandeis, Weizmann, and American Zionism* (New York: Oxford University Press, 1987).

Samuel Halperin, *The Political World of American Zionism* (Detroit: Wayne State University Press, 1961).

August Heckscher, *Woodrow Wilson* (New York: Scribner's, 1991).

Will Herberg, *Judaism and Modern Man: An Interpretation of the Jewish Religion* (New York: Farrar, Strauss & Young, 1951).

Edwin Hodder, *The Life and Work of the Seventh Earl of Shaftesbury, K. G.*, 2 vols (London: Cassell, 1887).

Irving Howe, *World of Our Fathers* (New York: Simon & Schuster, 1976).

Albert Hyamson, *History of the Jews in England* (London: Methuen, 1928).

Roy Jenkins, *Truman* (London: Collins, 1986).

David S. Katz, *Philo-Semitism and the Readmission of the Jews to England, 1603–1655* (Oxford: Clarendon Press, 1982).

C. W. Kegley, and R. W. Bretall (eds), *Reinhold Niebuhr: His Religious Social and Political Thought* (New York: Macmillan, 1956).

Max Kleiman (ed.), *Roosevelt: The Tribute of the Synagogue* (New York: Bloch, 1946).

Franz Kobler, *The Vision Was There: A History of the British Movement for the Restoration of the Jews to Palestine*, published for the World Jewish Congress, British Section (London: Lincolns-Praeger, 1956).

Walter Laqueur, *A History of Zionism* (New York: Schocken, 1989).

David M. Leith, 'American Christian Support for A Jewish Palestine', Senior thesis, Princeton University, 1957.

Beth M. Lindberg, *A God-Filled Life: The Story of William E. Blackstone* (Chicago: American Messianic Fellowship, 1985).

Arthur S. Link, *Wilson*, 5 vols (Princeton, NJ: Princeton University Press, 1947–65).

Arthur S. Link, *Woodrow Wilson and the Progressive Era, 1910–1917* (New York: Harper, 1954).

Arthur S. Link, *The Higher Realism of Woodrow Wilson and Other Essays* (Nashville: Vanderbilt University Press, 1971).

Louis Lipsky, *Thirty Years of Zionism* (1927; reprinted, New York: American Jewish Historical Society/Arno Press, 1977).

Yona Malachy, *American Fundamentalism and Israel* (Jerusalem: Hebrew University, 1978).

Frank E. Manuel, *The Realities of American–Palestine Relations* (Washington, DC: Public Affairs Press, 1949).

George Marsden, *Fundamentalism and American Culture: The Shaping of Twentieth-Century Evangelicalism, 1870–1925* (New York: Oxford University Press, 1980).

Alphaeus Thomas Mason, *Brandeis: A Free Man's Life* (New York: Viking, 1946).

Robert K. Massie, *Dreadnought: Britain, Germany, and the Coming of the Great War* (New York: Random House, 1991).

David McCullough, *Truman* (New York: Simon & Schuster, 1992).

John McDonald, *Isaiah's Message to the American Nation* (Albany, 1814). Reprinted as one of three items in *Call to America to Build Zion* (New York: Arno Press, 1977).

Albert J. Menendez, *Religion and the US Presidency: A Bibliography* (New York: Garland, 1986).

Paul Merkley, *Reinhold Niebuhr: A Political Account* (Montreal and London: McGill-Queen's University Press, 1975).

Isidore S. Meyer (ed.), *Early History of Zionism in America* (1958; reprinted, New York: American Jewish Historical Society, 1977).

Merle Miller, *Plain Speaking: An Oral Biography of Harry S. Truman* (New York: Berkeley, 1974).

Richard Lawrence Miller, *Truman: The Rise to Power* (New York: McGraw-Hill, 1985).

Henry Morgenthau III, *Mostly Morgenthaus: A Family History* (New York: Tichnor & Fields, 1991).

John M. Mulder, *Woodrow Wilson: The Years of Preparation* (Princeton, NJ: Princeton University Press, 1978).

Bruce Allen Murphy, *The Brandeis/Frankfurter Connection: The Secret Political Activities of Two Supreme Court Justices* (New York: Oxford University Press, 1982).

Emanuel Neumann, *In the Arena: An Autobiographical Memoir* (New York: Herzl Press, 1976).

Reinhold Niebuhr, *Love and Justice: Selections from the Shorter Writings of Reinhold Niebuhr*, ed. D. B. Robertson (Philadelphia, PA: Westminster Press, 1957).

Reinhold Niebuhr, *Pious and Secular America* (New York: Scribner's, 1958).

Ursula M. Niebuhr (ed.), *Remembering Reinhold Niebuhr: Letters of Reinhold and Ursula M. Niebuhr* (San Francisco, CA: HarperCollins, 1991).

Iris Noble, *Firebrand for Justice: A Biography of Louis Dembitz Brandeis* (Philadelphia, PA: Westminster, 1969).

One Hundred Years of Blessing: The Centennial History of the American Messianic Fellowship (1887–1987), Including a Biographical Introduction to its Founder, William E. Blackstone (Lansing, IL: American Messianic Fellowship, 1987).

Raphael Patai (ed.), *Herzl Year Book*, vol. IV (New York: Herzl Press, 1962).

Ernst Pawel, *The Labyrinth of Exile: A Life of Theodor Herzl* (New York: Farrar, Strauss & Giroux, 1989).

Frances Perkins, *The Roosevelt I Knew* (New York: Viking, 1946).

Michael Pragai, *Faith and Fulfilment: Christians and the Return to the Promised Land* (London: Vallentine Mitchell, 1985).

David A. Rausch, *Zionism within Early American Fundamentalism, 1878–1918* (New York: Edwin Mellen Press, 1979).

Daniel G. Reid (ed.), *Dictionary of Christianity in America* (Downers Grove, IL: InterVarsity, 1991).

Norman Rose, *The Gentile Zionists: A Study in Anglo-Zionist Diplomacy, 1929–1939* (London: Frank Cass, 1973).

Norman Rose (ed.), *Baffy: The Diaries of Blanche Dugdale, 1936–1947* (London: Vallentine Mitchell, 1973).

Norman Rose, *Chaim Weizmann* (New York: Viking, 1986).

Abram Leon Sachar, *A History of the Jews* (New York: Knopf, 1975).

Howard M. Sachar, *A History of Israel: From the Rise of Zionism to Our Time* (New York: Knopf, 1979).

Howard M. Sachar, *A History of the Jews in America* (New York: Knopf, 1992).

Ernest R. Sandeen, *The Roots of Fundamentalism* (Chicago: University of Chicago Press, 1970).

David Schoenbaum, *The United States and the State of Israel* (New York: Oxford University Press, 1993).

John M. Shaftesley (ed.), *Remember the Days: Essays on Anglo-Jewish History Presented to Cecil Roth* (London: Jewish Historical Society of England, 1966).

Robert Donald Shapiro, *A Reform Rabbi in the Progressive Era: The Early Career of Stephen S. Wise* (New York: Garland, 1984).

Regina S. Sharif, *Non-Jewish Zionism: Its Roots in Eastern History* (London: Zed Press, 1983).

Naomi Shepherd, *The Zealous Intruders: The Western Rediscovery of Palestine* (San Francisco, CA: Harper & Row, 1988).

Neil A. Silberman, *Digging for God and Country: Exploration, Archeology, and the Secret Struggle for the Holy Land, 1799–1917* (New York: Knopf, 1982).

John Snetsinger, *Truman, The Jewish Vote, and the Creation of Israel* (Stanford, CA: Hoover Institution, 1975).

Leonard Stein, *The Balfour Declaration* (1961; 2nd edn, Jerusalem/ London: Magnes Press, Hebrew University, 1983).

Alfred Steinberg, *The Man from Missouri* (New York: G. P. Putnam's, 1962).

Richard P. Stevens, *American Zionism and United States Foreign Policy, 1942–1947* (New York: Pageant, 1962).

Desmond Stewart, *Theodor Herzl* (Garden City, NY: Doubleday, 1974).

Philippa Strum, *Louis D. Brandeis: Justice for the People* (New York: Schocken, 1984).

Harry S. Truman, *Memoirs*, 2 vols (Garden City, NY: Doubleday, 1955–56).

Harry S. Truman, *Mr Citizen* (New York: Geis Associates, 1960).

Margaret Truman, *Letters: The Truman Family's Personal Correspondence* (New York: Arbor House, 1981).

Margaret Truman (ed.), *Where the Buck Stops: The Personal and Private Writings of Harry S. Truman* (New York: Warner, 1989).

The Truman Tapes. Recorded interviews with HST, during 1963–65, by Ben Gradus. Caedmon Records, New York. n.d.

Dan Tschirgi, *The Politics of Indecision: Origins and Implications of American Involvement with the Palestine Problem* (New York: Praeger, 1983).

Barbara Tuchman, *The Bible and the Sword: England and Palestine from the Bronze Age to Balfour* (New York: Ballantine, 1956).

Rexford Tugwell, *The Democratic Roosevelt* (Garden City, NY: Doubleday, 1957).

Alice Felt Tyler, *The Foreign Policy of James G. Blaine* (Minneapolis: University of Minnesota Press, 1927).

Melvin I. Urofsky, *American Zionism, from Herzl to the Holocaust* (Garden City, NY: Doubleday, 1975).

Melvin I. Urofsky, *Essays in American Zionism, 1917–1948* (*Herzl Year Book*, vol. VIII) (New York: Herzl Press, 1978).

Melvin I. Urofsky, *Louis D. Brandeis and the Progressive Tradition* (Boston, MA: Little, Brown, 1981).

Melvin I. Urofsky, *A Voice That Spoke for Justice: The Life and Times of Stephen S. Wise* (Albany: State University of New York Press, 1982).

Pierre van Paassen, *Days of Our Years* (New York: Hillman-Curl, 1940).

David Vital, *The Origins of Zionism* (Oxford: Oxford University Press, 1975).

Carl Hermann Voss (ed.), *Stephen S. Wise: Servant of the People: Selected Letters* (Philadelphia, PA: Jewish Publication Society of America, 1969).

Carl Hermann Voss, *Rabbi and Minister: The Friendship of Stephen S. Wise and John Haynes Holmes* (New York: World, 1984).

Arthur W. Walworth, *Woodrow Wilson*, 2nd edn, revised (Boston, MA: Houghton Mifflin, 1965).

Timothy P. Weber, *Living in the Shadow of the Second Coming: American Premillennialism, 1875–1982*, enlarged edn (Grand Rapids: Zondervan/Academie, 1983).

Allen Weinstein and Moshe Ma'oz (eds), *Truman and the American Commitment to Israel* (Jerusalem: Magnes Press, Hebrew University, 1981).

Meyer W. Weisgal (ed.), *Theodor Herzl: A Memorial*, published by *New Palestine* (official magazine of ZOA) (New York, 1929).

Chaim Weizmann, *Trial and Error: The Autobiography of Chaim Weizmann* (London: East and West Library, 1950).

William II, former Emperor of Germany, *My Early Life*, trans. from German (New York: AMS Press, 1971).

William II, *The Kaiser's Memoirs*, trans. from German (New York: Harper, 1922).

Justine Wise Poliet and James W. Wise (eds), *The Personal Letters of Stephen Wise* (Boston: Beacon Press, 1956).

Stephen S. Wise, *Challenging Years: The Autobiography of Stephen S. Wise* (New York: Putnam's, 1949).

Index

Titles of Related Interest

Cultures of Ambivalence and Contempt
Studies in Jewish–Non-Jewish Relations

Siân Jones, Tony Kushner and Sarah Pearce (Eds)
University of Southampton

This collection focuses on the concepts of tolerance and intolerance as it celebrates the life of the man who pioneered the study of antisemitism. It is a rich collection bringing together the best of interdisciplinary work including literary and cultural studies, history, political studies, psychology, sociology and religious studies. Yet whatever their approach or the period under study, the authors are united in their exploration of the importance of ideology and language in the formation of attitudes, responses and behaviour towards the Jews as well as the construction of identities, Jewish and non-Jewish. Many are inspired by the wide-ranging and pioneering work of Parkes himself. The cohesion of the collection is further enhanced by the editors' introductory essay, which highlights the career of Parkes and puts the essays into the context of his work. They divide it into three major themes: Judaism and Christianity; Jewishness and national identity; and antisemitism.

Contributors: Siân Jones, Sarah Pearce, Professor Colin Richmond, Professor James Shapiro, Claire Jowitt, Paolo Bernardini, Professor David Cesarani, Frederic Raphael, Dr Elisabeth Maxwell, Dr Tony Kushner, Michael Ignatieff.

336 pages   1998   0 85303 324 2 cloth   0 85303 325 0 paper
Parkes–Wiener Series on Jewish Studies
Vallentine Mitchell

The Jewish Exodus from Iraq, 1948-1951

Moshe Gat
Senior Lecturer, Department of General History and
Political Studies, Bar Ilan University, Israel

'The most important assessment in English. It is highly recommended.'
Choice

*'a well researched and documented three years drama of the decline
and fall of a 2,500-year-old community'*
Middle Eastern Studies

In 1950 and 1951, more than 120,000 Jews left Iraq for Israel, most
coming by air in the largest airlift in history. Scholars give various
reasons for this exodus. Some point to the strength of Zionism
amongst the Jews in Iraq whereas others blame the anti-Semitic
policies of the Iraqi government. Yet others see the cause as a
combination of Iraqi oppression and Zionist education.

Moshe Gat makes extensive use of the available official documents
and primary sources to produce a thoroughly researched study of
the extraordinary operation known as 'Ezra and Nehemiah'. He
provides a background to these events and argues that both Iraqi
discrimination and the actions of the Zionist underground in
previous years played a part in the flight. The Denaturalization law
of 1950 saw tens of thousands of Jews registering for emigration, and
a bomb thrown at a synagogue in 1951 accelerated the exodus.

224 pages   1997   0 7146 4689 X cloth   0 7146 4223 1 paper

Jews, Christians and Muslims in the Mediterranean World After 1492

Alisa Meyuhas Ginio (Ed)

The articles in this volume discuss the aftermath of the crucial historical events that took place in the Mediterranean world in 1492, focusing on the social, economic and cultural consequences of these occurrences.

294 pages   1992   0 7146 3492 1 cloth
A special issue of the journal Mediterranean Historical Review

War, Jews, and the New Europe
The Diplomacy of Lucien Wolf, 1914–1919

Mark Levene
University of Warwick

'*Mark Levene's impressive study... has implications well beyond the exploration of one man's diplomatic activity on behalf of British and British-Jewish interests*'.

David Cesarani, Jewish Chronicle

352 pages 2 maps   1992   0 19 710072 4 cloth
The Littman Library of Jewish Civilization

Printed in the United Kingdom by
Lightning Source UK Ltd., Milton Keynes
137573UK00003B/170/P